GREENSPIRIT

Bill & Shelley Jr
Every Blessing
in & on World

Greenspirit

Twelve Steps in Ecological Spirituality
An Individual, Cultural and Planetary Therapy

Albert J. LaChance
Foreword by Thomas Berry

First published by Element Books Ltd 1991
© Vega 2002
Text © Albert J. LaChance 1991

ISBN 1-84333-285-X

A catalogue record for this book is available
from the British Library

Published in 2002 by
Vega
64 Brewery Road
London, N7 9NT

A member of **Chrysalis** Books plc

Visit our website at www.chrysalisbooks.co.uk

Printed in Great Britain
by Lightning Source
Cover designed by Design Revolution, Brighton

In each generation there are a few great teachers
through whom a creative future flows.

To Thomas Berry

I do not propose to write an ode to dejection, but to brag as lustily as chanticleer in the morning, standing on his roost, if only to wake my neighbors up.

— Henry David Thoreau

TABLE OF CONTENTS

ACKNOWLEDGMENTS

Grateful acknowledgment is made for permission to reprint excerpts from the following works: Ezra Pound: *Confucius*. Copyright 1947, 1950 by Ezra Pound. Reprinted by permission of New Directions Publishing Corporation. *Indefensible Weapons* by Robert J. Lifton and Richard Falk. Copyright 1988 by Basic Books, Inc., Reprinted by permission of Basic Books, Inc., a division of Harper-Collins Publishers. "The Answer" from *The Selected Poetry of Robinson Jeffers* by Robinson Jeffers. Copyright 1937 and renewed 1965 by Donnan Jeffers & Garth Jeffers. Reprinted by permission of Random House, Inc. *The Presence of the Past* by Rupert Sheldrake. Copyright 1988 by A. Rupert Sheldrake. Reprinted by permission of Times Books, a division of Random House, Inc. *Religions of Man* by Huston Smith. Copyright 1958 by Huston Smith. Reprinted by permission of HarperCollins Publishers.

In addition, excerpts have been taken from the following works: *The Collected Works of C.G. Jung*. Copyright 1957 by Princeton University Press, Bollingen Series. *Letter to the American President* by Chief Seattle, Ives Street Press (no copyright). *The Pregnant Virgin* by Marion Woodman. Copyright 1985, Inner City Books, Toronto. *Memories, Dreams and Reflections* by C.G. Jung. Copyright 1963 Routledge, Kegan and Paul.

FOREWORD

One hundred million years ago, as far as we can determine, the vegetation of the Earth was all green. Then the flowering plants in all their brilliance appeared with their enclosed seeds; then the grasses, the berries and fruits and nuts appeared. These plants survived the great extinction that took place some sixty-five million years ago and were a determining factor in the wave upon wave of life developments that began at this time in what came to be known as the Recent Life Period — the Cenozoic. The Earth, as we experience the Earth, took on its shape and brought forth its distinctive life forms. Out of these, humans began to appear a few million years ago.

It is necessary to get such a time perspective to understand just what is happening now; for we are involved not simply in the decline of a western civilizational process or even of the human process. We, also, are involved in the closing down of the major life systems of the Earth that came into being during the past sixty-five million years. The devastation we are witnessing now is primarily due to the plundering industrial economy that has developed in the past few hundred years. Its root causes, however, reach far back into the most basic religious and cultural traditions of our western world.

The enormity of the changing environment surpasses comprehension. We think about its causes, but so far without the depth of insight or the level of psychic energy that would enable us to alter our present modes of action. That the disintegration of the planet is intertwined with the disintegration of the human personality, and the disintegration of the social order, is vaguely felt but seldom considered in any significant way.

The purpose of this book is to articulate the deeper causes of our distraught society and their relation to the larger issues of our religious and cultural heritage, and even more deeply, their relation to the disturbances being wrought upon the Earth's physical and biological functioning. The unifying cause can best be understood in terms of "addiction."

Not only are our individual personalities addictive, but our society is addictive. We could deal with our personal addictions much more effectively if our deeper addictions were not ultimately supported by the entire array of our spiritual and cultural institutions. We are dealing with cultural pathologies that have long been accepted as the normal expression of the human. The best example of such an addictive society from western history may be the addictions we discover in our studies of Rome -- Rome cosmopolis that became Rome necropolis. In this period the masochistic pathologies associated with the Coliseum were such that even now they still escape human understanding. So now, our consumer pathologies leading to the devastation of the life systems of the Earth, are not only acceptable models of human behavior, they are necessary for the functioning of our social and economic institutions.

Consumerism seeks to subordinate the entire Earth, all its energies, and all its functioning, to exaggerated or trivial human purposes. Just as addictions know no limits, so too, the disintegration of the Earth for human purposes knows no limits. The presumption is that everything in heaven and on Earth exists for human convenience.

We resent the basic conditions under which life is granted to us. There seems to be a deep hidden rage in the western psyche against the human condition. This resentment of the fact that we must endure some afflictions as the return due for the wondrous existence that is granted us, arises primarily from our religious traditions. A millenium − a period of a thousand years − is promised when the human condition itself will be transformed and we will live in a world of peace, justice, and abundance.

Because this millenium has not arrived by divine means, we are determined to raise it up through plundering industrial processes that see the Earth not as a community of subjects but as a collection of objects, put here for limitless consumption by humans until the whole is exhausted and this green and fertile planet is reduced to ashes. That this is happening we cannot admit for we are presently in what is usually designated as the "denial phase" of addiction.

We examine the situation and find that it is "not so desperate" as some of us indicate. Those concerned with the survival of the life systems of the planet are identified as "extremists" by government officials, with a heartless disregard for the need people have for "jobs," even when these jobs are destroying the planet itself. The government cannot see the degradation that is being inflicted on the Earth by the functioning of the modern economy. It wishes to save the human economy by destroying the Earth economy, as though a human economy could survive and even prosper when the basic life systems of the Earth are being extinguished.

We are now so integral with a plundering economy that we must plunder in order to survive, though our way of survival today means death tomorrow. Just as the alcoholic or drug addict must have the next drink or the next injection, even though "survival" today brings death closer tomorrow, we are in a state of psychological and even physical dependency on our addictions.

Generally, the solution for the addict comes in the form of a "crash" which confronts a person with the terror of imminent death unless the addiction is eliminated. The real difficulty is that a "crash" at the present order of magnitude involves a crash, not only of the human, but of many of the major life systems of the Earth itself. This crash is one from which the Earth would not likely recover with any splendor as long as humans remain present. That a crash, with all its uncertain consequences, is already happening is clear enough from the devastation that is taking place on every continent. The air, the water, the soil, and indeed all the major life systems of the planet are profoundly disrupted in their most essential functioning.

Still there is denial. There is even a general commitment in our society to plunge ahead into more devastating processes in the belief that a rising industrial economy is the proper way to security and well-being. In this suicidal situation, denial is extremely difficult to overcome because of our overemphasis on the well-being of the "human" regardless of the stress that we are placing on the larger community of life. Other beings are considered as "things" to be conquered and used, not as realities whose well-being is integral to our own.

Essentially, we may not be any better or worse than earlier generations. The issues we are dealing with, however, are infinitely more deadly and infinitely greater in their scale and their implications for the future survival of the planet. No other generation has been able to extinguish living species in such an extensive manner. Nor has any other generation been able to so poison the atmosphere, the soil, and the waters of the entire Earth. We have been able to extinguish the vast expanse of rainforests in a few decades, turning immensely fertile areas into desert, with utmost assurance that this is the proper way for humans to act in relation to the other forms of life.

Here, in this book, the multiple addictions of our times are brought together for the first time so far as I am aware. Personal addictions, social addictions, and consumer addictions all reinforce each other and lock the human community into a destructive relation with itself within the planetary community, and ultimately in relation to that mysterious origin whence all things emerged into being.

At this ultimate stage where can we go? Our addictions are all reinforcing each other. No longer can any of our therapies provide the answers on the scale needed by the larger society. Even though the drug addict can go to a clinic and the alcoholic can get into a recovery program, the rising rate of addiction continues. The culture is creating the addictions it seeks to heal.

Where do we go to remedy such a situation? Where can an entire culture, or the entire human community, go for therapy? Ordinarily the culture has its religious traditions, its educators, its cultural critics to guide the society in most of its adjustments to itself, to the surrounding universe, and to the ultimate mysteries of the universe. That our religious and cultural traditions have failed us so totally at this time constitutes one of our greatest difficulties. Indeed, it is within these traditions that the context of our present dissolution of the planet takes shape. It is no wonder for even now the colleges and universities of the eastern part of the United States advertise over a thousand courses and programs but offer no adequate programs that deal with the disintegration of the Earth.

An even greater wonder is that the religious establishments of western civilization have shown almost no concern for the fate of the Earth. There are pastoral letters for economics and critiques of nuclear war because of their threat to human well-being, but no equivalent pastoral concern for the fate of the Earth or for the integrity of its basic life systems. Concern for Peace and Justice in the human order have eliminated serious concern for Peace and Justice in human-Earth relations.

The type of change taking place and its order of magnitude are both incomprehensible to our basic religious and cultural institutions. These institutions were born into a functional world ever renewing itself in its seasonal cycles. They cannot understand a universe passing through a vast sequence of irreversible transformations and eventually producing Earth as a privileged planet. A planet so intimately woven together that all its members are immediately present to and dependent on each other. So, it can remain and renew itself indefinitely if only the parts each fulfill their own proper role in the functioning of the whole.

By some mysterious guidance deep within themselves the components of the planet found their inner dynamism in relation to each other. Each found its niche. But, then came the human — a being that must find its proper niche not simply through instinctive processes or limited forms of natural selection but, to some extent at least, by reasonable choice.

In the earlier stages of development, humans seemed to be capable of responding to the demands made upon them in the functioning of the whole. The planet was a community of beings speaking to each other in a vast sharing of existence. Each member of the outer world was addressed not as "I" but as "Thou" with the reverence always due to a power presence. Everything lived in communion with a Spirit Power present as an ultimate controlling force throughout the entire range of phenomenal appearances. That early humans lived in a certain intimacy with the surrounding world was due to their splendid intuitive insight and the comprehensive range of their vision. They were not yet afflicted with the analytical reductionism of rationalistic science. They knew that all beings were dependent on each other.

This situation was disturbed rather early in the course of the civilizational process although it did not reach its virulent phase until the industrial period of the past few centuries. When industrial plunder reached its climax in the twentieth century, we began the definitive termination of the Cenozoic period. It is one of the strangest moments in the entire history of the planet.

We are creatures of that lyric Cenozoic age when, for sixty-five million years, a sequence of life transformations took place that shaped the most beautiful forms that the Earth has yet known; the world of flowers and birds and insects, the mammals, then the anthropoids, and finally ourselves — the latest of the species brought into being at the end of this remarkable phase of Earth development. Creatures of the Cenozoic, we became destroyers of the Cenozoic.

We could have found our niche and accepted the limitations of Earthly existence. We could have advanced our human mode within the Earth's community of life systems. To some extent this was done, but from an early period, there seems to have been an inability for humans to expand their civilizational structures within the harmonies of the surrounding world. We soon began to assume that human well-being, or assumed human well-being, could exist only by a progressive stress upon the natural life systems of the planet.

All of this brings into question the conditions under which the human is a viable species:

- the possibility of human technologies that would be integral with Earth technologies
- a population level of humans that would not exceed what the natural systems of the planet could sustain
- an area suitable for human habitation that would allow the abundant territory needed by the other living species
- occupations that would provide the proper outlet for the creative talents of people
- a level of conflict that might be acceptable between various social groups
- a possibility of moving from a humanly controlled democracy to a fully participatory *geo*cracy — a government that would accept full participation by every component of the Earth community.

The ultimate challenge to our present human situation is the possibility of establishing a functional community based on qualitatively differentiated allegiances. Above all there is need for allegiance to the integral functioning of the planet. This will depend on our capacity for accepting the universe community as our primary referent with regard to reality and values — for Earthly beings the Earth in its integral functioning must be our immediate referent. Also, there is a need to realize that each being in the universe has multiple modes of experiencing itself.

So, for the human, there is the self of the individual, the family self, the community self, the human self, the Earth self, and the universe self — all of which are the multiple modes of a single person. An individual oak tree has its individual mode of being, and it is also a mountain being or a valley being according to its geographical position. It is also a life being and an Earth being as well as a universe being. Yet it remains one being throughout this variety of modalities.

In each instance, the higher self is the higher reality and the higher value. The ultimate order is that of mutual dependency. The well-being of the Earth is a condition for the well-being of everything on the Earth. Correspondingly the well-being of the various components of the Earth is a condition for the well-being of the Earth. The economic well-being of the Earth is a condition for the well-being of the human economy, and a disordered human economy will surely disturb the Earth economy. From this it is clear that a disturbance anywhere in any sequence of relationships is felt throughout the entire life pattern. It is no wonder that our assault upon the Earth is associated with an assault on the entire society to which we belong as well as with an assault upon ourselves — addiction.

Presently all the creative forces of human society have begun to move from the terminal Cenozoic into an emerging *Eco*zoic as the only context for human survival. The basic supposition is that we recognize and accept our own position as a dependency. It has been the supposition of people everywhere that we live in an entrancing universe, but that we cannot deal with life simply with our own powers. We need the more ultimate powers of the universe as these are manifest in the vastness of the sky above and by the magnificence of the Earth with its expansive land and its turbulent seas, with its awesome mountains and its luxuriant valleys, and with its arctic ice as well as its tropical forests.

If this ultimate power pervading the universe has its benign aspects, it also has its terror — its volcanic eruptions, its clashing and rifting of continents, its violent winds, its droughts, and its starvation. The seasons of life and death. But amid all of the destruction experienced by the Earth, the planet flourishes with overwhelming grandeur. Both life and death are caught up in the entrancing experience of existence itself.

There is, indeed, an inescapable price to be paid. Death is the price for life. Yet, there is unending celebration that we witness in the soaring flight of the birds, the quiet drifting of the fish through the sea, the springtime blossoming of ten thousand varieties of flowers, the exuberance of people everywhere — their endless songs and celebrations, their ritual dances, their art and poetry. All these express not exactly the triumph of life over death but the assertion of the deepest mystery of things that is beyond life and death, beyond calculation by humans. The urgency of celebration is the primordial spontaneity in every mode of being.

It is this primordial and sustaining awareness that is referred to in this book as the Originating Mystery that must be accepted as the ultimate referent in our efforts at recovery from our addiction. We must accept 'this primordial Spirit presence as the ultimate governing force within us, which expresses itself within us through the archetypal world of the collective unconscious. This cultural DNA expressed in all cultures is not contained fully or exhausted by the full complex of cultures. It is always available — immediately available. It offers the guidance and evokes the psychic energy needed at this time. We only need to respond to its presence. Often this guidance comes to us in dreams — sometimes our nocturnal dreams and sometimes in those extraordinary visionary moments while we are awake, mostly when we witness some of the more dramatic phenomena of the natural world.

In any case the ultimate force at work is that same Spirit sought by the Plains Indians in their Vision Quest. Only when we experience this transforming presence and awaken to its symbolisms are we likely to receive the psychic energy we need to give up our addiction and to proceed with the renewal of our individual lives, the revitalization of the human social order, and the inauguration of a mutually enhancing human presence to the Earth community.

When these events take place, we will have begun a successful transition from the terminal phase of the Cenozoic into a new age of individual fulfillment, cultural creativity, and planetary renewal. The emerging *Eco*zoic period of Earth history will have begun. As with origin moments generally, this is a supremely sacred moment.

Thomas Berry
Riverdale Center
for Religious Research
New York, New York
July 1990

PREFACE

NOTES TO THE READERS

Concerning gender-biased language — while I have made every effort to use inclusive language throughout the text, I do not feel justified in changing the language in the quotations that I have used. I ask the reader to understand that wherever inclusive language is not used in the writings of others, *my understanding* of those statements is inclusive. I therefore ask the reader to "translate" those quotations into inclusive language.

When this book goes into print, I shall be in the thirteenth year of recovery from an addiction pathology. During that time, I have gained a deep insight into the nature of addiction. The second half of those years was spent studying with Thomas Berry at his Riverdale Center in New York. The two experiences come together in this book. It is the joining of those two experiences that has given me, I think, a somewhat unique viewpoint concerning western culture — a viewpoint that I am trying to share with others here.

I admit that I am trying to encourage you to see and experience in a particular way. I think all authors are attempting to do the same in one way or another. In our day, it has become stylish to pretend that we are simply "providing information" and thus not attempting to influence our readers. In light of our new cosmology, this pose of objectivity is exposed as the fraud that it is. Even when we "just present information" our subjective choices of what information we present betray our purposes in presenting it — we and our beliefs are part of the process.

I would rather own up upfront that I am attempting to show you something. What is that something? It is threefold:

1. I believe that the one common denominator in symptoms of our cultural pathology is a lack of respect for living things and for the living planet that brings them forth.
2. I believe that most cultures have lost their spiritual moorings

which would have guided them into a deeper respect for the multiplicity and autonomy of living things.

3. I believe that western cultures are functioning within the context of addiction. Those cultures that are not yet addicted will become addicted unless we own up to the "bankruptcy" of our value system and become willing to be changed by an individual and collective spiritual experience.

In reading the *Twelve Steps of Ecological Spirituality*, the reader might come up against issues that s/he disagrees with. I encourage you at first to take what fits and leave the rest. One cannot understand this book by reading it. In taking the Steps, and only in taking the Steps, can we come to understand. I trust that, having taken the Steps, many will come to see the objectionable issues in a new light. In that new light, I also trust that the reader will come to see why I included all of the seemingly disparate issues that I have grouped together here.

In his brilliant and timeless poem "Theory Of Truth," Robinson Jeffers asks this question:

Why does insanity always twist the great answers?

Then he answers it himself:

Because only tormented persons want truth.

This book is the product of two personal torments of mine, and the search for truth predicated by them. The first is the pain of my own recovery and growth from addiction. The second is the knowledge of the sort of planet my children will inherit. So, I offer you the product of the search. That which is helpful, please consider your own — that which might be twisted by my own insanity, please forgive.

ACKNOWLEDGMENTS

To the Originating Mystery, the universe, the Earth, wind, rain, sky, and soils. To the lessons positive and negative learned from family. To people like Manny Silva whose decency could go unnoticed. To Kent and Lynne Evans and to many of their colleagues. To Matt Fox who broke new ground. To Brian Swimme and to Thomas Berry who helped me to make the story my own. To Andrew and Brian Wallas for their financial help. To my editors, Ginny Borden and Brian Wallas. To Brian and Shirley Wallas for so many kinds of help in so many different ways for so many years. Most of all I thank them for their first born daughter. To Sal and Jim. To Pat and Moo. To so many "friends of Bill" who have helped over the years. To Pat and Richard Payne.

To those who have opened doors throughout the years both to their hearts and to opportunities. To my present neighbors who share life day by day. To poor man Stan who serves the poor of Francis. To Ernest Boaten and Marlene Sheridan. To John Morin and Bill Ready and all those who have supported *Greenspirit*. To Dan Deveau, Ed Allen, Lex Kirk, and Gerry Auger.

To Carol, my best friend, who laughs with me and who has brought me most of what is good in my life, especially my children, I love you so. And to my children . . . to Becky whose birth into my hands opened the divine feminine to me and whose tender and burning heart has taught me more of compassion than all the scriptures I have ever read, I love you so. To Katie, offspring of my soul, born into my hands, whose bright blue eyes are a window to Paradise, Daddy loves you so.

To one and all
and to the many I have not mentioned by name . . .
Thank You.

THE TWELVE STEPS OF ECOLOGICAL SPIRITUALITY

1. We admit that we are powerless over an addicted society, that our lives and all of life have become degraded.
2. We come to acknowledge the existence of an Originating Mystery accomplishing the evolution of the universe. We accept that, if allowed, this Originating Mystery will reveal to each of us our natural relationships to self, to others, to other species, to the Earth and to the universe.
3. We decide to surrender our lives and our wills to this Originating Mystery, whatever we choose to name it.
4. We examine ourselves, listing all our attitudes and actions that damage the created order, thereby stopping or impeding the emergence of this Originating Mystery.
5. We acknowledge to ourselves, to that Originating Mystery and to another person, the specifics of our illusory thinking, attitudes, and behavior.
6. We become entirely willing to have all habits of illusion removed from our thoughts, our attitudes, and from our behavior.

7. In humility, we request that this Originating Mystery remove all our habits of illusory thought, attitude, and behavior.
8. We make a list of all persons, all other species, and all the life systems of the planet we have harmed and become ready to do everything in our power to heal them all.
9. We make a strenuous effort to heal all phases of the created order — human, animal, or planetary — injured by our illusory thinking, attitudes, or action.
10. We continue on a daily basis to go on examining our thinking and our actions as to whether they foster or impede the emergence of life. Where they impede this emergence, we admit it and become willing to be changed.
11. We continue through physical-mental-spiritual disciplines to so change ourselves as to improve our own ability to foster the emergence and health of the whole created order.
12. Having experienced a reawakening to self, to humanity, to all species, to the planet, and to the universe, we try to spread this awareness to others and to practice these disciplines in all phases of our lives.

THE TWELVE STEPS OF ALCOHOLICS ANONYMOUS

1. We admitted we were powerless over alcohol — that our lives had become unmanageable.
2. Came to believe that a Power greater than ourselves could restore us to sanity.
3. Made a decision to turn our will and our lives over to the care of God *as we understood Him.*
4. Made a searching and fearless moral inventory of ourselves.
5. Admitted to God, to ourselves and to another human being the exact nature of our wrongs.
6. Were entirely ready to have God remove all these defects of character.
7. Humbly asked Him to remove our shortcomings.
8. Made a list of all persons we had harmed, and became willing to make amends to them all.
9. Made direct amends to such people wherever possible, except when to do so would injure them or others.
10. Continued to take personal inventory and when we were wrong promptly admitted it.
11. Sought through prayer and meditation to improve our

conscious contact with God, *as we understood Him,* praying only for knowledge of His will for us and the power to carry that out.

12. Having had a spiritual awakening as the result of these steps, we tried to carry this message to alcoholics, and to practice these principles in all our affairs.[1]

The Twelve Steps are reprinted with permission of Alcoholics Anonymous World Services, Inc. Permission to reprint and adapt the Twelve Steps does not mean that A.A. has reviewed or approved the contents of this publication nor that A.A. agrees with the views expressed herein. A.A. is a program of recovery from alcoholism — use of the Twelve Steps in connection with programs and activities which are patterned after A.A., but which address other problems, does not imply otherwise.

INTRODUCTION

The industrial world is a kind of entrancement, a pathology.
It's addictive. We become addicted to automobiles. It's paralyzing, because once we're totally caught up in it, we think
we can't do anything about it. We have a type of religious
commitment to the industrial world. And that's the difficulty
now: these new movements to strengthen the corporate enter-
prise by what they call "humanizing" it are giving it a human
mission, a mythic dimension. All their advertising goes deep
into the deepest motivations of the human psychic sense; they
use children, the home, religious festivals, everything is used
– but that moves us from disaster to disaster, because the
process itself is pathological, suicidal.

Thomas Berry[1]

There is only one problem: everything! We like to talk about the
ecological problem, the nuclear problem, the drug problem, the
family problem, the violence problem, the alcohol problem, the
species extinction problem, and so on as though each of these
were separate and distinct pathologies, each unrelated to the other.
There's really only one problem. It's the way we live. The Earth
has only one problem. It's the way we live. We suffer from a deep,
cultural pathology.

Industrial culture has a bad chemical dependency problem.
Internally, within our bodies, we call it the drug and alcohol
epidemic. Externally, outside our bodies, it's the pollution problem — the two faces of one problem, a toxic human on a toxic
planet. Our attempts at detoxifying individuals and returning them
to a sick culture can be compared to wringing out a sponge and
tossing it back into the sea. We know how to treat individual
addiction. Alcoholics Anonymous (A.A.), and the programs
spawned by it, can provide us with individual answers. We have
come to understand the family systemic problem. Adult Children
of Alcoholics (A.C.O.A.) can provide help there. However, we
need to move into recovery *as cultures*. We need to detoxify the
planet! **Greenspirit** is that final stage of recovery. **Greenspirit** is a
cultural therapy and therefore a planetary therapy.

Addiction and perhaps all obsessive/compulsive disorders are the
"tip of the iceberg" of a potentially fatal malaise. The disease is

plagueing western culture and indeed the whole planet. It expresses itself in a pernicious relationship between western culture and the planetary life systems within which our culture has its context. This is also true of eastern and African cultures to the extent that they have adopted western economic procedures and the addictive lifestyle that results from those procedures. Addicts are merely the first, and most obvious signs, of this illness — the first cells to exhibit the disease when the whole body is becoming sick. Addicts are the whistle preceding the freight train that is about to collide with our whole way of life. Western culture is addicted to consuming. Western culture has an illness of spirit, mind, and body. Its name is *consumerism*.

Chronic intoxication of the bodies of many addicts eventually results in secondary diseases of the spirit, mind, and body. Most of these, like the parent disease, are progressive, ending eventually in death. Cynicism, depression, despair, hatred, violence, rape, suicide, crime, liver and heart disease, and stroke are a few of the diseases associated with chronic substance abuse. The chronic toxification of the planet, and the meaningless consumer lifestyle that engenders it, are creating secondary diseases as well. Among them are: loss of authentic functional contact with religious traditions, fundamentalism, an inability to believe in anything beyond the self, as well as many other spiritual and moral autisms. Sadly, these are just a few of the secondary maladies associated with cultural addiction: rabid nationalism as well as the inability to have any pride whatever in one's national heritage, television stupor, boredom, a life spent in fantasy, negative humor and deep cynicism, selfishness, infantile dependence on spiritual, economic, or political leaders, divorce, birth defects, sexual irresponsibility, child molestation and other sexual dysfunctions, loss of the ability to parent, abortion on demand, nuclear suicide, topsoil loss, smog, polluted water, plundered habitat, scorched forests, and a spasm of species extinction. Each of them is progressive and potentially deadly to our spirit, our culture, and even to our planet.

For more than twenty years, the industrial nations have been aware of the vast damage done to our planet. We know that consumerism spreads and increases every year, that increased consumption leads to increased production, and that increased production leads to increased plundering of an already exhausted planet as well as to further pollution of the planet. We know that increased pollution leads to poisoning and death. Still we go on. Why? We can't stop. We are addicted. We are at a place in history where, if the planet is to survive, we must all cry out for survival. But to whom? To what?

Alcoholism, and the other names for addictions, might be misnomers for this illness of spirit, mind, and body. *Denialism* might be a better word for the real problem. Addictions of all kinds, alcoholism included, are symptoms of denial. Then, too, denial becomes a symptom of addiction. Denialism is an illness in that it is involuntary. People do not choose to die horrible, alcoholic deaths. Denialism and the addictions that result from it are not a *refusal* to admit to what is real, denialism is the *inability* to do so. Alcoholism results when a person denies reality by the use and abuse of alcohol. Consumerism results when individuals and nations deny reality, in particular planetary reality, by the use and abuse of all "consumer goods."

When people are conceived in, carried in, born into, and brought up within the context of denial, how can they know that? Confronted with the notion that they are not living in reality, what can they do but deny it? Denial is built into the very structure of their personalities. It is part of the very pattern of their thoughts and feelings. The pain of reality denied is the "reality" of addicts — that pain is handled by numbing. The drug of choice might be alcohol, compulsive overeating, compulsive shopping, or cocaine. Numbing of the pain, however, is always the unconscious goal. When we are not living in reality, we cannot form a real self. When addicts say "I," they are referring to the emptiness where an ego was supposed to develop. The word *ego* means *me*. What addicts experience in an addicted family is the denial of an ego — "I am not me" is closer to their truth.

My feelings don't matter.
My needs are unimportant.
I don't need to be held or encouraged.
I don't need to be loved.
I don't need to be told that my mother finds me handsome.
I don't need to be told that my father is proud of me.
I don't need anyone to stay with me when I'm sick.
I don't need bedtime stories.
I don't need lullabies when I am frightened.
I don't need to be tucked in.
I don't need protection from those big boys in the school yard; I'm a
  coward.
I don't need to have time for baseball.
I don't need encouragement when I'm rejected.

I don't need to feel included.
I don't need help and support in dealing with this pregnancy.
It doesn't matter that I'm being beaten breathless, and even bloody, by
my father.
It doesn't matter that my mother pretends to be unaware of what happens
to me.
I don't mind that my teachers call me stupid.
I must be stupid; I can't concentrate on anything.
I don't mind that the priests and brothers who teach me punched me
silly because I couldn't do my homework last night.
It doesn't matter that my teacher put his hand in my pants.
I'm not ashamed that I was relieved this morning when my mother beat
my sister instead of me.
I'm not hurt that my father told me not to bother him when I was telling
him that I wanted to be just like him when I grow up.
I'm not ashamed that he keeps telling me those jokes that I don't under-
stand.
I don't mind laughing over my feelings of confusion and disgust so as
not to hurt his feelings.

These and similar denied needs of a child brought up in an addicted
home are the underlying signs of a sickness that will eventually
bloom into full-fledged addiction in later life. Many addicts are
asked to believe in a God whose name means *I am*. How are they
to identify with, or cry out to, a God like that? Early on many find
that alcohol and/or drugs can take away the pain of "I am not."
    I wrote the following poem during my own drinking years.

ALCOHOLISM
A black hole in inner space
waiting
the size of a grapefruit
waiting
sheathed in many skins
like an onion
waiting
sheathed in many skins
like a cancer
waiting
spending my life
and
waiting
to be born.

When a child's very processes of thought and feeling are formed
in countless daily interactions with addict parents, a predisposition

to addiction is built right into that child's personality. That predisposition is the main way in which addiction is passed along from generation to generation. An adult child of addicts will feel most comfortable, *familiar*, in a marriage to another adult child of addicts. Their offspring will inherit the predisposition as their personalities are shaped within the environment of addiction. It is passed from personality to personality and thus, is contagious.

As it was denied in the parent's personality, so will it be in the child's. With denial in place, and all the pain attendant to it, another potential addict is born. Once the diseased mode of thinking is a part of the personality, it's only a matter of time until a substance or behavior is discovered that provides temporary relief. It is neither a crime nor a weakness to want to feel good — addiction is an attempt to do just that. It takes great strength to live in unreality. A bumper sticker puts it comically: "Reality is for people who can't handle alcohol." But there's nothing funny about addiction. It is *hell*.

ECOLOGICAL REALITY IS FOR THOSE WHO CAN'T HANDLE CONSUMERISM!

Because the whole syndrome of addictive thinking/feeling is built right into the personality of its victims, it is nearly impossible for addicts to "see" the illness. It is a disease that tells its victims that they don't have a disease — the disease of denial. It is like getting into your car to go looking for your car. What is needed is to realize that the way we think about driving must change; one must first stop, get out, look, and then realize that, in fact, one has found the car. Addicts must realize that *they* are their problem. They must come to see that their world, their whole mode of being, is deluded and is built on deluded assumptions. But all the while, their thinking is denying this! To realize that their thoughts are not to be trusted, that their perceptions are the cause of their difficulties, that their feelings are triggered by assumptions that are faulty at best, and that their "reality" is not real requires that they experience something more real than their experience of themselves. They need to get a glimpse "over the top."

I have spent ten years looking long and hard at my own addictions, as well as at addiction in general. I am convinced that the underlying precondition of all addiction, the "original sin" of every addict, is the dysfunctional family environment within which the addict experienced him/herself. This is true whether or not actual addictive drinking and/or substance abuse was taking place. Again, these are just symptoms of the cultural pathology that we all suffer from. This diseased thinking is passed on in active abuse or in unrecovered abstinence.

Addiction is a slow form of suicide — suicide on the installment plan. But death is as absolute whether it comes from a gun, a kitchen stove, an exhaust pipe on a car, a razor blade, a bottle, a needle, environmental pollution, or a nuclear explosion. Beneath all these forms of addiction-related suicide lies the perverse pleasure the addict feels in the destruction of the self. That pleasure comes from the internalized dysfunctional parents, experienced in the alcoholic/addicted family. Often the only approval that alcoholics/ addicts can give themselves is associated with their own self-destruction. This is as true for those who learn obsessive greed, consumerism, and competition as it is for those who learn substance abuse from their parents. It all ends in individual, cultural, and planetary death.

Again, I believe that the underlying cause of most addiction is dysfunctional relationships with one or both parents. It is very painful, though not impossible, to tamper with the relationships that provide the very foundation of a personality. The unconscious phenomenon of denial intervenes to provide a barrier that shields individuals from facing the possibility that their parents did not, or do not, love them. Worse, it sets up a barrier between the person and the realization that addiction is happening — the real dependency is on the denial. The drug or behavior of choice is used in order to deal with that first denial. To lose that drug is to feel the dreaded truth. So, a secondary denial is set up around the drug in order to prevent the truth about it from surfacing.

As the need for the substance(s)/behavior(s) of addiction becomes absolute, further denials take root in the dynamics of the personality. The loss of spiritual/emotional value is denied as the drug comes to be seen as the ultimate good and supply becomes the mono-value. The spouse leaves, blaming the addiction; the truth of that loss is denied. The children become afraid; that is denied. The job is lost and addiction is cited as the cause; that is denied.

With the loss of all values that could serve as healthy assumptions upon which to anchor the thought process, mental illness sets in. Not only is that denied, but with the daily blunting of the mind by use of the substance of addiction, the very ability to perceive the truth at all is diminished. Finally, the body gives out. If that is denied, then death is the only way out. And that is, in fact, the way most addicts die. Again, death is absolute, regardless of the means of death.

In a functional home, when the male and female phases of a child's psyche are loved into being by good parents — not perfect parents . . . good parents, most children develop normally. When they reach adulthood, there is a great likelihood that their internal male will identify with a loving God experienced as father. The well-loved internal female dimension of the psyche will identify with birthing and nurturing and will discover her identity in the Earth process experienced as mother. While the emphasis on one or the other might be different, this is true for both men and women. In other words, adult humans properly nurtured, have within the very structures of their psyches the potential necessary for a healthy faith in God and in the Earth. That person will love and feel loved by "Our Father Who Art in Heaven" as well as by "Our Mother Who Art the Earth." ("Our Father" has a maternal dimension and "our Mother" produces males as well as females. Our Father and Mother are really two aspects of the same Mystery.) The unfortunate souls who do not find that love, whose internal parents were not evoked by love, will spend life in a hostile world and in an empty universe. They will feel orphaned both by God and by the Earth. In attempting to comfort themselves, such people are in danger of becoming addicts. A society of such people is a society of addicts.

COLLECTIVE OR CULTURAL ADDICTION THE DILEMMA OF THE WESTERN WORLD

Addiction! There is simply no other way to accurately describe America's energy habit.
                                                            — Jeremy Rifkin[2]

The western industrial world is caught in the vortex of cultural addiction. The substance of abuse is all "consumer" products. We have lost our spiritual moorings, which, like it or not, are patrifocal. Our heritage is Judeo-Christian. But we have also lost our spiritual inheritance from our Mother. In the name of patriarchate, we have destroyed the native cultures under the sign of "progress." Father-spirituality mediates our relationship with Father. The native peoples and their cultures mediate our relationship with Mother. We, in the West, have for the most part lost both and find ourselves orphans. We deny that these losses are the real cause of our problems. To admit it would mean feeling the full brunt of our agony.

With the loss of our spiritual values, we are becoming mentally ill, autistic as a people. Governments have fed us paranoic visions of enemies that promoted our willingness to build defense systems that have threatened to kill, not only these supposed enemies, but ourselves as well. We have lived in denial that our weapons could mean suicide, preferring to believe in fantasies of survivable nuclear war. In these opening years of the 1990s, the nuclear threat seems an issue of the past. Still, we should remember that there are still thousands of warheads aimed in all directions. We should not let our denial creep in until *all* nuclear weapons are removed from the face of the Earth. We have been destroying the planet, believing all the while that a ruined planet doesn't mean a ruined human. The advertising industry has served as the denial mechanism here, always promising that the next product, the next "fix" will do the trick.

We watch the Earth sicken and die. Yet we know that we are the Earth, we are the soils, we are the water, we are the air. We see our children die of maladies directly related to poisoned water, soil, and air, and we deny. The medical establishment serves our denial here — it keeps promising a cure. We avoid the following question: "How will a species born of a healthy planet find a cure for itself within the context of a poisoned one?" We deny and deny and deny. We consume in order to forget. But, as we consume, we eat the poisons of our prior consumption. When we drink, we drink the poisons of our chemical waste dumps. When we breathe, we breathe the exhaust from our last dream car. Yet, because we need to consume more and more to dull the pain of our degraded existence, we are forced to drink our own death, eat our own death, and breathe our own death. Worse, we must deny while we watch our children eat, breathe, and drink their death. That calls for still other denials like these.

Everything's going to be O.K. This planet can take more than we've dished out.

The air really isn't poisoned; it's just over the cities. It's not the cause of lung disease.

It doesn't matter if all the water is polluted, we can buy filters. That way the poisons can't wash through my blood or get stuck in my liver.

It doesn't matter if we've lost two thirds of our topsoil. Science will be making artificial soils soon.

You can't tell me that cancers come from poisons in food.

It doesn't matter that we lose ten thousand species every year. Most of them were horrible insects anyway.

It doesn't matter that there are fewer and fewer beautiful places. I'll just move further north.

It doesn't matter that the rainforests are disappearing. People just like to make a fuss.

Sure the governments have been holding a nuclear gun to our heads, but they won't let it happen.

So what if I hate my work, I have two Japanese cars and a T.V.

It doesn't matter that I've had the psychic equivalent of a lobotomy in losing my imagination. The President says that things are getting better.

Teenagers commit suicide because they're lazy and can't take it.

My consuming, and the resultant pollution, isn't causing changes in the genetic code that results in wild increases in birth defects. Besides, with new in utero technologies, we can abort any imperfect people.

I didn't kill the native peoples.

I'm not miserable living like this.

I didn't make the world. I only work here.

It's not my fault.

In misunderstanding our Father, we destroy our Mother. But the planet is not only our body, she is also our psyche. She is the matrix of all that lives, the womb, the tomb, and again the womb. To use a Jungian term, the planet is the collective unconscious of the whole human family, of all of life. As we destroy the unconscious mind of the planet, we have less and less ability to interpret the signs that would lead us out of *hell* and into the *truth*. We arrive at the state wherein denial is not the *refusal* to tell the truth about reality, it is the *inability* to do so. We have built a culture against life, against the planet. The result is the same as in all addiction-pathologies: *pain*. The more we feel the pain, the more we consume. The more we consume, the more we are in pain. We are an addicted culture!

As a culture, too, we have considered the quick way out via nuclear suicide. We experience the "nothing," the emptiness, the lack of parents; we watch helplessly while we destroy ourselves as well as our beautiful planet. The advertising industry spends billions in a frantic attempt to keep us consuming. Our governments spend billions convincing us that the real problem is "over there." The religious establishment tiptoes around, enculturated and addicted, turning out the same old tune about justice as the equal distribution of goods among rich and poor. The real problem goes much deeper. What goods will there be left to distribute on a ruined planet? If we are to serve the poor, we must first serve them water — clean water. If we are to feed the poor, we must feed them untainted foods grown in untainted soils. If we are to see them thrive, we must serve the air they breathe, making the quality of that air our own responsibility. Especially if we are people who "believe in God, the Father almighty, *the Maker of Heaven and Earth*," we must begin making our actions conform to that belief.

Perhaps the only way out of our hell is to *see* the cancer that eats our bodies, our minds, and our spirits. It is the same cancer that eats the Earth. We need to break through our denial; we need to cry out from this planet, for this planet, as this planet. We need to see that in the same way that the psyche of any addict is formed, shaped in daily interactions with addict-parents, so have all our psyches been shaped by addicts to the consumer economy. We have been brought up to consume. We have been brought up to believe that more "goods" is the greatest good, when in fact, more goods might mean the death of the planet, which is our only good. The death of the planet would mean our own death as individuals, as cultures, and as a species. To bring up our children in the consumer society is to build their addiction and death right into the fabric of their personalities. We might just as well nurse them on heroin!

It is clear that the overproduction of everything that sustains consumerism is not only robbing the Earth of her raw *mate*rials, but also her ability to sustain future generations of humans, animals, and plants. Worse, overproduction is poisoning the very systems upon which the present population depends for life and health. Worse still, the present level of toxicity, which grows each year, is interrupting the genetic code in its ability to even produce healthy individuals in this or in future generations. Birth defects are on the rise in many species. Our sins are carved into the very flesh of all generations to come. Here are the real "sins of the flesh!" More is not better — more will end in none!

The next deodorant will not make us better people, it will destroy the ozone layer and give us skin cancer. The next automobile is not a sleek feminine seductress that will bring us to the very spasm of driving pleasure, it is a pollution-producing machine that is choking us as well as animals. The fast foods we are encouraged to overeat are killing us while eating them is killing the soils from which we are trying to feed the poor. The beer we drink seldom brings us to the mountains, more often it brings us to the gutter. Consumerism is killing us in mind, in body, and in spirit. The fantasy we buy from the advertising industry will not bring us to the promised land. Rather, it leads us from the promised land to a desert.

Consumerism, the addiction to consuming, is not making us happy; it is killing us. What we need to be happy is our Father and Mother; what we are getting is a degraded life on a desecrated planet. Like all children, we are happy when we are loved and miserable when we are not, regardless of how many "goods" we have. So the most pressing question becomes: "How do we find our Mother and Father again?" There is an answer: through an experience of transcendence, a rising above our pathology, a glimpse past our individual and collective denial. The next question is: "How will this be done?" The *Twelve Steps of Ecological Spirituality* will provide this experience and will guide us out of the addiction/neurosis in which we are trapped. But a word of warning: we must have arrived at a certain willingness to grieve in order for this to happen.

If the industrial process is a manifestation of cultural pathology, what is the way out? Father Berry gave his second and more surprising answer. "We need a deep cultural therapy."

Therapy for a stricken planet. Planetary therapy. Once I'd gotten over the surprise, it seemed a sensible answer. The source of our problems lay, after all, inside ourselves.

Anuradha Vittachi[3]

We must have reached the ability to acknowledge the deep disgust we feel for our way of life. We must wake up one day and realize that things are too crazy to go on. We must look at our children and grieve the loss of all the beautiful places that have been destroyed for a quick profit. We must be willing to feel the deep revulsion we deny for the way we have mauled and "malled" the land. We must weep for our teenagers who don't have the beautiful places we had in which to court. We must grieve the hideous world we have built for ourselves — a world of garish plastic shining through the filthy haze that we and all the animals are condemned to breathe. We must grieve the taste of our tap water. We must grieve the eroded soils; we must grieve the farmlands desecrated for profit. We must hit bottom, cry out for help, and admit the truth about western culture. We must see that individual, cultural, and planetary therapy is a "sensible answer" to our woes. Then, and only then, will recovery begin — this recovery will be nothing less than the *Second Western Renaissance*.

We can spark that renaissance, but it will not be a return to antique cultural forms. This Second Western Renaissance will be a moral reawakening to the life processes of the planet Earth. We will awaken to ourselves, to the other species, to the sunlight pouring through revivified air, and to the huge turning galaxy with its 250,000,000 year cycle. We will awaken to the whole universe of evolving and intelligent matter as well as to the generous and benign Mystery that engendered and is present to it all. In awakening to the Earth and to the Mystery, which engendered the universe, we will have found our Mother and Father again and will become happy children at home in our garden.

This renaissance can begin when we begin to come together in **Greenspirit** therapy groups. In those groups, the *Twelve Steps of Ecological Spirituality* can help us to gain the experience of transcendence — the "glimpse over the top" that we so sorely need. Such an experience will provide the hope of recovery from consumerism, individually as well as collectively. Then we can go forth into this Second Western Renaissance as friends of the Earth and friends of the universe. Thus, we shall go forth able to believe in the future of life.

CHAPTER ONE

The American mind resembles a glove compartment jammed
tight with useless junk that no one pays any attention to until
we consider cleaning it out; and even then, even as we wonder
why we so needlessly clog up our lives, unable to part with it
all, we just jam it back in its place.

Brian Swimme [1]

STEP ONE: WE ADMIT THAT WE ARE POWERLESS OVER AN
ADDICTED SOCIETY, THAT OUR LIVES AND ALL OF LIFE HAVE
BECOME DEGRADED.

Imagine the Earth without humans. In our fantasy, there are no
nation states, there are only continents and ocean. The sea is
muscular with life — turgid and swarming. Whales, too numerous
to count, spray fonts of ecstasy into the air. Schools of fish darken
the water and move, like the shadows of clouds move over the
April meadow. The water leaps, sparkling in the sunlight. Lush
foliage tumbles to and fro with the grand rhythm of the tides.
Everything eats everything else in this sea. Everything becomes
dung, composts, and is born again. All is pure and sweet. Daily
new profusions of life are flung upon the scene with a generosity
and abandon that is recklessness itself.

Imagine the air as clean and fresh as an April morning, totally
receptive to the entry of the light. Imagine a sky peppered with
the great birds of prey: falcon, hawk, condor, eagle, and many
others that we have never seen. Imagine flocks of smaller birds
moving across those skies like swarms of locusts, blanketing entire
landscapes when they alight. Imagine the din of numberless insects,
flashing and darting in the dawn of life — an endless abundance
of shapes and sounds, eating each other and in their turn, giving
themselves as food. Imagine the sun-sparkled fins of numberless
fish, leaping from water to light in the seas, the lakes, and the
rivers, taking their food in mid-air, and then splashing back into
the froth.

Beside a roaring stream, bears and cats wait. Then the fangs and
claws . . . a fish is flipped, flopping onto the bank. Deer and moose
move to the lake to drink. Their tongues and teeth froth green
from their Earth-breakfast. As their necks bend toward the blue

life-wash . . . as their tongues and lips feel the first coolness, a cat leaps! There are groans; there is blood. The great muscular hulk becomes food for mother and cubs. In the meadow, a mouse darts to and fro, shrieking in alarm. He is caught in the diving eye of a hawk. In seconds, the mouse has become food. By afternoon he'll be dung — by next week, grass in the belly of a bison. The planet is food. The whole of life eats herself and is eaten by herself.

There are herds on the plains that are so huge, their movement causes dust storms that block out the sun. They move over the land like a blanket, like the rippling skin of a horse. Wolves prowl the margins of the herd, pruning — eating the old, the sick, and the lame. These become wolf dung and then grasses to feed the young of the herd. The grass in the bison's belly is his grandmother. Other animals hop, crawl, or run . . . and there are millions of all of them. There are animals that move in sunlight; there are others that move in moonlight. There are nests, dens, aeries, and lairs that chirp, growl, and purr. In all of them, life is born, screams, sings out, and dies; it is eaten and is born again. Everything limits and is limited, balances and is balanced. Everything is the fulfilment of everything else. Everything educates, heals, and nourishes everything else. Everything is clean, edible, drinkable, and breathable. Everything acts in the great drama. All the voices sing in the planetary choir. Everything is both beautiful and dangerous.

Only the human can imagine a world without the human; only the human can reflect upon the whole of life. In fact, the human is just that — the whole reflecting upon itself. We are that species in which the Earth reflects upon herself. Isn't it sad that we must imagine a clean, vibrant world? Wouldn't it be wonderful to live in one? Perhaps it is the great calling of the human in the present age, to make our dream become our reality? Could the dream of the human be the dream of the Earth? What else is the human for?

Like all that lives, humans, and therefore human cultures, depend upon the life systems of the planet Earth. This might appear obvious, but as cultures, we seem to have forgotten it. Humans are a creation of the planet, not the other way around. In fact, the human is a very recent creation of the planet — an infant species. We are the baby of the Earth! But, in our short tenure on the planet, we have disrupted — severely disrupted — all the life systems of the Earth. This, in some ways, appears normal given the disruption any newcomer causes in any family system. However, in most families, the baby grows up and in so doing takes a place within the context of family life in a less disruptive manner. Most babies eventually make their contribution to the family into which they are born, enhancing the other members in some way. But the human does not seem to be growing up. The human seems to just keep on taking. In fact, the human seems to be a baby that can take the very life of its mother and is bent on doing so.

In our present mode of industrial exploitation of the Earth, we have built an economy against life. It has, for the first time in the Earth's history, become possible for one species to destroy all the life systems of the planet. Overproduction of "goods" — fueled by the overconsumption of "goods" — threatens the very systems we rely upon for life itself. We are children who demand more than their mother can provide; we are working her to death. It is as though we have taken our mother, opened up her veins, and are intent on living by sucking her blood until she dies. As individuals, many of us feel powerless to do anything, even as we watch the relentless assault on the planet take place. When the consumption of something, anything, is killing us and we cannot stop consuming it, we are addicted. Addiction is degrading. Addiction is slavery. Addiction is *deadly*.

Nearly everyone I know is aware that something is dreadfully wrong. We feel it individually, but the problem is collective — cultural — in its order of magnitude. We know that being aware is not enough. Pointing to a hundred ills and stopping there does not produce a single cure. The demonic lure of addiction is more powerful than knowing. The self-destructive impulse that lies at the root of all addictions condemns addicts to slow, ugly deaths. The chief pleasure that addicts experience in this living death is the perverse self-approval they feel in the self-affliction of it. Addiction takes everything from its victims.

Addiction is fourfold in nature.

1. It is *spiritual* in that it produces a progressive breakdown in the value system of the addict.
2. It is *emotional* in that it produces a progressive schism between the cognitive and affective phases of the psyche — feelings are denied.
3. It is *mental* in that it produces progressive dysfunction in the intellective phase of the psyche, and ultimately, insanity.
4. It is *physical* in that it produces progressive illness in the body, and ultimately physical death.

In other words, it is a progressive disease of the whole person.

Addicts *must* have the substance(s)/behavior(s) of addiction. Whatever values guided an addict prior to addiction must be abandoned if they conflict with the need to supply the addiction. Supply becomes the mono-value. No longer anchored to permanent values, addicts begin to exhibit bizarre behavior and other signs of mental illness. Wherever there is hope that the addict will acknowledge the real situation, ever-present denial will be there to cover it up. Most of the painful feelings, which would serve to signal the malady, are repressed. If the instinct for self-preservation is at the root of life, then we must consider insane those who systematically inflict this slow suicide upon themselves. If surrender of control does not take place, the advanced stage of addiction sets in — physical breakdown. Liver failure, obesity, internal bleeding, heart attack, rectal bleeding, stroke, overdose, chronic diarrhea, auto accidents, and suicide are just a few of the ways in which addiction destroys the body. No one is able to sustain the brutal beating of addiction indefinitely. In time, even the most rugged, the most hardy, will begin to go down to sickness and death. It is predictable and inevitable.

Deep, semi-conscious feelings of inferiority torture most addicts. These are accompanied and enhanced by feelings of fear, anxiety, defensiveness, impending doom, impotence, vulnerability, and ultimately of total despair. The typical compensating attitude is one of pride, egotism, and anger — functions that mask the addict's real situation from himself. Here is a person, ruined on every level of human life, insulted that someone would insinuate that there is a *problem*!

What of collective, or cultural, addiction? In their fine book *The Emerging Order,* Jeremy Rifkin and Ted Howard say this:

The massive overconsumption of the middle and upper classes is merely a symptom of a deeper disease. That disease is materialism in its truest sense.

— Jeremy Rifkin [2]

I think the word "overconsumption" is the name of our individual and cultural addiction. While I understand what they are getting at, the deeper disease — "materialism" — is I think, misnamed. If we were true *Mater*ialists, we would care about *mater*ials. Our very first concern in all decisions, individual or collective, would be the materials of the planet — the soils, the waters, and the air. The sad fact is that we care little for the materials because we care little for *Mater Earth.* Our rabid overconsumption of everything betrays our deep hunger for *Mater*. *Orphanism* is the name of the underlying cultural pathology. *Consumerism* is the addiction/symptom of that disease.

No permanent help can be given to an addict until withdrawal from the substance(s) of abuse is complete. This is obvious. The addiction/symptom masks the disease/cause. We must take away the mask in order to see the disease. When withdrawal is complete, the underlying pathology begins to express itself. Only when the pathology begins to "speak," from below the addiction, can therapy begin. Until then addicts, like everyone in Dante's hell, think they are pursuing their own greatest good.

Consumer-addicts believe that the freedom to consume is the true measure of success or a measure of personal worth. The smog gathers overhead, and still they insist that the automobile is essential to their well-being. They fear the taste of tap water, but insist that a better life will result from chemistry. In the United States alone, we lose five billion tons of topsoil each year. We know in our guts what that means, but insist that chemically stimulated agricultural processes are the way it has to be. All of this is denied and repressed, along with the wailings of the millions, mostly children, who die in the dust of dead soils.

Our shared body/soul, the Earth, is the ultimate referent for all productivity. Pure water becomes blood. Pure air is brought by that blood to all cells of the body. Pure soils become plants, and the flesh of the animals become our flesh. We are the Earth, and the Earth is becoming toxic — in*toxic*ated. We know that the poisoning is the result of the overproduction of "goods," and that overproduction supplies overconsumption. Still, we proceed because we do not know how to stop — we are addicted.

In the same way that an individual addict will resort to mugging in order to protect the vital supply of drug(s), so, too, do we as nations build ever more insane weaponry in order "to protect our vital interests" globally. What are these "vital interests?" They are the raw materials of underdeveloped countries. This cultural arrogance is the compensating attitude for our deep feelings of uneasiness about the way things are going, not only with soils, water, and air, but also with the cultures of our planet. "Protecting our vital interests" is a polite way of saying that we are willing to "mug" any country that will not give us a "fix".

As I mentioned in the introduction, the personalities of addicts are shaped, or even engendered, in daily interactions with addict parents. They are predisposed to, or programmed for, addiction.

If we are brought up by consumer addicts in the consumer culture, then our world is the world of the addict. We are told early on that the acquisition and consumption of "goods" and comforts is for our own greatest good. In fact, it is communicated to us at the level of unquestionable assumption. Growing from that assumption, our schooling trains us for twelve or more years to compete bitterly for goods and comforts. Meanwhile, our parents are slaving in the markets of the consumer society. We are given consumer goods instead of the presence of our good parents. When "goods" replace mother and father, we begin to suffer from *Orphanism* and become addicted to the "goods". We become addicted to *Consumerism*.

There are rituals surrounding all addictions. The collection and arrangement of bottles, the use of special glasses, the special seat, and the readying of the room are all associated with alcoholism, not to mention the gathering at a special place. The rolling of joints, the lighting of incense, and the sharing of special foods are associated with the smoking or use of drugs. Consumerism too has its rituals. "To go shopping" is to buy things that we do not need at the mall — the "cathedral" of consuming. There is the short-lived spasm, the "rush" or the "glow," associated with buying things that is not unlike the experience we have when using drugs.

"Shopping" is a recreational drug. We titillate ourselves by reading the ads, fantasizing all the while about how we will feel with our new things. We place in layaway the things we know we cannot afford. We go out in droves during the "high holy days" of consuming — Washington's Birthday is one; all the days of advent are others. The day after Christmas is very holy. There are Fourth of July sales, New Year's sales, Easter sales, back-to-school sales, and the list goes on. The whole notion of pilgrimage is present as well — the trip to New York, Paris, or London.

We must pay for what we overconsume. We are, therefore, forced to choose jobs that will enhance our ability to buy. Few of us can afford to choose jobs based on the desire to serve. The human service jobs or teaching jobs, low on the consumer ladder, are jobs for "suckers," for those who "can't do anything important."

Like the next drink for the alcoholic or the next fix for the junkie, we imagine that the next thing we buy will fill the aching hole within. Always, too, there is the morning after when we find ourselves deeper in debt and emptier than before. The sum total of our buying binges is to find ourselves feeling swindled. The missing father and mother within are still missing — the advertising was a lie. Worse, yet, what we really need — the internalized presence of "Our Mother Who Art the Earth," and "Our Father Who Art in Heaven," the two aspects of the one Originating Mystery — are no closer to home. So, we begin to think of buying the next thing.

As individuals, as nations, even as cultures, we are losing our values. Our churches, the cultural conscience, try to preach against consumerism, but many preachers are themselves consumer addicts and have no authority — no calling power. Many television preachers even measure God's love for us by our ability to consume. They associate arrogant, militant nationalism with God's will for the nation. In this way, they bring the power of religion to bear not on the protection of the planet, but on its destruction, and therefore, on the destruction of all who dwell therein. In doing so, they fuel the evil of consumer addiction. As we lose our values, we become more willing to do almost anything to each other and are willing to make almost any nation our enemy in order to protect our supply. Competition, the compulsive component of consumer addiction, is bred right into us. Competition and compassion do not easily cohabitate.

During the economic boom of the post-World War II era, marketing experts set out to get American consumers to buy and toss. In the mid-fifties marketing consultant, Victor Libow, wrote in the *New York Journal of Retailing*, "Our enormously productive economy demands that we make consumption a way of life, that we convert the buying and use of goods into rituals, that we seek pure spiritual satisfaction in consumption. We need things consumed, worn out, burned up, replaced, and discarded at an ever-growing rate."[3]

We are brought up to think of ourselves as consumers. This is the obsessive component of consumerism. A consumer is one who consumes, as though we were eating/defecating machines! No wonder so many of us feel bad about ourselves! We are taught that "to consume is to live." To lose one's job is the ultimate misfortune, a kind of death — the supply is cut off. More and more we become the pawns, the slaves of the pusher, and the employees of the multinationals. We become ever more willing to subvert our skills, talents, and creativity to assure ourselves of a job. We become ever more willing to live without roots as well.

To live uprooted means to live without contact with the deeper zones of ourselves — the places of wisdom. A "promotion," however, means an enhanced ability to consume. We leave our friends and cause our children to lose theirs. We move them from school to school, keeping them uprooted, training them to live without depth. In so doing, we teach them that consuming is, in fact, the mono-value. As wants become needs, the addiction in our thinking tells us that we need still more . . . and more! Our values become subverted to the mono-value, *money*. Personal values, familial values, communal values, and even national values are denied when they conflict with our craving to consume. So, when we find ourselves thinking about buying, unable to stop buying, unable to stop thinking about buying, terrified by the thought of losing the ability to buy, willing to do almost anything not to lose the ability to buy, willing to slave away in the name of debts that only grow larger, we would do well to give up and admit that we are powerless over consumerism — addicted — and that our lives have become degraded.

The following quotation from the *Bhagavad Gita*, a Hindu scripture, makes this clear:

Thinking about sense-objects
will attach you to sense-objects;
Grow attached and you become addicted;
Thwart your addiction, it turns to anger;
Be angry and you confuse your mind;
Confuse your mind, you forget the lesson of experience;
Forget experience, you lose discrimination;
Lose discrimination, and you miss life's only purpose.[4]

Our minds become diseased by consumerism. Consider the frantic, even hysterical, pace of the modern city. We have come such a distance from the natural rhythms of the planet that we actually think of ourselves as separate from them. We live crazed, so that once a year we can line up in the sweltering heat and carbon monoxide, in thousands of cars, bumper to bumper, in order to "get back to nature." We spend two weeks in the country, leave the landscape a desert of litter, and then line up again for our return.

While in the country, we insulate ourselves against the intrusion of any natural sounds that might cause us to remember. We bring radios and tape decks that blast noise pollution over all the beaches, the lakes, and throughout the forests. We crowd the lakes with speedboats that stink, pollute the water, and are noisy and dangerous. Because the madness is in our thinking, we bring the madness with us wherever we go. We cannot imagine life without our junk — we are junkies!

Yet there is a worse dimension to the madness. Like all addicts, we consider suicide. We do so individually. Suicide among the young increases as their experience in the natural world — their planet — decreases. Individual suicide, however, is only one symptom of our love of death. We consider suicide as a culture, as a species, as a planet! Even now, with the threat of war with the Soviet union less likely, we continue to amass weapons and brood over them as we consider their use. We have adapted to living life with a gun at our heads. The only limit to the insanity of addiction is death. Our leaders test that limit — nuclear policy, whether for bombs or for "peaceful purposes," is logical madness.

Our bodies are breaking down under the strain of the intoxication of our shared body, the Earth. We know that poisoned air, water, and soil will kill us and our children, as well as the animals and their offspring. We know that cancer and many other degenerative diseases are epidemic. We are stunned into silence while "developers" (ponder the denial in that word!) destroy the natural habitat nearly everywhere for a quick profit. There are fewer beautiful places, and the ones that remain are more crowded and grow filthier. While insisting that the drug we are using helps us to live well, we are addicts who watch ourselves bleed and atrophy. We need to wake up, come out of our coma, and admit that our mythic fixation with "progress" is turning the entire planet into a garbage heap. We must admit that we are powerless over consuming, and powerless over the consuming society — addicted.

Powerless? Are we really powerless? Can you provide your own food? Can you provide your own fuel? Can you provide yourself with clean water? Can you provide you own clothing? Can you live without an automobile? Can you provide your own music? We could go on and on, but it is unnecessary. The point is clear; we can neither provide for our needs nor for our wants. Nor am I saying that I think we should be able to do so. I am well aware that the division of labor is fundamental to civilization, and am merely pointing out how dependent we really are upon what others provide and how they provide it. Still, a final question should be asked. Do you feel any sense of personal power over your life by trying to stop the nuclear threat — bombs or power plants?

Is Our Life Degraded? *Look Around!*

We must surrender to the obvious if we are to live. The beginning of the cure is in the naming of the illness. In his daring book *People of the Lie*, M. Scott Peck says: "We cannot even begin to deal with a disease until we identify it by its proper name. The treatment of an illness begins with its diagnosis."[5] The name of the addiction that is killing the Earth is *consumerism*.

When we admit that we are addicted, a huge burden is lifted from our shoulders. We become released from denial and freed to do something about getting well. No longer are we doomed to wander, lost, knowing that something, that everything, is wrong but not knowing what to do about it. We are able to move toward the answer. As we do so, we will be moving toward a renewal of the vision we shared at the opening of this chapter. We will be building a world in which our children can wander in the woods, enchanted by the sounds of birds and insects. We can walk along streams with them and scoop water to drink up into our hands. As they splash it to their mouths, we will see them stare skyward through the trees, stunned and overwhelmed with the goodness of being young and healthy on a young and healthy planet. They will need to be protected from the larger animals in the forest, for these too will be in a state of renewal and revivication. Cats and wolves and other animals of prey will prowl again. Life will be life again. The Earth will be radiant again. Our first concern will be the safety of the children and the animals. Only after that will we even consider the comforts of those already pampered.

We need not fear that there will be no cure, or that it is "too late." We can look back over some fifteen billion years of evolution, four billion years of the Earth's evolution, and see the stupendous creativity which engenders it all. And not only that! We shall come to understand that the creation itself rests upon an infinite uncreated potential. And . . . we shall come to see that we — humans — are the valve through which the uncreated becomes actual! We are co-creators with the Originating Mystery.

We will be able to see that there has been something beautiful in our own unfolding, from the joining of two cells to adulthood. In seeing that, it will be easy to admit to the existence of some sort of Originating Mystery, or whatever we wish to name it. With this dawning hope, we can move on to Step Two.

The day is not far distant when humanity will realize that biologically it is faced with a choice between suicide and adoration.

— *Teilhard de Chardin*[6]

In taking STEP ONE we say before our group: "I admit that I am powerless over an addicted society, that my life and all of life have become degraded."

CHAPTER TWO

Allah has brought you forth from the Earth like a plant and to the Earth he will restore you. Then he will bring you back afresh. He has made the Earth as a vast expanse for you so you may traverse its spacious paths.

The Koran[1]

STEP TWO: WE COME TO ACKNOWLEDGE THE EXISTENCE OF AN ORIGINATING MYSTERY ACCOMPLISHING THE EVOLUTION OF THE UNIVERSE, AND ACCEPT THAT, IF ALLOWED, THIS ORIGINATING MYSTERY WILL REVEAL TO EACH OF US OUR NATURAL RELATION-SHIPS TO SELF, TO OTHERS, TO OTHER SPECIES, TO THE EARTH, AND TO THE UNIVERSE.

We admitted in Step One that we find ourselves in an evolutionary impasse. The human, as a species, is pitted against the planet, and is being sucked into the vortex of individual and cultural addiction. We can now move on toward the solution to the problem. Be clear, *there is a solution!* In Step Two, we admit and accept that there is some Originating Mystery responsible for the marvelous unfolding of all the forms of evolution: cosmological, geological, biological, psychological, and cultural. It makes little matter what name we use for this Originating Mystery. The Originating Mystery seems much more tolerant of the different names than some theologians, and would-be theologians, would have us think. We have good reason for hope, and we begin to feel it.

If the impasse — or the denial of it — is broken and evolution is unblocked, this Originating Mystery can and will provide answers. These answers will lead us out of our present dilemma. If we consider, even for a moment, the vast creativity expressed in twenty billion years of evolution, the problems we face on this planet that loom so ominous, shrink to near insignificance. If the universe can create the Earth, then the universe can heal the Earth. For this to happen, however, it is necessary that we humans know the whole story — the story of the cosmos, of the Earth, of life, and of culture. We need to know the "New Story."

THE "NEW STORY"

> In the cosmos as I describe it here, it becomes possible, strange though the expression appears, to love the universe. It is indeed in this act alone that love can develop in boundless light and power.
>
> — *Teilhard de Chardin*[2]

Before the beginning there must have been a potential, an uncreated universe in the dark nothingness of the beginningless and endless sea of the Originating Mystery. Out of this fecund and plenary emptiness there emerged, some twenty billion years ago, a stupendous explosion of light. This explosion of light, the *fireball*, erupted into being from plenary nonbeing and began expanding into being, creating by its expansion both time and space — space/time. Within seconds this energy began to cool into matter, creating the energy/matter that we know as the "stuff" of the whole universe, ourselves included.

> What is implied by this proposal is that what we call empty space contains an immense background of energy, and that matter as we know it is a small "quantized" wavelike excitation on top of this background, rather like a tiny ripple on a vast sea.
>
> In this connection it may be said that space, which has so much energy, is full rather than empty.   — *David Bohm*[3]

Energy/matter was a manifestation of the Originating Mystery. In fact, this energy/matter, the universe, is the primary revelation of the ultimate mystery that we are here calling the Originating Mystery. All other revelations of the Originating Mystery are functions of this first revelation: *the universe itself*. This revelation continues to express itself at this moment in you.

So, as the energy of the fireball cooled into energy/matter, this inherent Originating Mystery continued to express Him/Her/Itself in the phenomenon called self-organization. Tiny particles of this energy/matter — quanta — began to organize themselves into communities called atoms. Now, these tiny communities were not, as is often imagined, dead balls of matter bouncing off one another, indifferent and inert. Rather, they were tiny psyche/particles that grouped together not out of blind determinism, but with a certain freedom. True, this freedom was circumscribed by probability, but not just any quanta would group with just any other quanta. Furthermore, not just any proton/neutron couple would accept just any electron into their company. But when they did join, the proton joined to the neutron became one, a new kind of psyche/particle! The new particle had properties about it that caused it to welcome only certain electrons into the community. When this happened, again, a new particle was the result! We call this an atom.

The newborn universe continued to expand from the common point of its emergence. The billions and billions of particles of primordial matter began to self-organize themselves into gigantic nations called *galaxies*. A galaxy, like an atom, though huge, exhibits a psychic as well as a material phase. Another way of putting it is, galaxies have souls. We can "see" the underlying shape, or field, or soul, because we see the particles that exhibit that shape. So, the Originating Mystery exhibits its being in the shape of things.

Within the great nations of the galaxies, cities of primordial matter began to take shape; stars were born. This self-shaping we call gravitational accretion. "To accrete" means to gather to one-self. A star is an accretion of particles, which, as more and more are gathered, begin to be highly compressed. The more the numbers multiply and are compressed, the more the whole city begins to heat up. When a certain threshold of compression is reached, the city erupts into fire. In its burning we see the return of energy/matter into energy. This accretion-compression-burning is the process through which the stars are willed aflame.

As the star burns, much of the energy/matter is converted back into energy. The remaining "ash" of the star begins to flare up in the same way as when a piece of wood or coal gets hottest — it releases the most energy just as it is about to become ash. In this way, the ember-star flares up and gives off a tremendous amount of energy. This is called the *nova* phase of the star. Soon after this flare-up the ash begins to collapse upon itself and turn to dust. In this collapse a wonderful process takes place. As the ash gathers tighter and tighter into a fist, the ash "composts" into all the minerals that we know are necessary to life: carbon, calcium, zinc, magnesium, and so on. Finally, gold is formed at the very core of the compost-star. When the fist can no longer gather itself any tighter, it explodes "gifting" the universe with its whole self, strewing the metal-rich soil of itself into space in great clouds of psyche/powder.

In time, the psyche/powder begins to self-organize again. Once more, we see the Originating Mystery begin to exhibit itself. These great clouds of metal-rich dust, these cities within the nation of the galaxy, begin through accretion, to reshape themselves into new, second-generation stars. A once dead star has risen from the dead.

Our nation, in the great empire of space, is called the Milky Way. Our sun and solar system, the local neighborhood, were all formed together from the dust of a dead first-generation star. The sun/planets system was formed of a single cloud, and was the resurrection phase of a former star. We call this one cloud the proto-solar nebula — a fancy name for a pre-sun dust cloud. The nucleus of this swirling cloud became the sun. The remainder of the dust formed into ten belts of dust whirling around the sun. Nine of these belts formed planets. One of them became the asteroids. The third planet out from the sun is our house and home, the good Earth. In imagining the sun and Earth forming from a single cloud, we can learn a great deal about ourselves.

In each of us, regardless of sexual identity, there seems to be an active as well as a receptive characteristic. In Jungian psychology, the active is called Animus and the receptive, Anima. The proto-solar disk exhibited these same characteristics. Out of *one* disk made of *one* substance, the sun, or active principle, expressed itself. From the same dust cloud, the Earth, or receptive principle, emerged as well. The sun gives light and the Earth receives it. Then the Earth fashions life from light and becomes active in birthing life. Life *is* the relationship between the Earth and sun in the one solar system. We are the conscious phase of that relationship. Back to the story . . .

When a sufficient amount of energy/matter had self-organized at the nucleus of the proto-solar disk, it again began to heat up. This heating up resulted in the sun that we see, feel, and love in our sky — a sun that gives light and life to the whole Earth. Each of the planets also tried to become suns. They were too small and couldn't get hot enough. But, they did heat up — the Earth's center is still hot. They tried but eventually gave up the hope of stardom and became the planets we know and love today.

Our house is the third up the street from the sun, and a beautiful home she is! From the moon, we saw her face, young and radiant behind her blue-and-white veil. She's the nicest house on the block, the only one that is a real home for life. Look at her! See how radiant she is? That radiance is her soul, the self-organizing Mystery that gathered so much primordial matter to form her body. The other planets have their own beauty, each and every one, but only ours lives.

How clever she is — she gathered herself in space. She literally "pulled herself together"! As the primordial matter accreted in space, her core was formed. As more and more was gathered, the weight pushing down upon the core increased, causing it to heat up. When still more was added, the heating up became explosive. In fact, the whole infant-Earth was boiling hot.

But, in time, the outer surface of our Earth began to cool in the surrounding coldness of space. Her heart remained afire nonetheless. Over and over again, tantrums of hot lava came splashing up, smashing the thin crust. Another thin shell would form . . . barely . . . and then . . . crash! Still, in time, the surface did cool enough to allow a permanent crust to form. Beneath this crust, the mantle of the Earth remained warm and pliant like dough. Even today, the hot heart of the planet sends up spouts of fury from the volcanoes that break through mantle and crust alike and pour over the crust of the Earth to cool and become new soil.

During this time, when the great shouts of heat were screaming up from the core, some other things were happening. The sun was growing brighter and brighter. The moon was turning cooler and cooler and finally turned cold. On our Earth, wonderful things were going on. Just as in January when you yell to a friend and see your own breath go white before you, in the same way, volcanic shouts from the hot Earth gave off steam and gases with every tantrum. This steam rose from the hot body of the Earth and ascended to cool in the surrounding winter of space. As this happened, clouds formed and the rains came, further cooling the crust and causing it to wrinkle and buckle into mountains and valleys. The deeper wrinkles became the ocean basins and were, in time, filled with rain. The steam and other gases became the primitive atmosphere of the Earth. The body/soul of Earth "knew" how to form air and water and did so.

In the same way that the quanta, subatomic psyche/particles, knew how to self-organize into tiny atomic communities in the early universe, so too, these same atoms knew how to form more complex communities called molecules. The fields of the whole group of atoms would co-join to form a new field — the "soul" of a molecule. Again, the Originating Mystery revealed itself in the material organization of the molecule; then molecules began to attract other molecules and mega-molecular communities resulted. Matter was complexifying and, therefore, so was the Originating Mystery exhibited in that complexification.

At some point, and no one can say for sure exactly how or when, another phase of complexification/evolution was evoked. Most

think that a combination of geo-thermal, solar, and lightning energies sparked the mega-molecules into life. In other words, the
complexification of psyche/matter "boiled over" into a new phase
of the evolution of the universe — life. The Originating Mystery
revealed itself as capable of living. The earliest forms that life
assumed were single-celled beings called *prokaryotes*. These
nucleus-free beings would alter the entire atmosphere of the Earth
preparing the planet for the higher, oxygen-breathing life forms.

The emergence of life was the next phase in the fabulous
creativity that began when the potential universe erupted into
actuality in the fireball. Where have we come so far?

1. Potential, nothingness changed state when actuality, some-thingness
   erupted from it as a fireball.
2. Energy changed state and cooled into psyche/matter.
3. Psyche/matter arranged itself into galaxies.
4. Within galaxies, stars were formed, burned, died, and rose from the
   dead to form second-generation stars such as the sun/planet system.
5. Our planet took shape along with the other planets in the presence of
   the gathering sun.
6. The Earth shaped herself, her landmass, her seas, and her air.
7. Life emerged from pre-life, probably in the seas.
8. Life began to co-evolve with pre-life.

The pre-living forms of the Earth shaped life while life changed
the pre-living Earth. Most important: *it was all one unbroken process.*

At first, life reproduced itself by division — one cell dividing
and making of itself two. Living matter was attracted to living
matter in the same way that nonliving matter had been. In time,
cells grouped into communities and began to function as a single
community. With the passing of still more time, these groupings
of cells learned to form internal subgroupings with each subgroup
performing specialized functions within the larger community.
Here, we see the roots of the division of labor. These specialized
functions became fins — now, psyche/matter could swim. Others
became eyes — now, psyche/matter could see. Some became lungs,
liver, and other organs. The Originating Mystery was learning to
move freely through water. Soon, it would walk and fly as well.

It wasn't long before matter became sexual in both plants and
animals. New life began to emerge from the union of two — a
male and a female — and the exchange of genetic material between
them. Thus, from one male component and one female component,
a new being with qualities of both, and something new as well,
came into being. With the emergence of sex, the Earth also

invented death. Otherwise, the constant emergence of new life would overpopulate the planet with too many members of all species. Death was not a punishment. It was an invention of the Earth, necessary to keep life fresh. But, as with the attraction of psyche/matter to psyche/matter since the beginning, so it was with sexuality. In the human, this attraction is called love. It is the truth of the human, as gravity is the truth of the whole cosmos.

In time, some fish were able to walk from the sea onto the land. So now the Originating Mystery was not only able to see but to walk. By now, the *prokaryotes* had prepared the air for breathing, and the land was a rich carpet of green plants that had themselves crept ashore earlier. In the green plants, the planet invented photosynthesis, allowing the Earth to capture and to hold the energy she absorbed from the sun. Life was explosive. The walking fish were able to eat the green plants, thereby eating the sun. In the same way as life began to be formed by the sexual union of one male and one female, so all of life was, and is formed, by the union of Father Sun and Mother Earth. The Earth seems to have exulted in all of this. Her exultation was expressed in the birth of flowers. In a very short time, the whole Earth was covered with the laughter of flowers.

The walking fish became lizards of various sizes, and the reptiles were "born." Earth went through her great reptilian youth and soon matured into marsupials and mammals. Earth-ecstacy was not confined to flowering plants — the reptiles too flowered into flight. The families of birds came to be, not to mention the myriad of flying insects. Soon, the great whales were shooting fonts of water skyward as they too experienced the exultation. All of this was a profuse outpouring of creativity and joy. The sun was eaten by the plants, the primary eaters ate the plants, and in turn were eaten by the carnivores. The omnivores ate flesh and plants. The whole Earth was eating the sunlight. All the beings of the Earth were eating the Earth. It was as though the Originating Mystery was saying through the planet: "Take, eat, this is my body. Take, drink, this is my blood."

All this time, while life was shaping itself in the one to two million or more species of plants and animals, the planet herself was also evolving and changing shape. At first, all the land mass that we know as the continents was gathered into one continent called Pangaea. There was only the rocking sea and one great continent, but, beneath the surface of the planet roared the old fires of the beginning. This central heating system of our house kept the mantle hot, plastic, and in a state of movement. It rippled over the core like the pelt of a puppy. This movement beneath the crust caused the crust to crack in the way the shell of an egg cracks when the chick is ready to emerge. In fact, the Earth at this time was like a not-completely-cooked boiled egg. The center was liquid, the mantle was sort of rubbery, and the thin shell was cracking. Between the cracks of the crust, the hot "yolk" of the planet would pour up from time to time. The several plates formed because the cracks were forced apart as the hot lava forced its way up between them. The various plates became the carriers of the continents.

On the surfaces of the continents, life arranged itself into large interacting systems called bioregions — regions of life. There are arctic and tropical, coastal and inland, mountain and flatland, river valleys, and desert bioregions. Each of these has its distinctive geological formations, climactic conditions, and living beings. Each bioregion is coherent within itself, while at the same time intimately related to all the others. Each bioregion is comprised of multiple *eco*systems — systems of life. These are areas wherein hundreds and frequently thousands of species of plants, insects, and animals interact as a mutually enhancing system. Ecosystems can be thought of as the organs in the greater body of the bioregion. Bioregion is another name for *biome*.

All ecosystems within bioregions are intimately related to all other ecosystems. Species evolve within the context of the eco-system, and thus, the ecosystem co-evolves with them. Species can be thought of as cells within the organ of the eco-system. While ecosystems evolve, so must the bioregions that contain them. While bioregions evolve, so must the continents that contain them. While the continents evolve, so must the planet on which they have their being. The evolution of the Earth is the evolution of the sun/planets system. The evolution of that system is the evolution of the galaxy. The evolution of the galaxy is the evolution of the universe. The evolution of the universe is the evolution of the immanent Originating Mystery that willed it into being. So, the Earth, within the solar system, is a self-emergent, self-nourishing, self-educating, self-governing, self-healing, and self-fulfilling community. All particular life systems, in their being, their nourishment, their education, their governing, their healing, and their fulfillment must integrate their functioning within this larger complex of mutually fulfilling Earth systems.

At this point in our story, we find the Earth a throbbing cell of life. Life moves in great swarms through the waters and the air, and stampedes over the land. Father Sun gives of his light and Mother Earth takes it in. She then turns light into life and pours it back again. The whole planet is covered with a carpet of life attracted to life, eating and creating life. The Earth is profuse, boiling with life. She is barking, belching, screeching, hissing, lowing, farting, purring, burping, howling, trilling, croaking, and more. Life is heating up . . . and . . . heating up. Suddenly, probably somewhere in what we call Africa, this heating up expressed itself in two or more individuals among the primates. Life was about to add laughter to her symphony of sounds.

Here, the evolution of the universe went through another phase change. Suddenly a species, and therefore the Earth and universe, emerged into self-reflection. Now, the Earth could think, and the universe curved upon itself to view its own beauty in the human. The Originating Mystery had evolved a species gifted with a freedom of will, a species that could make choices, a species with the power to decide. More incredible still, this species had the ability to call the vast uncreated universe into being. This being was to be a sort of valve through which the uncreated universe could flood into being. This being was created to be co-creator with the Originating Mystery.

Humans lived, like most primates, in clusters of families called tribes. Females were largely responsible for the birth and nurturing of the young as well as all other matters of the cave. The males were responsible for providing food from the hunt as well as for protection of the women and the young. All of this was adaptive behavior in that it provided for everyone's needs for food, protection, and nurturing. In most tribes, there emerged a priest called a shaman. These shamans had direct access to the Originating Mystery. They experienced this access within their own psyches. Thus, they were very powerful figures — priests by authority rather than by ordination. It was as though the shaman was a flute to be played by the Originating Mystery. The music, thus played, gave the whole tribe access to the Originating Mystery. This access gave the tribe an intimate connectedness with, and relationship to, the Earth — experienced as Great Mother — and also to the universe as a whole. So, with the shaman as leader and initiating priest, the whole tribe experienced that peculiarly human phenomenon – wonder. Religion has its roots in wonder at the planet, at life and death, at the stars, and at the universe.

The Tribal/Shamanic phase of human cultural development can be considered the "inner child" of human culture. During this period, the life of the tribe was still intimately interwoven within the context of the changing seasons, the land, water, and air, as well as the other animals. In short, within the context of the living Earth. But self-reflection meant the creation of culture. Culture is the exteriorizing of the human psyche, reflecting upon itself. Put another way, a culture is a biological niche exteriorized — culture is the *Uncreated*, frozen in forms. Living cultures are cultures in which the *Uncreated* is still flowing into being. Humans understand their niche by exteriorizing it. Then, by building cultural structures based on what was reflected upon within, human individuals could be born into, pass through, and die into these structures.

Cultural structures enable the self-reflecting individual to make sense of birth, life, and death. Human culture, like all other creations of the universe, is a creation of the Originating Mystery in the human. Put another way, human cultures are an invention of the Earth. Like languages, cultures and the religions which form their nuclei, are different. None of them are more or less important, more or less right or wrong than any of the others. Each of them tells us something unique about the Originating Mystery engendering them of the Earth process. In order to see any of them correctly, each of them must be looked at in the context of all the others.

Time passed, and men learned to husband animals rather than to hunt them. Women learned to cultivate crops by discovering the relationship between the planting of seeds and a higher yield the following year. These two discoveries allowed humans to enter into a cultural period characterized by settled village life. Husbanding and agriculture assured a more dependable supply of foods. The Originating Mystery was still worshipped in the feminine aspect as the great Mother Earth. In fact, we can think of this period as the period of the Great Mother. This period created the "inner mother" of the cultural psyche. Shamans and Shamanesses guided the human community in its worship of the Mother in her threefold aspects of Virgin, Mother, and Crone. It was in this neolithic period of settled village life that the men began to gather in secret societies which would cause them to formulate a new image of the Originating Mystery.

This new way of seeing the great Mystery was as Father. It was this period that gave us the "inner father" of the cultural psyche. Because the idea of Father was associated with the sun, it had about it an enormous creative energy. All over the Earth, great civilizations emerged with new and different names for the Originating Mystery. The Originating Mystery was called Zeus,

Yahweh, Allah, Logos, Holy Spirit, Tao, Buddha-Mind, and many others. Perhaps because many males had greater muscular strength with which to enforce their wills, or for some other reason, in some instances Mother began to be viewed with contempt and even hatred. When this happened, male humans began to abuse the shrines where the Mother was venerated. Along with this came a certain denigration of women, but worst of all, "Mother Earth" came to be seen simply as *mate*rials to be used and abused according to the whims of men. They perfected their technologies of exploitation to such a degree that Mother began to weaken toward death. In time, they became addicted to the *mate*rials they exploited. The age of the great classical religious cultures began to decline, and a new age was born. This was the age of the "inner divorce" of the cultural psyche and the age of *orphanism*.

This new age, an addictive age, can be referred to as the industrial/technological age. We can date its beginning to the time of the industrial revolution, but its roots reach back into the age of the great religious cultures. However, it must be pointed out that neither industry nor technology is, in itself, bad. Like alcohol, they only become dangerous when they are abused. They are only abused when they are used to fulfill needs in the human that they cannot fulfill. Presently, we are addicted to *mate*rials because we have lost our relationship, individually and culturally, with the inner child, the inner mother, and the inner father of our cultures. We have lost the joy and spontaneity of the inner child, we are lonely for our inner father, and we are hungry for Mother Earth because we have desacralized Her. Therefore we try to consume Her and become addicted to consuming. Addiction is deadly.

Our addicted culture can, and is, threatening the very life of Mother Earth. Ironically, addiction has caused a loss of functional contact with Father as well. Humans have no Father and no Mother at the moment; we are orphaned and anxious. In our loneliness we overconsume; we are addicted and are dying of pollutants even as we have considered nuclear suicide as a way out of this hell. Even while we're in hell, our individual, and collective denial forces us to pretend to believe the advertising that tells us we are bound for heaven. When we attempt to smile at one another, our grimaces betray the truth. We have tried to create heaven by cluttering our lives with things, but we awaken to find ourselves in hell — paradise having become a trash heap.

As we begin to admit the truth of our dilemma, something new begins to emerge. We are beginning to realize that we cannot "patch things up." It is an impossible and hopeless task. To try to deal with the problems of technological addiction with more technology is like trying to solve alcoholism by having another drink. We would do better to look back over the twenty billion years of cosmic/Earth/human evolution and allow that creativity to have its way in refashioning ourselves and our culture in a manner that causes us to be in a more appropriate relationship to the planet. We call forth the Uncreated so that we might be vehicles in the recreation of our cultures.

If we acknowledge the existence of an Originating Mystery that is accomplishing the evolution of the universe, and accept that, if allowed, this *Intelligence* will reveal to each of us our natural relationships to self, to others, to other species, to the Earth, and to the universe, we will be on our way toward the answer. We will have moved into the *Ecological Age*, the age of the great "inner wedding," when Father, Mother, and Child are reunited as one "Inner Family" for our cultures.

It is the story of all life that is holy and is good to tell, and of us two-leggeds sharing it with the four-leggeds and the wings of the air and all green things; for these are children of one mother and their father is one spirit. — *Black Elk*[4]

STEP TWO is taken by saying the following in the presence of our group: "I have come to believe that there is an Originating Mystery accomplishing the evolution of the universe. I accept that, if allowed, this Originating Mystery will reveal to me my natural relationships to myself, to others, to other species, to the Earth, and to the universe."

CHAPTER THREE

To compromise in this matter is to decide; to postpone and
evade decision is to decide; to hide the matter is to decide . . .
there are a thousand ways of saying no, one way of saying yes,
and no way of saying anything else.

— Gregory Vlastos[1]

STEP THREE: WE DECIDE TO SURRENDER OUR LIVES AND OUR
WILLS TO THIS ORIGINATING MYSTERY HOWEVER WE CHOOSE TO
NAME IT

We have come to a place of decision, of cutting away from old
modes of thinking and being. We are moving into a new reality,
the outlines of which we can only barely behold. This decision will
"blow the cork" of our repression and denial. This is a great leap
into an unknown world. We might be in hell, but a familiar hell
is often less threatening than an unfamiliar paradise. Recall that
the whole universe unfurled from a dark and empty potential. So,
too, must our answers emerge. The "light" of reason brought us
to our evolutionary impasse. We must again turn our hopes to the
Uncreated, to the darkness of feeling and intuition, to the groping
of the universe, and to wisdom.

Everything presses for change, but we humans resist change.
Evolution is dammed up within us, still we say no. The pressure
builds . . . we feel crazier and crazier and crazier. Our lives, our
institutions — our entire culture is characterized by panic, frantic-
ity, and hysteria. Much of this is held in check by denial and
repression. Relief can only come when we say *yes!* We must say
yes to using our wills properly: by opening them to the greater
will of the Originating Mystery unfolding within all creation. We
must say yes to the Uncreated.

> What is man's will
> And how shall he use it?
> Let him put forth its
> power to uncover the Atman:
> Man's will is the only
> friend of the Atman:

His will is also
The Atman's enemy.
Bhagavad Gita[2]

A decision is a simple choice, nothing more, nothing less. We can make a decision regardless of whether or not our feelings are there to support that decision. In fact, for many of us, there will be no feelings present to support our decision; feelings will follow. If feelings are present, they will probably be feelings of doubt or even of dread. But, feelings of relief will follow if we make the decision.

In order to have some understanding of what is going on, it will be helpful to have a working model of the human brain and the psychic phase of the brain — the human psyche. They are both a product and a function of the entire universe process, in particular, of the Earth. The context of the emergence of the human, as with all known life forms, is the planet Earth. So, let's go back to our "New Story" and look closer at the Earth.

As I said in chapter two, the Earth accreted or self-organized in space. The field, or soul, of the Earth, exhibited itself in this self-organizational propensity inherent in all matter. The Earth, like the whole universe, has this psychic — or spiritual — as well as a material dimension. The Originating Mystery is the Source of the whole universal unfolding of forms. Mystery, or Mind, preceded matter while matter makes Mystery visible. They are each a property of the other. The body and soul of this planet are one being — Earth.

The oldest area of the Earth is her core. It was the first to accrete and is still hot. The next zone out is the mantle. While the mantle is not hot, we can think of it as warm, in that it is still malleable and kinetic. The third zone out from the center of the Earth is the crust. The crust is comprised of several tectonic plates, which move over the mantle and carry the continents on their backs. Life dwells on the crust and is the interface between the planet and the sun. Life *is* the relationship between the planet and the sun.

Human life, of course, emerged within the context of all other life. In fact, humans with their peculiar form of consciousness serve as the conscious phase of all life. In other words, the human is that being in whom life reflects upon and celebrates itself. In that life is a function of the Earth, the human is the Earth conscious of herself. In that the Earth is a function of the sun/planets system, the human is the solar system emerged into consciousness. In that the solar system is a function of the Milky Way, the human is the galaxy conscious of itself and the galaxy is a function of the universe. Thus, the human is that being in whom the universe reflects upon itself and its Origin.

The human brain is structurally similar to the planet. The core of the human brain, *the instinctive brain* — what some call the brain stem or reptilian brain — is the oldest zone of the brain, the first to accrete in life one might say. The psychic phase of the instinctive brain is what Jung calls, *the collective unconscious*. One could say that all vertebrates get the news from the universe through the symbol system, or archetypes, experienced in the instinctive brain. To be cut off from that zone of the brain, it seems, is to be cut off from the voice of evolution. This is the zone of the inner child.

The next zone out, the mantle of the brain, is called *the affective brain* — what some call the paleo-mammalian cortex. We share the affective brain with all mammals. This zone of the brain is "warm" like the mantle of the Earth, in that it is the locus of the feelings. It gives us, for instance, our warm relationships with dolphins and dogs. This is the zone of the inner mother. What Jung calls *the personal subconscious*, it seems to me, is the psychic dimension of this zone of the brain. To be cut off from the conscious experience of this zone of the brain is to live without the experience of feelings.

The outer layer of the brain, *the conscious brain*, is called by some the neo-mammalian cortex. It is the seat of that particularly human form of knowing called self-reflection, or what Jung calls consciousness. The animals know and feel; but by means of an evolutionary leap, humans know that they know, and know that they feel. The conscious brain, and its self-reflexive psyche, can be, and too frequently is, dominant over the affective brain. It represses and clouds it with the contents of that repression. This is the zone of the inner father.

The human brain is bi-hemispherical in its functioning. What this means is simple. In most motor functions, the left side of the brain controls the right side of the body, and the right side of the brain controls the left side of the body. However, there is a further function that is psychic, not physical, in its manifestation. The right side of the brain is where the functions of the affective brain are experienced. In other words, such functions as intuition, compassion, and mysticism are all right-brain functions. Cognitive functions, such as mathematics, speech, and logic, are experienced mainly in the left hemisphere of the brain. When the two are functionally balanced, we have a balanced person. A culture of balanced people is a balanced culture. Such, unfortunately, is not the case with the world at this time.

To continue outward from the brain to the human skull, we see that the skull is divided into plates, similar to the tectonic plates of the planet. On these plates is the scalp from which the hair grows. The hair/scalp is the interface between the person and the sun. So it is easy to see that, in some ways at least, the human head/brain is like a tiny planet itself, but one that has risen into self-reflexive consciousness. We could say that the human head is to the body what the planet Earth is to the universe.

A major problem facing us in the western world is one that could be explained by the preceding model. As a culture, we have over-valued such "left brain" functions as mathematics, logic, and technology. Many of us have allowed ourselves, singularly and collectively, to repress "right brain" functions and have become emotionally autistic — we cannot feel. Because we do not feel, we no longer receive the "news from the universe" coming from the even deeper zone of the psyche — the instinctive brain — wherein are experienced the imperatives engendered by the Originating Mystery and experienced in the symbol system called the archetypes. Because we feel neither of the deeper brain/psyche zones, we cannot feel the devastation we reek upon the planet. We have come to be addicted to anything that will numb the pain of our repression of these zones or distract us from any awareness of them. We now live on a dying planet but we can not feel it. Let's have a closer look at each zone of the psyche in order to try to determine some sort of explanation as to how we will come out of our "sleepwalk."

CONSCIOUSNESS

Consciousness is the most recent zone of the psyche to emerge into being through evolution. Like everything else in the universe, it is the creation of, and therefore a function of, the whole. Because humans, you and I, are members of an unbroken chain of being which began when the fireball emerged from the Uncreated and continues to this moment, we can say that in the human, the Earth, the solar system, the galaxies, and the whole universe emerge into self-knowing. As a species, our function in the whole is to celebrate the whole in conscious self-awareness. Self-reflexive consciousness is experienced in the conscious brain, the father zone of the psyche.

Human consciousness is no more separate from the Great Mother of the unconscious, than a flower is separate from its stem. If a flower could become so deluded as to consider itself separate from its stem, roots, and the soil of the planet, and thereby achieve a functional break with them, what would happen? The same is true for humans. The Originating Mystery has endowed the universe with the ability to create itself. Consciousness provides the human with a decision-making faculty, commonly called "free will." Free will is a manifestation of this basic self-organizing freedom within the universe process. Humans can make choices that serve the whole of life. Such choices are *"whole-y."* On the other hand, we can make choices that serve only the individual, only the human. Such choices are reductionistic — *"unwhole-y."*

> Great knowledge sees all in one.
> Small knowledge breaks down into the many.
> — Chuang Tzu[3]

Because the universe is able to perceive itself in the human, we are struck by the fact that the primary function of the human is to celebrate the whole universe. In realizing that and in remembering the fact that the whole universe stands beneath the feet of the human, we begin to see how insane it is to think that the human can possibly find happiness in plundering the planet for energy and metals in order to glut the individual with junk . . . in being junkies. If we are the conscious phase of the universe, then the universe is our unconscious phase. The unfolding forms of the universe, recorded in the psyche of the instinctive brain, remembered in us through self-reflection in the conscious brain are the Jungian archetypes. To assault the planet is to assault the locus of these archetypes. Therefore to assault the planet is to assault the human brain/psyche.

> Ah, what is man that you should spare a thought for him, the son of man, that you should care for him?
> Yet you have made him little less than a god, you have crowned him with glory and splendor, made him lord over the works of your hands, set all things under his feet?
> — Psalm 8[4]

The Originating Mystery finds expression of him/her/itself in the unfurling of the evolving universe. The whole universe finds expression of itself in us. To cut from our conscious awareness the deeper zones of the psyche is to cut ourselves off from feelings, from nature, from the universe, and from the Originating Mystery. To do so is to cut our heads from our bodies, to decapitate ourselves and all of nature. The ultimate *ego*centricity is our willingness to cut off our life support system rather than to change our minds, to make a decision. To build military or nuclear arsenals in "defense" of a particular ideology and to pollute globally so that a few tycoons can be criminally glutted with wealth is to be madmen walking about, knives in both hands, stabbing ourselves repeatedly in the stomach, chest, and groin while we try to smile, pretending to be happy.

How shall we use the conscious will of the human? What sort of decisions will we make? Will we dominate, plunder, slaughter, pollute, and ultimately destroy everything in the name of individual or national self-determination? *Or*, will we make decisions that will enhance all of life, and thus the human? Will we cling like children screaming, "Mine, Mine," or will we surrender our wills to that vast power we call the collective unconscious and allow it to once again breathe the *Uncreated* will of the Originating Mystery through us and our culture? Will we go on insisting that the individual is the measure of the whole? What we choose to block in ourselves will be blocked on the planet. What we choose to release in ourselves will be released upon the planet. The decision is yours . . . mine . . . ours.

> I will give you the keys of the kingdom of heaven: whatever you bind on Earth shall be considered bound in heaven; whatever you loose on Earth shall be considered loosed in heaven.
> — Matt. 16:19[5]

THE PERSONAL SUBCONSCIOUS

> For it is from within, from men's hearts, that evil intentions emerge: fornication, theft, murder, adultery, avarice, malice, deceit, indecency, envy, slander, pride, folly. All these evil things come from within and make a man unclean.
> — Mark, 7:21[6]

This is the zone "beneath" consciousness — the "mantle" of the psyche. It is only theoretical at birth, becoming actual when the process of repression/denial begins. Repression occurs when some thought or feeling is judged to be incompatible with either our conscious view of ourselves or with the collective values of our culture. We push such feelings/memories out of consciousness "down" into the *personal subconscious*. They don't die there, however, but are "buried alive," and then live a life of their own out of the light of self-reflection. In the darkness, they color, garble, or impede the entry of cosmic libido from the collective — Earth —

into consciousness. Whatever is judged to be "inferior," "bad," "guilt-ridden," "evil," or unseemly is simply pushed out of mind, denied, and ignored. As the process progresses, the conscious mind/personality begins to experience itself as a liar. A certain loneliness also sets in at this point as the individual begins to feel cut off from the whole. In the words of Jung,

It should be evident from the foregoing that we have to distinguish in the unconscious a layer which we may call the personal unconscious. The materials contained in this layer are of a personal nature in so far as they have the character partly of acquisitions derived from the individual's life and partly from psychological factors which could just as well be conscious. It can readily be understood that incompatible elements are liable to repression and therefore become unconscious. But, on the other hand, this implies the possibility of making and keeping the repressed contents conscious once they have been recognized. We recognize them as personal contents because their effects, or their partial manifestation, or their source can be discovered in our personal past. They are the integral components of the personality, they belong to its inventory, and their loss to consciousness produces an inferiority in one respect or another — an inferiority, moreover, that has the psychological character not so much of an organic lesion or an inborn defect as of a lack which gives rise to a feeling of moral resentment. The sense of moral inferiority always indicates that the missing element is something which, to judge by this feeling about it, really ought not be missing, or which could be made conscious if only one took sufficient trouble. The moral inferiority does not come from a collision with the generally accepted, and in a sense, arbitrary moral law, but from the conflict with one's own self which, for reasons of psychic equilibrium, demands that the deficit be redressed. Whenever a sense of moral inferiority appears, it indicates not only a need to assimilate an unconscious component, but also the possibility of such assimilation. In the last resort, it is a man's moral qualities which force him, either through direct recognition of the need or indirectly through a painful neurosis, to assimilate his unconscious self and to keep himself fully conscious. Whoever progresses along this road of self-realization must inevitably bring into consciousness the contents of the personal unconscious, thus enlarging the scope of his personality. I should add at once that this enlargement has to do primarily with one's moral consciousness, one's knowledge of oneself, for the unconscious contents that are released and brought into consciousness by analysis are usually unpleasant — which is precisely why these wishes, memories, tendencies, plans, etc. were repressed. These are the contents that are brought to light in much the same way by a thorough confession, though to a much more limited extent. The rest comes out as a rule in dream analysis.[7]

The reason why newborn babies are so powerful and beautiful and so able to center a room full of people onto them is that the collective energies of the universe are made manifest in them, unimpeded by denial and repression. To the degree that denial and repression are going on in the individual, that person is diminished as a center of being. We can speak of repression in the physical phase of the brain by saying that the left brain is dominating the right brain — the cognitive brain is overpowering and dominating the deeper zones of the brain. Still another way of putting it is that the head is dominating the heart, which might be the root cause of many heart attacks. Still another way of putting it is that the inner father is dominating the inner mother and child.

When "inferior contents" become the underbedding of the conscious mind, repressed "beneath" it, consciousness begins to experience itself as floating on a sea of inferiority. While the personality fears and denies all identity with these contents, the unfortunate truth is that identity with them becomes more deeply suspected. The individual caught in this "circle of denial" begins to sicken into feelings of inferiority that result in the need for more denial/repression, a worse self-image, more bad feelings, more denial, and so on. The need to numb the pain and anxiety of this horrible cycle of futility will lead the sufferer to the substance(s) or behavior(s) of addiction that will promise temporary relief from the symptoms. Now, the psychodynamics of addiction are in place. A fake or ideal personality will be built around the junk heap — the "dump" of the repressed contents smoldering in the native self. Beneath the dump, the native self will go on trying to manifest itself, straining to manifest the Originating Mystery to the conscious ego.

Nothing is more outwardly visible than the secrets of the heart, nothing more obvious than what one attempts to conceal.

— Confucius[8]

At some point, the native or real personality becomes identified with the "inferior" contents buried in it. It is abandoned by the ego in favor of the created or ideal self. At this point we can truly say that the sufferer has lost him/herself. Spiritual rebirth, "being born from above," is the experience of the ego reclaiming the real self and discarding its identity with the false self. This truly is a divine experience, for it is only through the real self that the Originating Mystery of the collective can manifest itself. But where this does not happen, where no decision is made in favor of the real self, more and more energies of the psyche are subverted away from the creative processes of the real self and are utilized in the

demands of repression and in the need to support and affirm the
liar-self.

The denial of the real self can only result in loneliness. The true
person — *Imago Dei* — lives a subterranean life, locked into a
casket somewhere in the psyche, spun off from ego-consciousness.
Instead of the healthy growth of the true person, the cheap sheen
of the liar-self is polished and polished some more. The false self
can neither love nor be loved — it is artificial. It is cut off and is
itself the denial of the very source of love. In vain will spouse or
children try to love or be loved by such a person. It will seem as
if an invisible barrier is between them. From time to time, the
inner rage of the real self will express itself in a sort of psychic
volcanism. The expression will take the form of ulcers, migraine
headaches, diseases of the skin, and violence of every kind. The self
will remind the sufferer that it is not dead — it lives in the shadows.

Now may you see the fleeting vanity of all the gods of fortune for which
men tear down all that they are to build a mockery.

— Dante[9]

If the ego/self axis finally breaks, the real self is abandoned and
the artificial creation of the ego becomes a mask. The false personality must be protected at all cost now — to show the real self is
too terrifying to even consider. Left unchecked by a moment of
honesty, the individual goes on making little choices which one by
one result in a slow slippage into the evil of addiction. We do not
slip into evil all at once. It happens in little steps, in little decisions
. . . or the lack of them.

In the same way that individuals create false selves when they
practice denial/repression, so do collectives of individuals — cultures. For instance, in a country where:

We hold these truths to be self-evident: that all men are created equal;
that they are endowed by their Creator with certain unalienable rights;
that among these are life, liberty and the pursuit of happiness; that, to
secure these rights, governments are instituted among men, deriving their
just powers from the consent of the governed.

— U.S. Declaration of Independence[10]

it is difficult to admit what has been done to native peoples, to
black people, to women, to the preborn. Worse, if all are in fact
believed to be equal, then everyone in every country are included
in that "all." What then of a nuclear technology that threatens to
end "all" life? The above quotation arose from the real self of a
nation. To live a life that is a denial of "unalienable rights," a false

self must be built. An idea such as "The American Way" becomes an ideal self, a cover-up for an addicted culture. Then, anyone who doesn't agree with the false self is quickly labeled "un-American."

The individual addict will try to hold up a socially acceptable liar-self. The right house, the right car(s), the right friends, the right schools, and so on, all become very important extensions of the cover-up. The destruction of the native beauty of our environment in order to construct an artificial one, hideous if it is anything, is the same phenomenon on a collective scale. We must hide from the truth of nature if we are not living in proper relationship to that truth. We build our arsenal of "defense" mechanisms around our false self, and threaten all life on the planet should anyone or anything threaten our supply — our "vital interests." When an individual abandons his or her real self to construct a phoney one, that person becomes a liar. When a nation abandons its founding principles for the sake of luxury, that nation becomes a liar.

To sum up: If we are ever to reconnect, to remember, the conscious zone of our psyches to the deeper zone of the collective psyche, we will have to rid ourselves of the blockage — the denial that keeps them separate. That blockage is the denied contents of the personal subconscious. When we make the decision called for in Step Three, we are deciding to end our exile from our real selves. We are deciding to "remarry" ourselves to our roots — the universe — and to give ourselves over to the Originating Mystery. When we do so, we will allow the upsurge of renewed creativity to gush forth from the collective psyche. That gushing forth will summon the Uncreated potential of the universe into being. Creation renewed can recreate us and thus renew the evolution of our cultures and of the Earth.

THE COLLECTIVE UNCONSCIOUS

We lived in good ways for many years, but eventually evil proved stronger. Some of the people forgot or ignored the Great Spirit's laws and once again began to do things that went against his instructions. They became materialistic, inventing many things for their own gain, and not sharing things as they had in the past. This resulted in a great division, for some still wanted to follow the original instructions and live simply.

The inventive ones, clever but lacking wisdom, made many destructive things by which their lives were disrupted, and which threatened to destroy all the people. Many of the things we see today are known to have existed at that time. Finally, immorality flourished. The life of the people became corrupted with social and sexual licence which swiftly

involved the Kikmongwi's (chief's) wife and daughters, who rarely came
home to take care of their household duties. Not only the Kikmongwi,
but also the high religious leaders were having the same problem.

— The Hopi Story[12]

There are great divisions in our lives. There are divisions in ourselves between inner child, inner mother, and inner father. There
are also the self-hatreds we feel. There are divisions we feel between
one another, the fear that governs our neighborhoods. There are
divisions between the born and the preborn. There are divisions
between nations. There is a terrible division between the human
and the other species, and even a division between the human and
the life systems of the planet. Ultimately, there is a break between
the human and the cosmos. Many of us feel lonely, anxious, and
fearful and many despair in silence. Many of us even fear our own
"leaders." But happily, there is a way to re-connect with ourselves,
each other, the planet, and the universe. We can do so by making
a decision, a conscious choice, to surrender to the vast powers of
the *collective unconscious.*

Again, like all species, we are engendered by the planet. The
planet exists in the community of the solar system, the solar system
exists in the community of the galaxy, and the galaxy in the great
tribe of galaxies that is the universe. We need to reconnect, to
remember the whole, the universe, our unconscious mind. Locally,
cosmologically speaking, we can think of the planet Earth as both
our collective body and mind — body/mind. We all share in the
life of this one planet. Sadly, it is that very life — the life of
Earth — that we are blocking. That missing zest for living is the
root cause of our individual and cultural neurosis as well as its
most obvious symptom. We block the flowering of that life by the
process of repression, by lying to ourselves.

The conscious mind does not embrace the totality of a man, for this
totality consists only partly of his conscious contents, and for the other
and far greater part, of his unconscious, which is of indefinite extent with
no assignable limits. In this totality the conscious mind is contained like
a smaller circle within a larger one. Hence it is quite possible for the ego
to be made into an object, that is to say, for a more compendious personality to emerge in the course of development and take the ego into its
service. Since this growth of personality comes out of the unconscious,
which is by definition unlimited, the extent of the personality now gradu-
ally realizing itself cannot in practice be limited either. But unlike the
Freudian superego, it is still individual. It is in fact individuality in the
highest sense, and therefore theoretically limited, since no individual can

possibly display *every* quality. (I have called this process the "individuation process.") So far as the personality is still potential, it can be called transcendent, and so far as it is unconscious, it is indistinguishable from all those things that carry its projections — in other words, the unconscious personality merges with our environment in accordance with the above named *participation mystique.*

— C.G. Jung[13]

Present in each of us is the complete history of the birth and evolution of the universe. The signature of the fireball is everywhere. Cut a kiwi fruit at its equator and look inside the halves. There's the Great Signature! However, for us to feel the hugeness of the universe, which is our life, our heritage, and our hope, we must remove the blockage that prevents the emergence of that life. Before we do so in Step Four, we must make the conscious choice, the decision to open ourselves to the universe process and to appeal to the Uncreated. We were the fireball, are the fireball, and will be the fireball. But, we are given the choice to be open to that greatness or to remain "infolded," to die in the bud state. The choice to open up is ours. We must face that choice as individuals — to not choose to is to choose not to.

No wonder so many of us feel sick, frightened, and out of sorts. When we pollute water, we pollute our own unconscious. We do the same when we cough industrial filth into our air. The destruction of the soil community is the destruction of the community of which we are all members. When we eliminate a species, which we do by the thousands yearly and the numbers accelerate, we diminish the vocabulary of our own unconscious. Because we are the conscious phase of the Earth's process, everything we flush into the Earth washes back to in*toxi*cate us. Would you swallow sulphuric acid, insisting it could only hurt your stomach and intestines but could never injure your brain? To think that we can hurt the Earth and not hurt ourselves is a similar folly.

If we want to be fully human, if we want to feel creative again — to feel "creative" is to feel the Uncreated emergent in creation — and if we want to feel at home on this planet, in this body, then we must allow the creative, unconscious mind of the planet to manifest freely through, with, and in us again. To cut ourselves off from the collective, individually or culturally, is to slip into *dis*ease. When we do so, it should not surprise us that psychic epidemics overwhelm us. If we eat, drink, and breathe poisons, it should not surprise us when tumors overwhelm us. However, if we choose to open ourselves to the unconscious, we will feel the creative and soothing warmth of the universe flow through us, our families, and our communities once again. We will begin to live again and cease merely trying to cope.

Following surrender we will begin to feel the depth of space. We will "see" galaxies within us and will experience the numinosity of the archetypes. We will feel the hot core of the fireball, the hot core of the Earth, and the hot center of ourselves. We will realize that the hot center of ourselves is not a wound to escape from but the spontaneity of a child to experience and channel. Stop now . . . feel the hot center of your own heart. Have you felt it before? Have you thought it peculiar to you? What did you think it was? Have you been running away from it? Feel it! It is the hot core of all that lives, the molten heart of the Earth, the *Uncreated* heart of the universe — the divine child.

Am I saying that choices made by the human will determine the course of evolution? Can the human choose to stop or to renew the unfolding of life on this planet? Am I saying that your choices, you, the reader, can determine the life or death of the Earth? *Yes!!!! Precisely!!!!* We are co-creators with the Originating Mystery. We have been given the choice to shape and direct the fate of the Earth.

Imagine a common garden hose. Imagine that the water flowing through it is the emergent Originating Mystery. The hose is cosmic history, and the source of the water is the *Source* the Uncreated. We are the decision making faculty holding the hose and directing its flow. The water is really the life within us, the history is the archetypes within us, and the decision is our own free will. Let's make the greatest decision ever made in the history of this planet and stop fighting our planetary problems. Let's surrender instead to the Source of the planet.

How do we do so? Sit or kneel in a meditational attitude, preferably in the presence of another person, for secrets spoken alone remain secrets. From your heart and using your name for the Originating Mystery say the following:

O— — — — — — — —, Originating Mystery, and creative power, emergent in the unfurling of the universe and the Earth, I decide here and now to surrender my life and will, once and for always, to your life and will, to make of me and to do with me what you will. Help me to remove any blockage that stands in the way of your will for me in the unfolding beauty of the universe, of the Earth and of life. Let me always be a vent for your creative energy.

CHAPTER FOUR

The task of prophetic imagination is to cut through the numbness, to penetrate the self-deception . . . . That task has three parts
(a) To offer symbols that are adequate to the horror and massiveness of the experience which evokes numbness and requires denial. The prophet is to provide a way in which the coverup and the stone-walling can be ended.
(b) To bring to public expression those very fears and terrors that have been denied so long and repressed so deeply that we do not know they are there.
(c) To speak metaphorically but concretely about the real deathliness that hovers over us and gnaws within us and to speak neither in rage nor in cheap grace, but with the candor born of anguish and passion.
— Walter Brueggemann[1]

STEP FOUR: WE EXAMINE OURSELVES, LISTING ALL OUR ATTITUDES AND ACTIONS THAT DAMAGE THE CREATED ORDER, THEREBY STOPPING OR IMPEDING THE EMERGENCE OF THIS ORIGINATING MYSTERY

How then do we become prophets? By becoming emptied so that the Originating Mystery can speak through us. This will provide the language with which we can discern the truth about our condition as well as the answers necessary to heal it. In order for this to happen, we must understand that Step Four cannot be avoided or skimped upon, nor can any of the Steps be done only once and then forgotten. There can be only a limited experience of *Ecological Spirituality* — a true greening of the spirit — without a thorough death of the false self and the rebirth of the true, natural self in each of us. To avoid Steps Four, Five, Six and Seven is to remain only superficially changed. Let's not paint on a smile; we must change our whole mode of being, little by little, if the planet is to survive. We will change, and continue to change, by making the *Twelve Steps of Ecological Spirituality* a way of life. Only when we have journeyed inward to confront ourselves naked and needy can we be made anew. Each journey will reveal new landscapes, which we could not have seen before.

Even when we are in touch with our real selves, alone and

unaided, we simply cannot rectify the situation that we and our planet face. Individually we cannot confront the evil in which we are engulfed. The problem is at an order of magnitude before which the mind balks, the heart shrinks, and the spirit whimpers. Never before have humans been forced to deal with geocide. We awaken to find that we have altered evolution, that we have little idea where we are headed, and that, wherever we are headed, things do not look very promising for anything other than catastrophe. It is all too much; it is all out of control. Many of us might have preferred to have died in our sleep.

However, we are not alone. If we have taken Step Three, we are at the service of a benign and beautiful power responsible for the birth and evolution of the universe. When we go inward, we are not going toward death, but through the dead land of the false self toward the rosy dawn of our beginnings. We are going to end our condition of loneliness and find out who we are. We will come to understand our *inner*ness, find out what makes us unique beings, and understand how to come into communion with all other beings, who are also unique and who also experience an innerness. We will rediscover our common origin and common destiny with all that is and cease to feel inferior, useless, and desperate. We will find release from the tension in our stomachs, the migraines, and the clenched teeth. We will find our hearts again, and with them the courage to stand again for what is decent and right. We will thaw out — hearts of stone will become hearts of flesh again. We will end our lives of coping and begin to live with zest again. Then, together, we will regain control over our national destinies.

Everything must be written down. We will need a pad of paper to be used for this purpose only. We will want to take one day each week or part of everyday, or a weekend or a week-long retreat, to go to some natural place to be surrounded by the very beauty we are seeking. We are going to consider our lives, confronting ourselves — our thinking, our attitudes, and our behavior. It might be helpful to begin by examining the year in which we find ourselves. Then, we can go back one year at a time as though we were descending a staircase toward our innocence. We are seeking our *original selves*. We are looking to become children again, radiant, whole, and "fresh from the Word."

Some of us will have spiritual experiences during the journey within. We might see things that will cause us to marvel or fill us with terror, as we are walk toward the soothing light of dawn. Whatever we see in the night will later seem like shadows or illusions. They are "boogey-men" that until now made us slaves of the empire of consuming. The dawn will come, and we will sense that we are approaching the answer to our dilemma. Our fears will evaporate as we come closer and closer to reality, to the source of the universe.

Only the most absolute sincerity under heaven can bring the inborn talent to the full and empty the chalice of the nature.

He who can totally sweep clean the chalice of himself can carry the inborn nature of others to its fulfillment; getting to the bottom of the natures of men one can thence understand the nature of material things, and this understanding of the nature of things can aid the transforming and nutritive powers of Earth and heaven and raise man up to be a sort of third partner with heaven and Earth.

— Confucius[2]

We need a second renaissance. We will die together unless we are reborn together. Nor can we be reborn by saying that we are. We can be reborn by going through the death of the false self and the rebirth of the real, *Original Self.* What we are doing is the bravest, most noble act we will ever do; we are facing ourselves. There is nothing more terrifying than that, but we are doing it to save the planet. We are bowing out of a diseased culture. We are disappearing beneath its surface, and plunging right into the underlying pathology beneath it. We will dive beneath that sickness until we find the new skin beneath the scab. Dante did so in the *Divine Comedy.* The Renaissance followed.

Rather than talking about what Jesus Christ and others did, we are doing it by descending among our own dead. The whole planet, the whole universe is calling us to do this. The Earth is waiting to reward us with the one prize that life has to offer: satisfaction. We will be, all of us, one by one, commissioned for the great work — to speak for the planet and for all of life. We will all be midwives to a new period of human/Earth history by declaring the death of *ego*logic and the birth of the ecological age. This will be the greatest moment in our lives as citizens of this planet. Let's be thorough.

Again, let's look at the planet in order to really understand that what we are doing truly has a planetary dimension. The Earth has several structural envelopes or spheres that have been named by Teilhard de Chardin. First, there is the *lithosphere*, which is the actual rock body of the planet — the core, mantle, and crust. Then, there is the *hydrosphere* — the waters of the planet including the oceans, rivers, and lakes of the planet. Next, there is the *atmosphere* of the planet — the envelope of air surrounding the Earth. We can speak of the *photosphere* of the planet, which is, of course, the light from the sun. The life of the planet is referred to as the *biosphere*. It includes all that lives. Growing from the biosphere is the *noosphere* — the sphere of thought. This is the thinking of the planet and is a function of the human. We can think of the noosphere as a sort of radiance surrounding the planet — the radiance of human thought. However, there is a dark side of the noosphere that I would like to name the *skotosphere* — the sphere of shadow. What is the skotosphere?

> See, darkness covers the Earth,
> and thick clouds cover the peoples;
> — Isaiah 60:2[3]

The skotosphere is the smog of the noosphere. It is the poisoning of the radiance of the noosphere with lies, which are the result of repression and denial. When individuals begin to practice denial — *re*pression versus *ex*pression—a certain poisoning begins to take hold in their inner lives. However, as we have seen so many times, the individual is not separate from the whole. When repression continues, there is a spilling over that takes place from the individual psyche into the collective psyche — cultural mind. When this happens, the cultural mind begins to poison, but cultures are not separate from the whole either. Cultural poisons spill out into the planetary mind, thus, slowly, the planetary mind or field begins to sicken. We can think of it in the way we think of air pollution. Toxins from any chimney poison the whole atmosphere however slightly.

> The world is dark, few only can see here;
> a few only go to heaven, like birds
> escaped from the net.
> — *Dhammapada*[4]

In time, the psychic hygiene of the whole planet comes into question. We are moving in the ambiance of our own lies, and we all feel the craziness and the lack of trust. We all assume the problem is "out there," "in them." The truth is that the evil we fear is our own. We have, by our own denial, polluted the mental/emotional/spiritual environment in which we must live. By emptying ourselves, we are beginning to cleanse the noosphere, and in so doing, we are, in reality, making the whole planet a better place on which to live. It is not an exaggeration to say that we are helping all humans to begin to trust one another again.

Traditional religious systems have given us a wealth of insight concerning relationships between humans. We should be grateful for this rich inheritance, use it, and build upon it. But this overemphasis on the human/human experience has caused a certain *homocentricity* to dominate our spiritualities. This homocentricity has limited us and has caused a certain superficiality to dominate our thinking. We can deal with homi*cide*, even geno*cide*, but our traditional wisdom has provided precious few categories within which to deal with bio*cide*, geo*cide*, and even omni*cide*. This one sidedness has resulted in a *de*-sacralization of nature, which brings us to the very brink of self-annihilation. A dead planet means dead humans. We must deepen and renew our relationship to the other species, and to the planet, if we are to survive. We must become "third partners with Earth and heaven." We must begin to question not only the human/human relationship, but the human/Earth and human/universe relationships as well. In so doing, we will rediscover the truth of human life and can begin to live accordingly.

Food and alcohol hold an overwhelming fascination for a vast majority in our society, and it may well be that the numinosity of food and drink reflects the central crisis in our twentieth century culture: the crisis in faith. We live in a predominantly Christian culture, which has lost its living connection to the symbolism of wafer and wine. Lacking spiritual sustenance there is a genuine hunger and thirst.

— Marion Woodman[5]

We are, all of us, given a number of very powerful drives. They are given to us by, and within, the context of an unfolding universe. Each of us is a function of the adaptive groping of the universe as it is experienced in us. We have a drive for security that causes us to build shelters from the cold and heat. We have a drive for food that causes us to make certain that we and our children do not starve. We have a drive for sex, guaranteeing the propagation of our species as well as calling forth in us a gentle fleshiness that enables us to identify with the pain and joy of all other living things. Problems arise when we demand more satisfaction from these drives than they were created to supply.

When we demand too much of everything, we begin to experience our excesses as *needs*. It is at this point that we can begin to speak of addiction. There is enough on Earth for everyone and for all the species. The present task of the human is to *re*discover that invisible line where wants became needs and needs became addictions. When we find that line within ourselves, we can begin

to move backward over it again. In doing so, we will again learn
to live with each other, with the animals, and within the context
of the life systems of the planet in a life-enhancing way. At present,
few of us in what is called the First World, know the difference
between wants and needs. Most of us need our wants and are
therefore addicted to them. It is because of this that the so-called
Third World exists. There is only one world, but too much is
consumed in the First World. So, we must begin to look at all our
excesses. To do so, we can look at the following seven common
dysfunctions in our mode of living.

1. *EGOCENTRICITY*

Another word for egocentricity is self-centeredness. It is the
attempt to get the outer world flowing toward the self rather than
to have the self flowing outward toward the outer world. It is the
attempt to have the whole serve the part. The outward flow from
the self is the flow of the Originating Mystery through us to others.
The self-centered person lives in a most unnatural way in that s/he
attempts to make the universe flow backward in some sense. Of
course, the unhappiness, the gross dissatisfaction of this sort of
living, is evident all around us. Egocentricity causes and must
cause deep unhappiness.

Egocentricity is often the fuel behind competition. It deludes us
into thinking that to have more is to be happier, but having more
means that others must have less and that some will have none.
Thus, egocentricity causes us to hurt other humans, other species,
and the Earth. All of this, of course, hurts us. In looking at
egocentricity in our lives, we will want to become aware of, and
write down, how we have been overly concerned for ourselves at
the expense of other people, other species, and the planet. Using
our notebooks, we can journal backward a year at a time looking
at this problem in our lives.

Truly, the human is a marvellous species. Who could record our
wonders from the moment we knew ourselves to be other than
apes until we landed on the moon? However, there has been a
price, a shadow side to all of this, and the price cannot be measured
in dollars. Everything we need comes from the planet and her
species. What has the human venture cost the other species? How
many species can we extinguish before the very fabric of evolution
collapses? At the time of the writing of this book, we are losing
about ten thousand species each year! We must ask how our atti-

tudes and actions affect this holocaust and write down our responses.

Many lakes are dead, and many rivers are open sewers, or chemical baths, in which the fish are forced to live, breed, and die. Many cities are darkened beneath clouds of smog. Children born in these cities are born into a darkened, degraded world. Billions of tons of topsoil are lost each year. How will we feed the future generations? How does egocentricity in my life contribute to all of this? Write down the answers.

2. LOVE OF MONEY

I am absolutely convinced that all the wealth in the world cannot move humanity forward, even in the hands of the most devoted worker. The example of great and pure individuals is the only thing that can lead us to noble thoughts and deeds. Money only appeals to selfishness and irresistibly invites abuse. Can anyone imagine Moses, Jesus or Ghandi armed with the money bags of Carnegie?

— Albert Einstein[6]

When money threatens to become a mono-value in our lives, we are suffering a pathology of the spirit. It takes a thousand forms and is difficult to root out. But, we are not trying to be perfect. Instead, we are trying to make a beginning.

As Europeans, North Americans, or any person in the industrialized world, we are subjected to the relentless pounding by the advertising "industry." We are encouraged to be greedy by every medium available to that industry. To succeed in the accumulation of wealth, we are told, is to "succeed" as people. However, if our "success" is achieved at the cost of the poor and helpless, at the cost to the other species, and even, at the cost of life itself, then just how successful can we *feel*? Remember, if anyone dies or agonizes anywhere, we all feel it.

Every living being participates in the same life/psyche — biosphere — in which we all participate. We feel the starving children. It is that niggling guilt that some of us feel around which we build the justifications of the false self. We feel the death of the animals, the slow degradation of life, and we feel estranged and uneasy in the natural world. When we build defenses around excessive lifestyles, we not only block out the cries of the dying children, but must, in order to do so, block out the cries and laughter of our own children. Thus, our families begin to die. Perhaps this is the root cause for our failed institution of marriage.

We are one family . . . all humans . . . all of life . . . like it or not. The starvation of a child anywhere has happened to me.

For He brought things into being in order that His goodness might be communicated to creatures, and be represented by them; and because His goodness could not be adequately represented by one creature alone, He produced many and diverse creatures, that what was wanting to one in the representation of the divine goodness might be supplied by another. For goodness, which in God is simple and uniform, in creatures is manifold and divided; and hence the whole universe together participates in the divine goodness more perfectly, and represents it better than any single creature whatever.

— Aquinas[7]

We are told from childhood that we have the right to get ahead, to have all we want as long as we are willing to work for it. Then the life-long advertising blitz tells us over and over again exactly what it is we're to want. Our own deepest dreams and fantasies tell us what we really want. "What I really want is life. What I really want is life for all people and for all living beings." It is then that the "divine goodness," which is my life, will be fulfilled. Deep down I want to be generous and to serve all of life, but what I find myself desiring is a new sports car. While my deepest wish is to see everyone with what they need, I find myself working for trinkets and slaving for baubles. In order to become a "successful consumer," I must train to be a successful exploiter. True success is success for the whole, not success for any of the parts achieved at the expense of the whole. So, where has the love of money dominated my value system? Write down all the instances beginning with this year and going backward.

3. SEXUAL SUPERFICIALITY

When we deny our depth, have no experience of our hearts, and are out of touch with our centers, we remain in a state of longing that cannot be fulfilled. With all the emptiness of consumerism, nothing is so much spoken of and nothing provides less satisfaction than sex. Our craving for sexual gratification becomes like the drinking of sea water — we just keep getting thirstier. The reason is that we have left unmet our deeper needs while chasing after sex with the consumer mentality, "more is better," in sexual matters. Without contact with our deeper selves, we experience sex in the head and genitals not in the heart. Thus, love dies. Seldom, if ever, do we connect with the depth dimension of our partner's or of our own personhood. Seldom do we experience our sexuality as a life-function of the planet. Seldom can we feel the cosmic mysticism of sexual union. Instead, many times we walk away emptier than before and condemned to begin craving again.

We discover the depth dimension of our sexuality when we begin to feel and participate in the cosmos/Earth dimension of ourselves. When we experience the connectedness that sexuality engenders, we are no longer alone. The whole planet is with us, laughing, playing, and joining in the ecstacy. Sex is participation in the dynamics of evolution. There is a triangle involved in all sexual exchange — human, animal or floral:

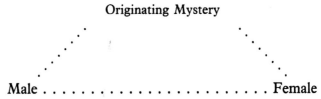

Originating Mystery

Male . . . . Female

When the whole is present in our sexual experience, then that experience is *"whole-y."* The joining of opposites in the unity of the Originating Mystery sparks new life and is a *whole-y* act. Sexuality is holy and needs to be treated in that way.

When we remain on the surface of life, we need not suffer much, consciously at least. But below, where the whole Earth suffers, we suffer also. Sex can be a method for us to deepen with another so that we can begin to feel the planet, and listen to her needs. Her needs are our deepest needs as well. It behooves us to go there. Concentration on the surface dimension of sex while denying a deep relationship with the whole person of our partner, or while denying responsibility for the possible offspring, drives wedges between different aspects of our own being. We separate consciousness from the unconscious, mental and genital affectivity from the heart, body from spirit, pleasure from responsibility, and heaven from Earth. All forms of pornography make millions fostering that split in us. It separates the body of the model from his or her person for the purpose of titillation, which clearly cannot lead to satisfaction or union. Paper dolls, whether male or female, cannot satisfy. Titillation itself is an addictive behavior. In time, that addiction can strip us of the ability to respond sexually to a real person. We lose our depth and become addicted to surfaces.

Within each of us is a vulnerable child, needing acceptance, touch, and nurturing. These are not luxuries; we need personal communion with others. We can experience *communion* — union with — when we have com*passion* — feel with. Many of us become so terrified of the shared suffering, which real compassion presupposes, that we protect ourselves from it, condemning that child within to loneliness. Real love is willing to go deep — journeying into hurts and ecstacies and feeling them together. To remain superficial is to experience only the exterior of life. While we can choose to have the endless variety of different exteriors, in doing so we deny ourselves the depth experience of another's inner self and the communion that arises from that experience. To refuse *inner*ness and its communion is to refuse to experience the joy of the child within. We then become disposable people for one another. Like disposable cigarette lighters, we can toss each other away when the fire is gone. As we do so, it becomes easier to dispose of our children as well — born or preborn.

Cultures, as we have said, are composed of individuals. Most cultures build monuments to what they consider to be their most important achievements or deepest held beliefs. Be they the pyramids of Egypt or the cathedrals of Europe, the underlying imperative seems to be the same. What then can we learn about ourselves by looking at our insurance skyscrapers — great ladders to the sky? What can we learn from the thousands of phallus-shaped missiles, tipped with their seeds of light, poised to destroy all cultures and even the planet herself? The problem is not between countries. The problem is between the human species and life itself, between "masculine" consciousness and the great depth of the "feminine" unconscious, the planet, the universe.

We must contact the mother planet within ourselves. We do so by emptying ourselves, by peeling off the scab of superficiality so as to see the new skin of depth beneath it. When we do so, we begin to feel *with* each other. When we feel with each other, we begin to experience communion with all the species that we presently mutilate and extinguish with indifference. When we feel with the other species, we begin to feel our shared support system, our shared habitat, our shared life, *and* our shared planet.

4. VIOLENCE

The whole universe has a conflictual as well as a creative aspect. In fact, conflict seems to be essential to creativity. Anger can arise out of conflict and is an emotion often associated with human conflict. As such, anger is a functional component of the human psyche, which, like everything else that is, is a component and function of the universe. Anger is not, therefore, some foreign, alien, sinful, or neurotic dysfunction in the personality. However, it can become any, and even all of these, when repressed or expressed in ways that violate self or others.

Rage and violence are dysfunctional expressions of anger or conflict. Anger can be functional, and even creative, when channelled in certain ways. For instance, Martin Luther King was probably very angry about the injustices done to his people over the centuries. But, rather than to express himself in rage or revenge, he channelled his anger into his famous "dream," which echoes yet. He used his anger as fuel for a social justice movement that is still emerging. He violated no one; he was *non*violent. Instead he allowed the blocked energies of the Originating Mystery to be expressed through him in a way that engendered change. Thus, his anger was the creativity of the universe and Earth expressed in human culture, the Uncreated potential of the universe made actual. Something new was born. Black America began to experience a new dignity.

So then, if we all have anger, how do we avoid violence? We begin by ending the denial of our anger. Then we admit how and to whom we have been violent. Next, we begin to seek òut ways in which we can express our conflict *non*violently and creatively. Violence is an obsolete way of dealing with conflict. All our thinking about individual and collective violence must change if we are to befriend the Earth and the universe and all the creatures therein.

5. OVEREATING/DRINKING

If we're not in the "here and now" no matter how much food we put in our bellies . . . it's never going to be enough. And that's the feeling of Western man. It's not enough.

He's got it all going in as fast as he can shovel it. He's got every sensual gratification he can possibly desire and it's not enough. Because there is no "Here and Nowness" about it. Here and now is the doorway to all that energy. Because if you're truthfully here and now, there's no more you.

— Ram Dass[8]

As I pointed out in the Introduction, the addiction to consuming, *consumerism*, arises out of the underlying pathology I have called *orphanism*. Orphanism is the condition of lacking internal parenting from "Our Father Who Art in Heaven" and "Our Mother Who Art the Earth." Both Father as well as Mother are two masks for the one reality, which is the Originating Mystery. Overconsumption could be the attempt to fill the inner emptiness with food and drink. We might do better by calling out to our *parents* in the following ways:

Our Father who art in heaven,	Our Mother who art the Earth,
Hallowed be thy name.	Hallowed be thy name.
Thy kingdom come,	Thy kingdom come,
Thy will be done,	Thy will be done,
On Earth,	On Earth,
As it is in heaven.	As it is in heaven.
Give us this day,	Give us this day,
Our daily bread.	Our daily bread.
And forgive us our trespasses,	And forgive us our trespasses,
As we forgive those	As we forgive those
Who trespass against us.	Who trespass against you.
And lead us not	And lead us not
Into temptation.	Into temptation.
But deliver us from evil.	But deliver us from evil.
For thine is the kingdom,	For thine is the queendom,
The power, and the glory,	The power, and the glory,
Forever and ever . . .	Forever and ever . . .
Amen.	Amen.

It is the express purpose of advertising to encourage us to overeat, overdrink, and overconsume generally — "It's good for business." The ads assure us that satisfaction and happiness, forever out of reach, will be ours if we can just consume more. Of course, these are lies — all lies — a grinning and sneering evil that keeps us in a perpetual state of desire for what we neither need or even want. In fact, the much awaited happiness is self-hatred and worse, even a slow suicide. It becomes ever more sickening when we admit to ourselves that millions are starving.

Once again, we all participate in one life system and share a common psyche. We all feel the low-grade sense of guilt and the self-hatred. However we muffle them, we all hear the cries of the dying and see the helplessness of the mother who watches the slow death of her children while on the same planet other children, who have no more or less of a right to food and drink, are satiated. We hear them all because we are them all and they are us. We are all responsible to all that lives all of the time.

Everyone conceived of and born to this planet, every animal born to this planet has the same right to eat of this planet, drink of this planet, and breathe of this planet. What a hideous thing it is for a minority of the human family to be gorged while most go without. What a hideous thing it is to be one of the "stuffed." We are all functions of one living organism. We don't "deserve a break today" while others are starving; we just don't. Gandhi said that if we have more than we need, we have stolen it from the poor. It's a good measuring stick for our use of the planet's resources.

It's sad to think of what gluttony has done to our own foods. We are hard put to eat anything that is not poisoned in some way. We frequently eat highly processed foods that are conducive to colon cancers and gum disease. We have taken the real joy, the real savoring out of eating in order to eat more and quicker. All of this is addiction to food and drink.

6. ENVY

Envy is a sourness of soul that is bred of competition, overconsumption, and *fear*. The word envy is defined by Webster's as "chagrin or discontent at the excellence or good fortune of another; resentful; begrudging." If we experience ourselves as units of competition and consumption, how can we hope to be happy if someone else does as well, or even better than us? If we are scrambling up the same ladder, can I afford to feel bad if my foot is in your face? If "to live is to consume," then we must be resentful and begrudging toward those with more to consume. Permeating every moment of competitive living is the fear of falling behind. But behind what? Behind whom?

> He then told the guests a parable, because he had noticed how they picked the places of honor. He said this, "When someone invites you to a wedding feast, do not take your seat in the place of honor. A more distinguished person than you may have been invited, and the person who invited you both may come and say, 'Give your place to this man.' And then to your embarrassment, you will have to go and take the lowest place. No, when you are a guest, make your way to the lowest place and sit there, so that, when your host comes, he may say, 'My friend, move up higher.' Then, everyone with you at the table will see you honored. For everyone who raises himself up will be humbled, and the one who humbles himself will be raised up."
>
> — Luke, 14:7–11[9]

Envy breeds tension in the heart and stomach. It is the longing for power over other people, as well as for power over economic and natural systems. Envy is the drive behind the craving that eats our hearts, minds, and souls. If envy is to be even partially replaced by serenity, competition must be held in check by commu*nity*. Communal bonds must once again replace economic bonds. In order to live in community we must live on a scale that allows for the needs of all, within the context of the life systems that support all. To accomplish this, we must first disengage from the obsessive/compulsive dynamic of envy. We must admit our powerlessness over it.

Most advertising is designed to make us envious of one another. We want this one's body, that one's car, this one's hair, that one's spouse. (The folly of it all!) The whole hideous multi-billion dollar advertising "industry" — another denial word to ponder — keeps us craving and envious unless we say no by surrendering. We do so by admitting that we are all powerless over the whole hideous thing.

7. APATHY

Apathy means "to not feel, to not suffer." It is a symptom of the numbing that comes with addiction. The apathetic refuse to feel with others, with other species, with the planet. It is a smallness of soul — a rickets of the spirit—and a shrinkage of the mind and heart alike. It is the denial that all of creation is groaning, poisoned, plundered, and still poised on a nuclear powder keg. It is the denial that the poisons produced during the production of weapons are soaking into our soils and water.

Apathy, and not hatred, is the opposite of love. It is that indifference, that laziness that allows and even encourages us to atrophy in our present condition rather than to stand up and change. Apathy is the capitulation of personhood, the refusal to grow, to become who we really are. It is the ultimate cop out — the insistence that things will never change so why should we. It is the willingness to watch our children's suicides, rather than to examine our thinking about our "Defense" Department. Apathy enables us to watch our children die of cancers, or live with birth defects, rather than to admit that our economies are poisoning them and altering their genetic inheritance. It is the willingness to pretend that the manufacture of genetically altered bacteria, which keep the frost off strawberries while threatening the dynamics of life on this planet, is progress! Apathy is the willingness to pretend to believe that "they won't let it happen" while "they" have prepared for "it" every day and with billions of "our" dollars. Even though "they" have made small moves to reverse the situation, "it" is still with us and "we" pay "them" to continue preparing for "it" every day.

Apathy is the willingness to sit silently before clergy who exhibit little or no insight or interest in the present state of the planet. These are clergy who are willing to allow real evils to go unnamed, while lulling us to sleep — literally and figuratively — with sermons claiming redemption separate from the creation at the same time they are saying that that creation came into being of a divine agency. Apathy is the refusal to show up for life. It is the willingness to let life happen while never really entering into it. Apathy is the willingness to live dead lives stuffed with dead things, sleeping away the afternoon while our children huddle to poison themselves with drugs and alcohol in an attempt to numb the pain of our indifference toward them. Apathy is the lowering of our ideals so that we never have to rise to meet them — the apathetic just don't want to know. They breathe, eat, and drink, but there are few other signs of life. The apathetic are the undead who label the living as "kooks," "odd balls," and "peaceniks."

You might ask, "Isn't this a little morbid and impractical?" Well, are pollution, nuclear war, and suicide life-giving or practical? Further, you might ask, "Isn't this depressing as well as frightening?" Yes, but is slow death by pollution or planetary death by nuclear end, encouraging or comforting?

The performance of these Steps throughout life is an act of heroism/sheroism . . . no less than that! The planetary problem is at an order of magnitude that requires heroism of us all. No longer can one hero lead a culture into renewal. We must all speak for the whole planet and for all of life. We must change or die. This is the truth that we are up against.

Planetary death is a personal issue. Radical action is the result of rootedness in the self, in the planet, and in the universe. When we confront ourselves in Step Four, we "weed" our lives and allow them to root and flower again. We become stronger, energized, and empowered. Can we expect an easy answer to a global dilemma? The goal is survival — we must come alive if we are to stay alive.

It did not happen in a day; we cannot cure it in a day. However, we can begin in this day — *today*! As we continue, more and more will be revealed. As we find ourselves, we will *re*discover each other. As we rediscover each other, the culture will change. When we change the culture, we change the world. When we have changed the world, we will have changed the Earth. When we have changed the Earth, we will have changed the universe. We must respond to the great call from the whole to the whole. We must empty ourselves so that the Originating Mystery can manifest through us.

Furthermore, the technological age is propelling us into a space quite unrelated to our instincts. We have forgotten how to listen to our bodies; we pop pills for everything that goes wrong with us; we can have an intestinal bypass or we can have our stomach stapled. We can turn ourselves over to medicine without ever questioning what the body is trying to tell us. To our peril, we assume it has no wisdom of its own and we attempt to right our physical ills without making the necessary psychic corrections. We may temporarily succeed but the body has its own way and soon another symptom appears, attempting to draw our attention to some basic problem. If we ignore the small symptoms, the body eventually takes its revenge. As a culture we are not in touch with our instinctual roots, and parents tend to treat their children as if they too were machines instead of human beings with feelings and fears. If the child is treated that way, consciously or unconsciously, it in turn treats itself that way and the malaise deepens with each generation until someone in the family becomes conscious enough to stop it.

— Marion Woodman[10]

STEP FOUR is taken by writing down all your responses to the information discussed above.

CHAPTER FIVE

The linking backward to the origin presents the possibility of
a new start.

— Erich Jantsch[1]

STEP FIVE: WE ACKNOWLEDGE TO OURSELVES, TO THAT ORIG-
INATING MYSTERY, AND TO ANOTHER PERSON, THE SPECIFICS OF
OUR ILLUSORY THINKING, ATTITUDES, AND BEHAVIOR.

In Step Four we linked backward, shattering our denial and
remembering all the repressed fragments of our histories. We listed
all the actions, feelings, and attitudes that we have for so long
denied. In so doing, we tried to journey back in time to the source
of our being — innocence is the source of our being. We are trying
to get back to the garden of our innocence, to the seed state so
that we can allow our entire beings to be born anew from that
place. We are trying to get back to what the Taoists call "the state
of the uncarved block."

Step Five is the act of uncovering, discovering Eden. In Step
Five we rake away all the dead leaves, trash, and debris of the
winter that has covered the fecund soils of the planet within. We
are linking back to where our souls arose from those soils. In
linking back to the soils, we are linking back to the solar system.
In linking back to the solar system, we are linking back to the
galaxy. In linking back to the galaxy, we are linking back to the
universe. In linking back to the universe, we are linking back to
its seed, the fireball. The soil of the fireball is the Originating
Mystery — the mystery from whence it sprouted into being. We
are linking back to the event of events, to the ritual of rituals, to
the source — the ground.

Consider the following dream of C. G. Jung:

I was in a house I did not know, which had two stories. It was "my
house." I found myself in the upper story, where there was a kind of
salon furnished with fine old pieces in rococo style. On the walls hung
a number of precious old paintings. I wondered that this should be my
house, and thought, "not bad." But then it occurred to me that I did
not know what the lower floor looked like. Descending the stairs, I
reached the ground floor. There everything was much older, and I realized
that this part of the house must date from about the fifteenth or sixteenth

century. The furnishings were medieval; the floors were of red brick. Everywhere it was rather dark. I went from one room to another, thinking, "Now I really must explore the whole house." I came upon a heavy door, and opened it. Beyond it, I discovered a stone stairway that led down into the cellar. Descending again, I found myself in a beautifully vaulted room which looked exceedingly ancient. Examining the walls, I discovered layers of brick among the ordinary stone blocks, and chips of brick in the mortar. As soon as I saw this I knew that the walls dated from Roman times. My interest was now intense. I looked more closely at the floor. It was of stone slabs, and in one of these I discovered a ring. When I pulled it, the stone slab lifted, and again I saw a stairway of narrow stone steps leading down into the depths. These too, I descended, and entered a low cave cut into the rock. Thick dust lay on the floor, and in the dust were scattered bones and broken pottery, like remains of a primitive culture. I discovered two human skulls, obviously very old and half disintegrated. Then I awoke.[2]

In Step Five we are going to uncover the soil of the beginning.

In his book *The Presence of the Past*, Rupert Sheldrake holds that the material universe has a memory that enables it to produce individual after individual within each of its mineral and animal species. He holds that this memory is inherent in morphic fields that are responsible for the engendering of species and individuals within species. In his book *The Universe Is a Green Dragon*, Brian Swimme holds that the planet has a memory, which is seen in the fossil record, that the human geologist "*remembers*" by studying those rocks. In that the universe itself is engendered of some Originating Mystery, it takes only a small leap of the imagination to realize that the whole universe must have a memory inherent in the field of immanence in which the Originating Mystery is co-extensive with the space/time continuum.

If this is so, then in the center of the universe-memory there exists forever the searing memory of the fireball. That memory also is stored in the Earth-memory of her core. Events such as the eruption of Mt. St. Helens remind us that the planet remembers the original heat. Furthermore, in the hot, conflictual/creative centers of us all, that memory perdures. The hot beginnings of the universe, the hot core of the planet, and the hot core of the human are the same memory. In linking backward to our own centers, we contact the primordial creativity that has engendered galaxies, two generations of stars, life, consciousness, cultures, you, and me. We can "plug into" the real circuit of creative energy — the unfolding ritual of the universe.

In his book, *The Self-Organizing Universe,* Erich Jantsch says this:

Creativity is nothing else but the unfolding of evolution. The question, where evolution will proceed to, occupies many people today. It may be posed in a meaningful way only where there is openness, where novelty has a chance to be woven into evolution.[3]

Step Five represents our attempt to achieve that openness.

When we clear away the blockages, the Originating Mystery can recreate us. We will become vents for the creative dynamics of a time/developmental universe that shapes itself. This, it seems to me, is the real meaning of the Zen concept — *sunyata.* It is usually rendered in English as "void" or "empty." We can think of it as the state of nonblockage or openness.

Without concepts, ideologies, memories, and repressed feelings blocking, or even shaping the creativity emanating from the hot core of the universe/Earth/heart, the Originating Mystery is given a radical freedom to recreate each of us and as a result of that, of course, our cultures. *Unimpeded* might be another good way to render the concept of openness. In our time, when most institutions and ideologies be they economic, political, or even religious, point to collective death, it is high time we consult the Originating Mystery responsible for willing the whole into existence. In Step Four we gaze down the historiscope to our beginnings, listing all blockages that blur the lens. In Step Five we remove them — we clean the lens. Warning: Steps Four and Five *must be experienced* in order to be understood. Knowing about them or reading them is not enough — we must do them.

> Who, being in the form of God
> did not count equality with God
> something to be grasped.
>
> But he *emptied* himself,
> taking the form of a slave,
> becoming as humans are;
>
> and being in every way like a human being,
> he was humbler yet,
> even to accepting death, death on a cross.
>
> And for this God raised him high
> and gave him the name
> which is above all other names.
>
> — Philippians: 2:6–9 [4]

Step Five is the emptying — the crucifixion of an old self. In the space thereby created, the Originating Mystery will "raise up" a new, an *Original Self*.

. . .

Most of us want to hide what we judge to be the worst of who we are. We hope "it will go away," "maybe no one will notice," or "maybe we'll just forget about it all." As a culture, we have done the same with our trash and chemical dumps. Whatever we bury in ourselves stays there until we confess it. Whatever we bury in the Earth stays there until we deal with it. In the first instance, we poison ourselves and those close to us, and in the second, we poison the whole planet and all that lives. Worse still, it seems that when we bury our lies, we also bury our truth. Then we are not only carrying the problem around in us, but we are also blocking the solution to the problem. The final result is the individual and collective poisoning that at this juncture threatens not only human culture but all of life.

The following quotation from C. G. Jung, while a lengthy one, is, I think, important enough to record in its entirety.

Treatment should really have begun with the mother, or rather with the relations between the father and the mother. I think that an all-round conscious realization of the situation and its implications would have had a salutary effect. Conscious realization prevents the unmentionable atmosphere, the general cluelessness, the blank disregard of the troublesome object; in short, it stops the painful content from being repressed. And though this may seem to cause the individual more suffering, he is at least suffering meaningfully and from something real. Repression has the apparent advantage of clearing the conscious mind of worry, and the spirit of all its troubles, but to counter that, it causes an indirect suffering from something unreal, namely a neurosis. Neurotic suffering is an unconscious fraud and has no moral merit, as has real suffering. Apart, however, from producing a neurosis the repressed cause of the suffering has other effects: it radiates out into the environment and, if there are children, infects them too. In this way neurotic states are often passed on from generation to generation, like the curse of Atreus. The children are infected indirectly through the attitude they instinctively adopt towards their parents' state of mind: either they fight against it with unspoken protest (though occasionally the protest is vociferous) or else they succumb to a paralyzing and compulsive imitation. In both cases they are obliged to do, to feel, and to live not as *they* want, but as their parents want. The more "impressive" the parents are, and the less they accept their own problems (mostly on the excuse of "sparing the children"), the

longer the children will have to suffer the unlived life of their parents and
the more they will be forced into fulfilling all the things the parents have
repressed and kept unconscious. It is not a question of the parents having
to be "perfect" in order to have no deleterious effects on their children.
If they were perfect, it would be a positive catastrophe, for the children
would then have no alternative but moral inferiority, unless, of course,
they chose to fight the parents with their own weapons, that is, copy
them. But this trick only postpones the final reckoning till the third
generation. The repressed problems and the suffering thus fraudulently
avoided secrete an insidious poison which seeps into the soul of the child
through the thickest walls of silence and through the whited sepulchres
of deceit, complacency, and evasion. The child is helplessly exposed to
the psychic influence of the parents and is bound to copy their self-
deception, their insincerity, hypocrisy, cowardice, self-righteousness, and
selfish regard for their own comfort, just as wax takes up the imprint of
the seal. The only thing that can save the child from unnatural injury is
the efforts of the parents not to shirk the psychic difficulties of life by
deceitful manoeuvres or by remaining artificially unconscious, but rather
to accept them as tasks, to be as honest with themselves as possible, and
to shed a beam of light into the darkest corners of their souls. If they
can confess to an understanding ear, so much the better.[5]

In order to make sure that there is no misunderstanding about
perfectionism, he goes on in the very next paragraph:

It is not, let me repeat, a question of the parents committing no faults —
that would be humanly impossible—but of their recognizing them for
what they are.[6]

Jung is encouraging us to acknowledge to ourselves, and to another
person, the specifics of our deluded thinking, attitudes and
behavior.

. . .

We know that the planet is in dire jeopardy. The very knowledge
of the situation can cause us to freeze with terror, and most of us
repress that knowledge in order to be able to go on day after
day. But again, when we numb out the problem, we numb
out the solution! The solution is to identify and break the
blockage that prevents our direct and constant contact with the
power that can break the evolutionary impasse. When we do so,
we will have the power to shatter the addiction to consuming
and its associated symptoms, particularly the desire for collective
suicide.

The *dis*ease is within us, and we can no longer run from it if we are to survive. The answer is also within us, and we must run to it if we are to survive. The one hope for genuine renewal of ourselves and our cultures, is to empty ourselves of repressions and lies and to reconnect with the deeper zones of the psyche — the collective unconscious — or, if you will, the planet and the universe.

In Step Four we took a long look into our own mirror. Our self-reflexive consciousness reflected on self. We listed with pen and paper our deluded thinking and actions. Now, we will shake off the delusion, and with it, the deluded selves we built to disguise it. This can cause an in-depth deflation of the ego. Remember, we are lancing the "sore" at the pit of the heart and allowing the poisons to drain out. When this is done, the liar-self will collapse and deflate in much the same way that the swelling of a boil goes down when the core is removed. But, as the swelling and its pain go down, we will rediscover our real selves, and our connection to everything and everyone else. With this, our sense of loneliness, isolation, and despair will evaporate.

Once again, C. G. Jung:

Nothing makes people more lonely, and more cut off from the fellowship of others, than the possession of an anxiously hidden and jealously guarded personal secret. Very often it is "sinful" thoughts and deeds that keep them apart and estrange them from one another. Here confession sometimes has a truly redeeming effect. The tremendous feeling of relief which usually follows a confession can be ascribed to the readmission of the lost sheep into the human community. His moral isolation and seclusion, which were so difficult to bear, cease. Herein lies the chief psychological value of confession.[7]

Next, a certain serenity will dawn upon the scene as we begin to realize that we have been running from ourselves across the landscape of the years. We will become conscious of a gentle light rising from the deeper zones of our psyches, dispelling the dark loneliness of our terror. We will sleep deeply again and have vivid dreams, and we will recall them. The various zones of the psyche will be fluid in their compensatory relationships, one with another. Our personality will settle into proper and natural relationship with itself, with others, and with the planet. We will experience this as connectedness.

We will feel connected to the inner world again. Our new integrity will cause visions, spiritual experiences, and insights that we never thought possible. We will feel connected to the outer world as well. The false personalities we might have built will dissolve, the masks will drop, and our real selves — our Original Selves — will emerge and smile in the light of day. For some of us, it will seem like the first time we have ever been able to risk being ourselves. We will feel our own worth — our preciousness. We will know ourselves and feel *with* others. The teaching of our and others' religions will take on new meaning, depth, and relevance. We will have new eyes to see, new ears to hear, new hearts, and minds with which to create.

Nonetheless, before these good things can begin to happen, we must humble ourselves to ourselves, to the Originating Mystery and to another human being. Some might ask, "Why is it necessary to tell another person our most painful secrets and failures?"

A general and merely academic "insight into one's mistakes" is ineffectual, for the mistakes are not really seen at all, only the idea of them. But they show up acutely when a human relationship brings them to the fore and when they are noticed by the other person as well as by oneself. Then and then only can they really be felt and their true nature recognized. Similarly, confessions made to one's secret self generally have little or no effect, whereas confessions made to another are much more promising.

— C. G. Jung[8]

There is another reason why we should confess to another person. When we sit before another human being and admit the realities of our lives, and find that they are not horrified, and indeed, have done many of the same things themselves, we begin to feel forgivable. Until we see that we have not been so unique in our manifold addictions and their coverups, we will go on in our isolation, hating ourselves and refusing ourselves the fellowship we so badly need in order to birth the *Second Western Renaissance* — the renewal of the vision and institutions of the cultures of the world. We cannot do it alone; the evils we face are unprecedented. It is either *co*existence or no existence; we must connect.

We will want to be very careful when choosing the person with whom we are to share our confidences. There are few things as painful as the attempt to be honest, in depth, with those who have not yet gone deep themselves. Superficiality is violent; it feels with no one. We will want to choose someone who has gone through this, or a similar process, him/herself. Counsellors, psychologists, priests and ministers are often trained for this sort of experience. As Jung points out in the following statement, Catholics, Orthodox Christians, and Anglo-Catholics have a sacramental vehicle for this purpose.

In treating devout Catholics, I always refer them to the Church's confessional and its means of grace.

— C. G. Jung[9]

If we have a deep friendship with our spouse or with someone else, then this might be the best person to share confidences with. But, be honest! If you suspect that you might feel ridiculed, compromised, or in any way unsafe, look for someone else. It is crucial to find the right person — someone who understands your vision.

Having made your choice of a person, be sure to give serious consideration to the environment in which you will do your sharing. You will not wish to be interrupted by doorbells, telephones, or unexpected guests. A comfortable and secure sitting room might be best for some. A pine grove deep in the forest might be best for others. Be sure to decide what is best for *you*. Make this very clear to the person with whom you will be sharing this experience. Remember, you are taking the risk of a lifetime; it is nothing less than that. You are about to do the one thing people fear most. You are going to admit to yourself, to the Originating Mystery, and to another person, the truth about who you really are. It is a singular act of human greatness. Do not allow it to be botched because you were too reticent to state your needs.

When you have found the right person and the right environment, begin. It is wise to invoke the presence of the Originating Mystery, using whatever name you choose. The healing presence will be felt if you ask. The Mystery responsible for creating the galaxies does not discriminate. Having done so, begin without fear. Take the list you prepared in Step Four and begin to share.

As may easily be imagined, the effect of such a confession on simple souls is great, and its curative results often astonishing. Yet I would not wish to see the main achievement of our psychology at this stage merely as the fact that some sufferers are cured, but rather in the systematic emphasis it lays upon the significance of confession. For this concerns us all. All of us are somehow divided by our secrets, but instead of seeking to cross the gulf on the firm bridge of confession, we choose the treacherous makeshifts of opinion and illusion. — C. G. Jung[10]

As soon as you begin, you will experience wave after wave of relief as holes are poked in the dikes of a repressed life. You will feel the fresh energies of the emerging universe begin to manifest within. It will feel new because it is new, and divine because it is divine. The emerging universe is new in every moment and in every place. You will feel that newness, that innocence. As you continue, it will become obvious to you that this feeling of newness is precisely what we have been searching for in the futility of all of our addictions.

We chased it in alcohol, in drugs, in promiscuity, in power, and in consumerism, and always, we came up emptier than before. We looked for it in office, position, and ordination and yet it eluded us. We chased it around the world, in and out of jails and marriages; we abandoned or aborted our own children, all to no avail. No matter how frantically we searched, the much-wanted insight seemed always just around the corner. When we thought we had it, it vanished yet again. We need only to stop, to confess, and thereby break the blockage that prevents us from feeling our younger self — the child within. When we do so, we discover — uncover — the child and mother we buried in denial, and we begin to live again. We come out of our tomb only when we gain access to the fiery creativity smoldering beneath its floor.

We admit into consciousness all the denied ghosts of years gone by. We face them all, one by one. We say calmly, "Yes I have done this. . . ." and "Yes, I have been that. . . . " and "Yes, I have wished this. . . ." and so on. When we notice that our companion has not walked off in horror, we can begin to believe in our own forgivability. With that, we can touch our inner self again and feel its connection to the outer world . . . to the planet . . . they are one.

As we begin to feel our own worth again, we begin to feel the worth of all of humanity, all of the animals, and the entire shared garden of the planet Earth. We begin a love affair with the whole planet — we befriend the Earth. We begin to sense the presence of the Originating Mystery in ourselves and in all things, living and nonliving. We begin to see that everything is one vast bath of innocence. Here is the kingdom of the God of Christians, the pure land of the Buddhists, the paradise of Islam. Here is the Garden of Eden. It is here, and now and in our midst. It also pre-exists and post-exists our brief individual transits on this planet. Time past, present, and future are all of one unfurling dynamic — the evolution of a time/developmental universe.

As though awakening from a bad dream, we sense the fact that all beings have the same claim on existence that we have. We see again, with eyes washed of the dross of delusion, the vast and varied beauty of our garden paradise. We experience a springtime in the cosmos. We experience the breath of the eternal blowing through the garden at all times and in all places, and most beautiful of all, we come to realize that we are that breath. We are not the illusions we have cherished; we are the Originating Mystery, conscious of and celebrating itself.

With the influx of new life, our personalities will again begin to evolve. We will begin to mature — ripen — into our full humanity. The silly toys offered up to us by an addicted culture will seem not only unimportant, but boring; we will not desire them. We will no longer be deluded into thinking that the amassing of great numbers of things can offer us any form of happiness whatsoever. We will already know what happiness is because we will feel happy. Never again will we be tricked into searching for happiness — happiness will be ours. We will be able to be still.

To feel good ourselves, and to feel *with* others, will become more important by far than the next pickup truck coming out of Detroit, Tokyo, or anywhere else. We will let go of the "my nation is #1" attitude, as though we were talking of a high school football team. We will not need to amass six thousand World War II's worth of explosives in order to feel like #1 either.

We will also let go of our equally arrogant insistence that our religion contains the whole revelation of truth, or that our name for the Originating Mystery is the only name. We will begin to see that all religions, past, present, pagan, polytheistic, or monotheistic are all languages of the divine, each of them saying something of truth about the Originating Mystery. We will see that the truth of human spirituality is only to be found in the whole expression of all the languages of the divine combined into the *Global Spiritual Tradition of the Human*. We will discover that it was the very same Originating Mystery that engendered the universe, formed the galaxies, shaped our Milky Way, willed the sun aflame, gathered the Earth, engendered life and conscious life, and all the languages of the divine. To befriend one religion is to befriend all religions; to befriend all religions is to befriend the universe.

We did not create the Earth; she is not ours to destroy. We are just visitors here and each of us is responsible for the health and beauty of the whole. Certainly we are responsible for cleaning up after ourselves. As we begin to come out of the dungeons of our repression and despair, it will begin to dawn on us that the problems facing the planet are not just our problems, not just human problems, but are the Earth's problems. In that we are the conscious phase of the Earth, she becomes aware of them in us. It is true that we have created them with our immaturity, laziness, and general dishonesty — we have buried our chemical dumps like our personal lies that we hoped no one would ever discover. However, having dragged all our folly out into the light of day, individually and collectively, we begin to realize that the healing will be done by the planet. The doctor dresses the wound, the body heals itself. If we change and get ourselves out of the way, she will heal. This is certainly good news! How could we ever do it alone?

Like the little boy in *The Neverending Story*, we must act or the whole, for which we are responsible, will die. Once we begin to experience the splendors of the emerging universe and the incredible powers of creativity latent in the Earth processes, we will begin to see that there are real reasons for hope. If we change the way we are living, then the planet will evolve beyond the present impasse. If we stop pouring poisons into the water, the water will heal, and the species present in the water will flourish again and new ones will appear. If we stop coughing poisons into the air, the air will heal. The species present in the air will flourish again and new ones will appear. If we stop destroying the soils and precious habitat, the soils and habitat will heal and the species present on the land will flourish again. Humans will flourish again! But, we must *begin* to change.

Having done a thorough job on Steps Four and Five constitutes our willingness to change. It will be because of the admission of the problems within us that we will hope to change in Steps Six, Seven, Eight, and Nine. In doing so, a new age of human/Earth history will be dawning. In us the blockage will be shattered — the blockage that has prevented our maturation as individuals, as cultures, and even as a species. In us the human will be learning to live among the animals, and among the nonliving components of the Earth's community, in a mutually enhancing way. In us the dawn will break, dispelling the darkness of our deluded relationship with our support systems. In us the Earth will begin to smile again.

Do not worry, however, that few others seem to be going through this process of change. You will become the teacher that they need. The time is now. This is the emergent moment when the universe can be born fresh, innocent, and in you!

The first beginnings of all analytical treatment of the soul are to be found in its prototype, the confessional.

— C. G. Jung[11]

STEP FIVE is taken by admitting to ourselves, to the Originating Mystery — however we might name the Mystery — and to another person all that we wrote about in Step Four.

CHAPTER SIX

We must reinvent the human at the species level.
— Thomas Berry[1]

STEP SIX: WE BECOME ENTIRELY WILLING TO HAVE ALL HABITS OF ILLUSION REMOVED FROM OUR THOUGHTS, FROM OUR ATTITUDES, AND FROM OUR BEHAVIOR.

In order to reinvent "the human," we must first reinvent humans — individuals. In truth, we can reinvent no other human beside ourselves. Thus, it is wise to concentrate on ourselves and allow others to be inspired by the changes they see taking place in us. We reinvent ourselves by becoming our *Original Selves*, the selves engendered of the Originating Mystery. The truth is, we cannot become our Original Selves simply because we want to. The reason for this is that, while I know that I need to change, the person who would make choices about change *is* the person who needs to be changed! In other words, if my thought is confused by habits shaped during years of living within the addicted culture, how can I think clearly about what I need to change about me? The secondary — addicted — personality looking at itself cannot know what the *Original Self* looks like. So, I must become willing to *be* changed *by* some other source — the Originating Mystery.

It is the false self, and the habitual delusions of the false self, that need to be removed, peeled away in the way a snake sloughs its skin. In Steps Four and Five, we admitted the particulars of our deluded thoughts, attitudes, and actions. Having done a thorough job on these Steps, we have emptied ourselves of our denial and repression surrounding our delusions. In Steps Six and Seven we will attempt to allow the Original Self to come to the fore. To do so, and to understand what we are doing, it is necessary that we find a way to think about the Original Self. To do so, we will refer back to "The New Story."

Before the beginning there was the Originating Mystery, which can never be described fully. Nonetheless, we can imagine an *Uncreated* but totally creative plenum or potential out of which everything emerges. We can imagine the entire universe as somehow enfolded or implicit within the plenary potential, the mind of the Originating Mystery. We can imagine the fireball of the beginning as a powerful thought or inspiration within the *Original Mind*. Thus, what we call creation, or the universe, can actually be thought of as unfolding from a state of potentiality into a state of actuality. This unfolding is called evolution.

The universe is a psychic as well as a physical reality. These are not separate or dualistic realities, though they can be spoken of separately in the same way that I can speak of my personality and my body as separate realities when in fact they are one reality, me. In this chapter I shall speak of the psychic phase of humans which I call our Original Selves. When I speak of an Original Self, I am speaking of that invisible dimension of myself, that self-organizing field that exhibits itself through my body and in which my body exhibits itself. So what is this field, this Original Self?

In Rupert Sheldrake's superb book *The Presence of the Past*, he describes the fields in this way:

Fields are non-material regions of influence. The Earth's gravitational field, for example, is all around us. We cannot see it — it is not a material object; but it is nevertheless real. It gives things weight and makes things fall. It is holding us down to Earth at this moment; without it we would be floating. The moon moves around the Earth because of the curvature of the Earth's gravitational field; the Earth and all the other planets move around the sun because of the curvature of the sun's field. Indeed the gravitational field pervades the entire universe, curving around all matter within it. According to Einstein, it is not *in* space and time; it *is* space-time. Space-time is not a bland background abstraction; it has a structure, which actively shapes and includes everything that exists or happens within the physical universe.[2]

We can think of the gravitational field of the universe as the Original Self of the whole universe, the immanent aspect of the preexistent/transcendent Originating Mystery. All other selves or fields are functions of this Original Self, which itself is a function of the Originating Mystery.

In the diagram overleaf, also taken from Sheldrake's book, we can imagine how the individual fields of the Earth, solar system, galaxies, and so on all function as whole fields within the greater whole-field of the universe.

Taken a step further, the diagram could refer to an individual, within a family, within a community, within a *bio*region, within a continent, within the planet, and so on. At every level of organization, there is an interdependent autonomy. Each and every field has a different function while at the same time being inseparably a function of the whole. The whole is engendered of the Originating

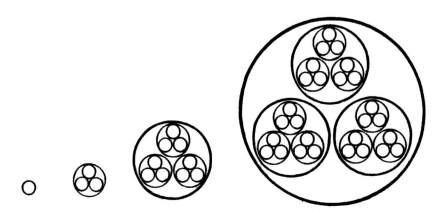

Successive levels in a nested hierarchy of morphic units, or holons. At each level, the holons are wholes containing parts, which are themselves wholes containing lower-level holons and so on. This diagram could represent subatomic particles in atoms, in molecules, in crystals, for example, or cells in tissues, in organs, in organisms.

Mystery and, therefore, so are each of the individual wholes functioning within the whole. You and I are, each of us, autonomous wholes functioning within and as functions of the whole.

This is the psychic phase of the "New Story," or rather the New Story told from the point of view of its psychic phase. Every subatomic particle has an associated field of organization, and every atom has an associated field within which the subatomic fields are nested. Every molecule has an associated field within which the fields of its constituent fields are nested, and every mega-molecule has an associated field in which its constituent fields are nested. Every cell has an associated field in which all of its material components' fields are nested, and every tissue has a field in which the fields of its constituent cells are nested. Every organ has an associated field in which the fields of its tissues are nested, and every organism has a field in which the fields of its organs are nested. Every human has a field, an Original Self, in which all the preceding subfields are nested. Another word for the Original Self is *the soul*. Every family has a field in which human individuals are nested. The same can be said for animal families, insect colonies, fish schools, and bird flocks. Every community has a field in which the fields of each of its members are nested; these fields are called cultures.

Every species has a field in which all of its members' fields are nested. Each *bio*region is a field in which the individual fields of several or many species of living beings are nested. Each continent has a field in which its constituent *bio*regional fields are nested. The Earth is a field in which all continental/*bio*regional fields are nested. Our solar system is a field in which the sun, planets, and moons are nested, and the Milky Way has a field in which our solar system is nested. The universe has a field in which the galaxies are nested. The whole universe, the solar system, and the planet Earth in themselves, and in their evolutionary emergence, constitute for the human community the primary revelation of that ultimate mystery whence all things emerge into being, the Originating Mystery.

Within every field, at every level of organization, inheres the memory of the Originating Mystery. Inherent in that memory is the will of the Originating Mystery for each and every one of those fields. In D.N.A. and R.N.A. the physical unfolding of the particular expression of the *Original Will* cooperates with the field in the unfolding of the whole body/self of a particular being. Each and every being in the universe has a differentiated being, an interiority or self, while at the same time being in ontological and perpetual communion with all other beings throughout the universe — there is a time and a purpose for all things. Knowing and expressing our Original Selves is what constitutes happiness. In knowing our Original Selves we are able to know and love the Originating Mystery, and we are able to befriend ourselves, the Earth, and the universe.

When the relationship to the maternal and paternal images, which constitute our Original Self, is severed, we often lose the experience of our connection to the Originating Mystery. Addiction often follows. No longer can the Original Will resonate within the field of ourself, so we become like leaves cut off from the unfolding tree of the universe. Being cut off we begin to atrophy and shrink. Addiction becomes the attempt to cool the pain of that shrinkage. Addiction has a will of its own, and has its own habits as well. The resonance of those habits can become built into our souls, replacing the resonance of the Original Will. Next, the resonance causes more addictive behavior to be desired — addiction becomes the will of our souls. It can condemn us to death.

CULTURAL FIELDS AND CULTURAL ADDICTION

Cultures themselves are fields of organization. When we speak of a nation-state, for instance, we are not really speaking of a geo-structural reality. Instead, we are speaking of an idea within which a body of people is organized. A flag is symbolic of the "seed" idea around which the nation organizes itself. Cultural fields self-organize around the "seed" of a great idea — a constitution or a holy book — in the way a magnetic field self-organizes around a magnet. Cultural clusters of many nations are known to organize around one holy book. The holy book represents not only the collective history of all these peoples, but also a collective code of morality and ritual. Judicial institutions, economic institutions, education, marriage, and many, if not all, institutions of a particular culture can refer back to a holy book for their authority. The holy book tells the whole story of the people/peoples. When confusion arises, the story within the holy book can be consulted for advice.

The holy book of most of western civilization, the Bible, is no longer functioning as the organizing "seed" of the western world. Because of this, we people of the west have lost our moorings. In losing the influence of, or the direction provided by, the Bible on the one hand, and having lost the connection to the Earth provided by the native peoples on the other, we have lost our Father and Mother. Being orphaned, we have slipped into addiction to the products and comforts of the Industrial Revolution. Our culture has lost its resonance with the Original Will and instead, self-resonates with its own memory of addiction.

In preliterate cultures, the story was not written down. It was passed on from generation to generation by the priests and priestesses of the culture. The holy ones, in those instances, were the "seed" of the culture — they were *The* holy book. The shaman was the seed around which the tribal field organized the members of the tribe. Rites of initiation and seasonal rituals served to integrate and organize the whole tribe within the field, and further, to integrate the functioning of the tribal field with the fields of the Earth. The holy one was the collective memory of the tribe — s/he made the past present. New members born into the tribe were shaped within the field of the tribe, and by fitting into the greater field of the tribe, the individual had access to support through all phases of life. Birth had its ritual as well as puberty, marriage, and death. To be outside of this support, to be without one's place in the tribe, was the ultimate terror, worse than death — to be outside was death in life. Connection to the whole was lost; one was orphaned, one of the wandering undead.

During the period of neolithic village life, the cultural fields were organized within the milieu of the seed notion of the Great Mother. In other words, the Originating Mystery was seen as female rather than male. This was the case in the earlier cultures mentioned above as well. With her many different faces and names, the Great Mother was, in fact, Mother Earth. Though the details of initiation differed greatly from tribe to tribe, bioregion to bioregion, continent to continent, the central notion was of a loving mother who gave us birth, sustained us in life, and took us back to herself in death. In native African religions, Native American religions, and native European and Australian aboriginal religions, the womb, the breasts and the tomb of Mother Earth were the dominant ideas around which tribal culture self-organized.

When woman lost her friendship with the Earth and with the universe, she lost a deep part of herself; she lost the mother of nature's beings — When woman regains her communion with the world and when she educates the human family in this communion, her cosmic purpose will be fulfilled.

— Mary Rosera Joyce[4]

During the age of the great religious cultures — Hinduism, Buddhism, Taoism, Confucianism, Judaism, Islam, and Christianity— entire cultures and sometimes several cultures self-organized around the teachings contained in one or several holy books. Painting, architecture, poetry, philosphy, theology, ritual, ethics, family life, the norms of commerce and government, and indeed, nearly every aspect of life in all these cultures could in one way or another be traced back to the holy book. Truth was thus "self-evident." Each of the cultures looked to the holy book for the resonant memory of its story. To know the story was to know one's place in the cultural field, and to know your place in the field was to know your place in the community, in the bioregion, in the Earth, and in the universe. To know one's place in the story was to *know*!

Many, if not most, modern individuals place little or no importance in knowing the Holy Story of this culture. Both Jew and Gentile alike seem to pay only a nodding acknowledgment to the Judeo-Christian story as a mode of life-organization. While we might enjoy the art, the music, and the poetry born of the Judeo-Christian experience, we experience it outside the living tradition from which it was born. To be outside of the context of the story is to forget the language of the divine, which is one's story. Every religion is a language of the divine, and once lost, we cannot "hear" the Original Will resonating within the cultural field. When the "hearing" of the story is lost, so are the initiating rituals articulated within that particular language of the divine. With the loss of our rituals, we lose our connection to the great ritual from which all rituals assume their power — the great ritual of the unfolding universe.

With the loss of the rituals of initiation, the young born into such a culture never hear the voice of the Heavenly Father or the voice of Mother Earth. Such persons are forced to live without the consolation of the *Original Voices* — they begin life orphaned. They begin life, and must live their lives, in the condition of terror mentioned above; they are outside the field of cultural memory. Worse, because they do not even know the language, they have no way of knowing that they are outside. Terror is the condition of their lives, and they don't even know that they are terrified. They must conform to the cultural mode in order to belong somewhere. The cultural mode is currently the mode of addiction. They mistake the substances and behaviors of addiction offered them by an addicted society for the real field of that society. They receive the teachings of the fathers and the mothers like birds with open beaks, and like the bird, they swallow the worm whole. In this case the teachings of the addict-mothers and fathers are competition, denial, consumption, consumption, and more consumption. Suffering from *orphanism* they begin the journey to hell and many never return.

In the absence of adequate rites of passage, ad-men become the high priests of initiation into the addictions of consumerism. Everywhere the ceremony of innocence is exploited.

— Marion Woodman[5]

In the same way that the field or soul of an individual addict takes on permanent distortions as a result of the habits of addiction, so, too, do the cultural or collective fields of such individuals. We, in the western world — it is probably the same with Eastern peoples — are born into cultural fields that lack the resonant memories of collective parents. Thus, they lack the connection with heaven or with Earth. Such fields are distorted by the habits of addiction and of consumerism. The addictive distortions are built into our souls as we develop as persons — male or female. In other words, we are all birth defective in the psychic dimension of our beings. The addicted culture has its own priests, priestesses, and heroes, its own memory, and its own rites — all of these are now part of our very being.

In Step Six we make a list of these distortions as we experience them in our individual psyches and become willing to have them removed. Note that we are not trying to remove them ourselves. Rather, we are becoming willing to have them removed.

In large part, our attitudes and behavior stem from the way we think about the world. Our world is the family into which we are born and the culture in which we are raised. To the extent that the "mind" or field of the culture is dysfunctional, so too will our assumptions be distorted. In Step Five we shared our dysfunctional stories, and in Step Six we return to the list we made in Step Four. Now we acknowledge to ourselves what the specific dysfunctions are. For example, if we found in Step Four that much of what we disliked about ourselves revolved around our willingness to violate others in order to make money, then greed and violence would be the dysfunctions we are trying to rid ourselves of. We would then say to ourselves, "I'm greedy and violent and would like these attitudes to be taken from me."

We might find that we are resistant to having the attitudes removed. If that is the case, we pray for willingness. If we are to change, we must find a new basis for living other than the basis of addiction. We must find a way to have the assumptions of addiction lifted from our souls. The new basis for living will be the original basis for living, the Original Self. We are as powerless over the powers within that drive us as we are over the outer powers of death that confront us. In fact, they are the same problem with both an inner and an outer aspect. Addicted individuals produce addicted cultures that in turn produce addicted individuals, and so on. We are trapped in the *hell*ish circle of addiction. In Step Six we are admitting our powerlessness over the thinking and attitudes that have brought us to the present impasse as a species.

The evils we face in the world are too monstrous for us, and we admit that. The compulsion to continue in those evils is built right into our thinking. "Seeing" the evils and naming them can lead us to surrender, which is the means of disengagement and change. We allow ourselves to be operated upon, to be changed, to be reinvented by the great unfolding mystery of the universe. Like all else in a relative universe, cultures are functions of that universe. By surrendering, we allow the universe as a whole to act within and upon each of us. Collectively, that will amount to the universe acting upon our culture and our cultural problem. If the universe can bring forth the planet, life, consciousness, and culture, then it can remake or renew our souls and, thereby, refresh our cultures. But this can only be done with our consent, our willingness. Autonomy is respected throughout all levels of the universe process. We must become willing or we remain stuck as persons as well as cultures.

On the other hand, if in our autonomy we become willing to allow the Originating Mystery to operate upon us from within, then we will be prepared for that operation. So this next question is crucial, and each of us must ask it alone: "Am I willing to be changed?" If we can answer "yes," then we can go on to some further questions. If we cannot answer "yes," then we must wait for the willingness.

The next questions will be: "Am I willing to have my concern for self changed into concern for the whole? Am I willing to fall in love with all people and with all the living and nonliving components of the planet Earth? Am I willing to befriend the Earth and befriend the universe?"

Let us live happily then among the greedy! Among those who are greedy let us dwell free from greed.

— *The Dhammapada*[6]

Am I willing to give up the mad scramble after money, along with all the root causes of that scramble? Am I willing to give up my desire for sexual superficiality, for titillation, and for exploitation of myself and the other sex? Am I willing to pursue the depth dimension of sexual union and bear responsibility both for my reproductive powers as well as for my offspring?

From lust comes grief, from grief comes fear; he [she] who is free from lust neither sorrows nor fears.

— *The Dhammapada*[7]

How about hatred and violence? Am I willing to have these pathological forms of anger removed from my soul? Am I willing to be emptied of denied anger and vengeful motives so that healthy anger can emerge again?

Let us live happily then, not hating those who hate us! Among those who hate us, let us dwell free from hatred.

— *The Dhammapada* [8]

We are violent when we seek to diminish diversity — when we

make our way the only way. Am I willing to be open to different ways of understanding the Originating Mystery? Am I willing to understand that my way is only one of the languages of the divine? Am I willing to be concerned with the whole?

Then Arjuna beheld the entire universe, in all its multitudinous diversity, lodged as one being . . .

— Bhagavad Gita[9]

Am I willing to stop hating myself? And am I willing to have my relationship to both food and drink brought into line with the needs of all life on this planet?

Hunger is the greatest affliction.

— The Dhammapada[10]

For I was hungry and you gave me food, I was thirsty and you gave me drink . . .

— Matt. 25:35, 36[11]

Am I willing to eat and drink bearing in mind all those who have neither food nor drink? Am I willing to be concerned with soils and water so that all might eat and drink?

Envy is the feeling we have when someone else gets what we crave. Am I willing to have envy removed from my soul with all its root causes? Am I willing to let go of all the suffering that comes from craving and envy? Can I admit to myself that there are certain perverse pleasures associated with craving and be willing to let them go? Buddhism offers us a spiritual therapy for dealing with the phenomenon of craving.

The Four Noble Truths Of Buddhism
1. All of life entails sorrow and suffering
2. The cause of suffering is craving
3. Suffering ends when craving ends
4. Craving ends when the eightfold path is followed.

Am I willing to replace craving with a burning desire that all people will have what they need? That the animals are left with their habitat? That the beauty of the planet is kept intact?

Apathy is the real opposite of love; it is indifference. Sloth is another word for apathy and laziness is another. It is a state of willful blindness and deafness. It is the choice to not see and hear the agonies everywhere around us.

O conquerer of sloth, this very day you shall behold the whole universe

Greenspirit

with all things animate and inert made one within this body of mine. And whatever else you desire to see, that you shall see also. But you cannot see me with those human eyes. Therefore I give you divine sight.

— *Bhagavad Gita*[12]

Am I willing to have divine sight? Am I willing to see the whole? Am I willing to have all my blindnesses removed and all my deafnesses removed so that I can see and hear? Am I willing to ask for new eyes, new ears, and a new heart?

We can now identify a certain psychological combination taking shape in many people, in something like the following sequence: Fear and a sense of threat break through prior numbing; these uncomfortable (potentially shattering) feelings in turn raise the personal question of whether one should take some form of action to counter the danger; that question becomes an additional source of conflict, associated as it is with feelings of helplessness and doubts about efficacy; and one seeks a psychological safe haven of resignation ("Well, if it happens, it happens — and it will happen to all of us.") and cynicism ("They'll drop it all right and it will be the end of all of us — that's the way people are, and that will be that!") That stance prevents one from feeling too fearful, and, equally important, it protects one from conflict and anxiety about doing something about the situation. If the situation is hopeless, one need do nothing. There is a particularly sophisticated version of resignation-cynicism that one encounters these days mainly at universities, which goes something like this: "Well, what's so special about man? Other species have come and gone, so perhaps this is our turn to become extinct?" This is perhaps the ultimate "above the battle" position. Again nothing is to be done, one is philosophically-cosmically detached from it all. All of these add up to a stance of waiting for the bomb and contribute to a self-fulfilling prophesy of universal doom.

— Lifton and Falk[13]

All of the above could be said about the environmental crisis as well. That "bomb" has already gone off. Am I willing to be changed? Am I even willing to be willing?

We take STEP SIX when we can say the following before our group: "I am entirely willing to have all habits of delusion removed from my thinking, my attitudes and from my behavior."

CHAPTER SEVEN

Nuclear awareness has certain specific requirements. It means breaking out of the illusory system we described, renouncing the illusions of limit and control, of the benefits of foreknowledge, of preparation, protection, stoic behavior of survivors, and recovery. It also means extricating ourselves from our deadly dependence on and worship of the weapons, extricating ourselves from nuclearism. The process is psychologically difficult in the extreme because our relationship to both nuclear illusions and nuclearism has had the quality of an addiction. Addiction is always a life-death pattern. That is, one's emotions become so invested in one's relationship (or 'connection') to a particular object that all vitality and attachment — one's existence itself — are at stake in that relationship. In the language of addiction, nuclearism and nuclear illusions are the "nuclear connection." Never has that connection been more malignant; nor has it ever been under more critical scrutiny. While one can feel the attraction of a "cold turkey" (immediate, total cessation of the use of the "drug") cure, a more gradual, incremental approach is undoubtedly more practical.

— Lifton and Falk[1]

STEP SEVEN: IN HUMILITY, WE REQUEST THAT THIS ORIGINATING MYSTERY REMOVE ALL OUR HABITS OF ILLUSORY THOUGHT, ATTITUDE AND BEHAVIOR.

The universe is a unity. When it acts in any or all of its parts, it acts as a unity, as a whole. If I feel an itch on my leg, the itch and my recognition of it are two functions of the unity that I am. My hand moving to scratch it is another function of the same unity, and the pleasure at relieving the itch is another. Whenever I act, I act as a unity.

It is the same with the universe. It emerged as a unity, a single multiform energy event called the fireball. It also evolves as a unity, and all functions within the universe are functions of that unity. This hand holding this pencil that scratches along this page spreading carbon lines that capture a certain language and a certain idea within that language . . . all of these are functions of the Earth/universe process.

Science has revealed for us four primordial forces inherent within the universe process that act upon all matter. We shall look at them and explain them, but though we speak of them separately, we must remember that they are not separate. They are four functions of the universe being observed by the self-reflexive phase of the universe. We have said that from its beginning, the universe is psychic as well as material. In looking at these four forces, we will be noting how the psychic — intelligent — dimension of the universe acts upon the material — physical — phase of the universe. They are phases of the same unity in the same way that my body and emotions are parts of one whole. In fact, everything is part of a single whole. Erich Jantsch puts it simply:

The environment of a cell consists not only of its neighbor cells but also of the total biosphere with its chemistry and energy flows, and even of the solar system with its radiation phenomena and its gravity.[2]

As we discussed earlier, the solar system is a function of the galaxy, and the galaxy of the universe. So, the environment of a cell is the universe. The universe acts as a whole in every cell.

THE FOUR FORCES

Gravity

What is gravity? We can't really say what gravity is — no one has ever seen gravity. We can say what gravity does, and we can observe its effects on matter. Pick up a pencil and hold it in front of you. Let it drop. It is drawn to the floor by gravity. The gravitational pull of the mass of the Earth acting on the pencil will draw the pencil down. That same force keeps one from floating around the room, holds the moon in orbit around the Earth, and holds the Earth in orbit around the sun. All heavenly bodies exert gravitional attraction upon one another no matter how distant they are or how slight the pull. So, we can assume that gravity acts similarly in all parts of the universe. What then is gravity? It is a function of the universe in each of its parts. If the universe is a function of the Originating Mystery, then gravity is a function of that Mystery in all parts of the universe.

Electromagnetism

When we look into the night sky and perceive the distant stars, the electrical charges in our eyes are oscillating in unison with an electromagnetic force field that originated from oscillating charges on that star many years ago. We are interacting with the past. In that we are a product and a function of this planet, the above interaction is between the Earth and a star. Again, the Earth is a function of the solar system, the solar system is a function of the Milky Way, and the Milky Way is a function of the universe. Thus, stargazing is a function of the universe observing itself in us. Whatever stars we could observe from whatever place on the planet, the description would be the same: Earth observes a star in us. We are the universe looking at itself. Therefore, electomagnetism is a function of the universe in all its parts, and we experience this function in several ways:

1. When we feel the warmth of the sun, our skin is interacting with light from the sun.
2. All of life's processes — thinking, digestion, muscular responses, growth, sexuality, chemistry, and optical phenomena — arise out of electromagnetism.

The Strong Nuclear Force

This is the force that glues together the particles comprising the nucleus of the atom. Protons and neutrons together form the core of the atom. Protons naturally repel one another in that they have the same electrical charge. A free neutron, left to itself, breaks down into a proton, an electron, and a neutrino in about half an hour. What holds protons and neutrons together in the nucleus is the strong nuclear force. We must remember that, as with gravity, we never see the strong nuclear force. What we see are the effects of the force. We deduce that this force is acting because we learn to see the *effects* of its action. The force itself, while exhibiting itself in matter throughout the universe, remains invisible, a *mystery*.

The Weak Nuclear Force

This interaction or force is little known, rather recently discovered, and is largely mysterious. In particular, the weak nuclear force accounts for the disintegration of atomic nuclei. We call this disintegration radioactivity. Like the other three universe dynamics we have mentioned, we perceive its effects only by detecting particles emitted from the atomic nucleus. Its nature — *the force in and of itself* — remains invisible, a mystery.

We can think of these forces as four aspects of the universal personality. As is the case with your personality, the whole personality of the universe acts in each of its parts. What we perceive as we come to know and befriend each other is our personalities as they are made manifest through our bodies. The personalities of each of us remain invisible and mysterious. As we befriend the Earth, it is the planetary personality that we experience everywhere, in each of her parts. As we befriend the universe, it is the personality of the universe that we experience in each of its parts. The truth is that these are all one personality; they comprise the personality of the Originating Mystery as it functions throughout the universe everywhere and in all things. So, everything we perceive anywhere in the universe is the result of an invisible function of the universe.

The human is that being in whom the personality of the universe comes to observe itself. In other words, the four forces we mentioned above come into self-reflection in the human. The act of being named by science as the four forces *is* the four forces coming into consciousness — self-awareness in the human. While they were present throughout the universe long before the human evolved, they came to be able to perceive themselves in us. Human self-reflection is itself a function of the universe/Earth. So, if human self-reflection is a function of the universe, and if the universe is a function of the Originating Mystery, then human self-reflection is itself a function of the Originating Mystery.

If this is so, then we should be able to trust the universe to act in the individual human personality/field/soul in the same way that it acts on the individual pencil we held up and dropped. Wonderfully . . . this is the case! When we have removed the blockage of denial, we open ourselves to the dynamics of the collective unconscious — the universe. In doing so, we experience the Originating Mystery rejoining the individual to the whole, thereby allowing the whole to act within the individual. In Step Seven we take the process another step further.

Now, as autonomous entities — fields — within the greater field of the universe, we request that the Originating Mystery "break the bones" of our habits of delusion and reset them according to the *Original Plan*. We are asking that the very structures of our psyches, formed by years of addictive distortions, be changed. We are asking to be remade according to the needs of the evolution of the whole. We are relinquishing our wills so that the *Original Will* can be manifest in and through us. So, we make our simple request in humility. Having done so, we can expect that the universe will act within us in wonderful ways and can expect to be changed, fundamentally.

Note that Step Seven calls for us to ask in humility. Humility comes from the same root as the word *humus* — or soil. Humility is an attitude that arises out of our recognition that we are members of the soil community. Humility is not meekness, it is true *Earthiness*. We are one of the organisms of the soil community; we are contingent. We plant, harvest, and eat the products of the soil. When we die, we compost into soil again.

> For you are dirt
> and to dirt you shall return.
> — Gen. 3:19[3]

We are as dependent on the soil as all other living things. We can think of ourselves as the conscious phase of the soil community, so to ask in humility is to ask as humus people.

As members of the soil community, we are members of the planet community. As members of the planet community, we are members of the solar system, and the solar system is a member of the Milky Way, and the Milky Way is a member of the community of galaxies. The community of galaxies is the universe, born of and revelatory of the Originating Mystery. When we ask in humility, we are recognizing the ability of the whole universe to act in each of its parts or members. We are asking that the universe reinvent the human — this human! — in a way that will enhance the survivability of the entire bio-planet Earth.

Like Steps One, Three, and Five, Step Seven is a surrender step. We are admitting that we do not know who we are supposed to be, and that someone other than ourselves will have to reinvent us. Not many people care to admit that they just don't know. Everyone wants to be an expert or to hire an expert.

> An expert is a person who used to be a pert!
> —Stanley Gorsky[4]

We are threatened as a species, indeed, as a planet. Our experts have no real plan, no overall strategy to deal with the problems we face. Each of them sees only a small part of the problem — a narrow slice of the dilemma that falls within the field of their expertise. We need people who see the whole, who surrender to the whole, and who are reinvented by the whole.

The very context within which our present programs are formulated, be they political, economic, legal, or religious, is itself the problem. Each of them is seen as a separate area of expertise. Seldom, if ever, are they seen in the context of the whole planet. Economies of each nation state are formulated without reference to each other, or to the planetary reality, while all are nonetheless totally dependent on the planet. Airtight departments at many universities guarantee the continuation of the problem. We must ask some new questions.

Has theology anything whatever to do with biology? Has geology anything whatever to do with economics? Has ecology anything whatever to do with political science? What is the paradigm, or underlying set of assumptions or ideas upon which our present system of thought is based? Presently, a paradigm of parts is being replaced by a paradigm of wholes. This therapy or spirituality will help readers to change the assumptions that ground their thinking. That change will be from a paradigm of parts to a paradigm of interdependent, but autonomous, wholes.

Governments must accept that all policies must arise from the knowledge that we all share one planet, and that we all have the right to life upon that planet. We must define our relationships to each other by inclusion rather than exclusion, and then deal creatively with the conflictual gap of our differences. We must stop preparing for collective death — no nation has that right! It is a criminal preoccupation, one that must be condemned with the same finality as Nazism. The arms race has been, and still is, an unprecedented evil. We must abandon forever the idea that the Earth will be gathered under any mono-ideology; we must accept and value diversity. That is the way the planet works. Humility predicates that we align ourselves with the dynamics of the whole planet. The nation-state can no longer be the primary referent for world order. Before I think of myself as an American, I must think of myself as a citizen of the Earth. In Step Seven I am asking that this change be effected in me, and then, we must go further and work to make the same changes in our institutions.

All plundering economies must be replaced with local, sustainable economies suited to local needs and resources. We are coming to see that quality of life is far more important than standard of living. In fact, the term "standard of living" can be considered part of the obsolete rhetoric of addiction. "Quality of life" refers to the health of the planet for all species. We have witnessed the cruel degradation of the planet. We, and all of life, have become degraded as a result. The health and radiance of the natural world is the only hope for a sustainable economy and must become the primary referent for all economic thought.

Natural systems compost the dead in order to support the living. Recycling and composting must replace the dump, the incinerator, and/or dumping at sea. Smaller ecosystems function within the context of larger ones which in turn function within the context of *bio*regions. Local economies must function within a comprehensive web of interdependent but autonomous economies. The multinational corporation is a "dinosaur" and must be encouraged to become extinct. The difference between local economies and multinational corporations can be compared to the difference between healthy cell growth and cancer. The present plundering economy is built upon assumptions that guarantee the ultimate destruction of the base upon which they are built. An economy that destroys its own base must inevitably lead to famine.

When money becomes the mono-value in addicted cultures, justice loses its relationship to fairness and becomes a scramble to win. Few lawyers build their reputations on the high ideals of protecting the innocent and the vulnerable. More often, the entire focus is on winning and on the size of the haul. Lawyers become hired liars, and individuals can seldom compete with big business and government in hiring an effective one. While the ideal is that all are equal under the law, seldom is that the case in reality. The wealthy and powerful seem equal under the law and are, more often than not, responsible for the exploitation of the planet and her beings.

Because there are few laws that name the crimes of biocide and geocide, the rich and powerful remain rich and powerful at the expense of the planet and her beings. New weapons systems are built and deployed; justice remains silent. The future of our children is ever more degraded on an ever more degraded planet; justice remains silent. Toxins burn our soils, besmudge our air, and malign our waters; justice remains silent. Justice will become just when it is locally administered. Then, lawyers will be defending people they know and who know them and will become servants of the law again, not servants of the lie.

Education must provide new visions of wholeness for our children. Children need to know the great story of the universe; they need to know the story of the planet, the story of life, the story of culture. When they know the whole story, they will know their place within the story. Knowing your place in the story is to know your place, and to know your place is to be at home. They need to see new opportunities for work . . . good work . . . work that brings them in touch with their own gifts, the gifts of others, and the gifts of the planet. Children of the addicted and plundering nations must be taught that the smaller nations will not tolerate the present gluttonous plundering of their resources forever. Children must be taught proper relationship to *their* soil, to *their* water, and to *their* resources. Americans need to be taught the real history and herstory of North America before, as well as since, "discovery" by Columbus. They should be taught *by* Native Americans so that they can finally come to learn how to live on this continent. All children need contact with the "mother" peoples of their *father*lands, as well as with the "father" peoples of their *mother*lands.

We must come up with a new vision for our "health" establishment. Presently, we do not focus on health but rather on curing disease — there's more money in disease. We must change our focus and spend our research dollars on ways of optimizing health. This must begin with the realization that only a healthy habitat can create and sustain healthy individuals. Next, health maintenance by such wholistic healers as chiropractors, nutritionists, and homeopathic healers would provide a focus on the healthy organism rather than upon the diseased organism. Only in extreme cases would doctors, as we know them, even be consulted. Hard science has given us or has at least exacerbated the cancer epidemic; why expect a cure from the same source? We need healers . . . real healers.

Too many marriages end in divorce — the family, as an institution, is dysfunctional. When more value is placed on the ownership of things than on time spent with the family, we can hardly expect the situation to be otherwise. We must begin, again, to focus our attention on protecting our children, instead of asking them to adapt to the selfish concerns of an addicted lifestyle. We have created a nation of orphans — that's the real "Pepsi generation." These orphans are only those that we have allowed to survive in the womb. It is unnatural for a people to kill their own offspring. In a smaller, more local mode of neo-village life, the community could become the extended family, providing welcome for unexpected children and support for their mothers. When the "unexpected child" is welcome, the "unwanted child" no longer exists.

It is unnatural for fathers to be careless concerning their reproductive responsibilities. When the fathers no longer initiate the sons into the ways of the "grandfathers," then the sons never integrate the morality of the grandfathers which includes the protection and nurturance of both mothers and children as well as of each other. It is unnatural for children to be brought up outside of the presence of their mothers. It is an unnatural economy that causes, implements, and supports such divorce. It is unnatural for women to be forced into circumstances that cause them to kill the life rooted in their own bodies. It is an unnatural culture that encourages and sanctions such practices. The child in utero is a function of the planet, and only the planet — *the unconscious* — has the right to terminate pregnancy. We need to understand and admit what families really need . . . *each other*. Consumerism, with all its emptiness and lack of true values, is the addiction responsible for the wholesale destruction of the family.

Beneath all the dysfunctions touched on above lies the "seed" dysfunction, the loss of relationship to the Originating Mystery brought on by a breakdown of the language of the divine. In the western world, where the relationship to the Book isn't lost, its most pernicious aspects are frequently overvalued. These aspects encourage and sanction the very plundering of the planet that is killing us all. On the one hand, the human is considered fallen — ontologically flawed. On the other, the human is given lordship over all the natural systems of the planet. Again, on one hand we are taught that we are dysfunctional by nature while on the other we are the chosen people. There seems to be a compensatory relationship between these polarizations. We need to understand that all people and all living beings are chosen by the Originating Mystery or they simply would not be here. None are ontologically dysfunctional either or they could not be here. With the destruction of the native "mother" peoples of the western world, we have become *hyper*patriated. Hierarchy seems to be the way men organize themselves. There is nothing unnatural in that. What is unnatural is *de*matriated hierarchy. When father loses mother he becomes hard to live with.

We are worn out with absolute paternal care. We need our Mother. We need a teaching authority that insists on the rights of the planet, on the divine rights of the planet. We are tired of feeling "fallen" and of compensating for that with the inflated attitude of being a "chosen people." We are tired of religious establishments that encourage cooperation with, and allegiance to, governments and economic entities that hold the planet hostage while plundering and destroying her. We are tired of funding our own suicide. We want to hear confrontation with empire preached, not cooperation with empire. When a religious establishment can no longer empower people to confront the evils that are destroying them, then that establishment can be said to be dysfunctional, and as such, an agency of those very evils.

In Step Seven we are humble — we are in solidarity with all souls and all soils. We are asking that all dysfunctional assumptions in each of us be removed. Collectives of individuals with functional assumptions will produce institutions with functional assumptions. We are asking that the universe restore us to soil-based assumptions. We are admitting that we do not even know what those assumptions will be. We are going to let the universe change us at its own pace, in its own time, and for its own ends. Of course, its ends are our ends. We will be the conscious phase of its unconscious ends. In other words, we will come to know.

Nor will we become perfected in our *Original Selves* overnight, if ever. While the greater part of the culture functions in an addicted mode, we cannot hope to be entirely untouched by it. That would be like taking a sponge from the ocean, wringing it out, and tossing it back while expecting it to remain dry. The addicted culture is our culture. We must depend upon the deeper dynamics of the planet to keep us well in a sick culture. We do so by continuing to surrender to those deeper needs, those deeper dynamics of the Originating Mystery present to us as Mother Earth. We ask to be shaped into more fitting vessels through which the energies of evolution might be expressed. There will be pain; it will be the pain of the Earth as she changes things. Old habits will be cut out, new ones will be born, and dead ones will come back to life again.

We will be remade into birth canals for a new culture. This will be a culture that made the decision — the cutting away from addiction and the lies of addiction. A culture that died and rose from the dead. A culture that reinvented itself in health, appropriateness, freedom, and truth. A culture that learned to live in harmony with the other creatures of the Earth community. A culture that learned to live in harmony within the life systems of the planet Earth. A culture that cared enough about its children to leave behind the superficial trivialities of addiction. A culture of people who reinvented themselves by allowing life to reinvent them.

In this new culture, all governments will have as their first concern, the condition of soils, water, and air. Economies will be appropriate to the natural systems from which they draw their resources. Sustainable prosperity will be their goal and not unchecked growth. Education will evoke within students an identity with, and a corresponding love of, the natural world. Wonder will replace competition in the classroom — a wonder born of being part of an unfolding universe that is new and fresh in every moment. Beauty will be at least as important as utility in the new educational establishments. The family — *home*rship — will be more important than ownership. Religions will be seen in relationship to each other rather than in opposition to each other. The *Global Spiritual Tradition of the Human* will be the basis for mutual respect and decency for all languages of the divine. Religions will evoke in the faithful a love of the Creator by evoking in them a love of creation and of their own creativity. All religions will be enriched by understanding and valuing all other religions.

Again, I want to remind the reader of the greatness, the nobility of the journey upon which we have embarked. The human is co-creator with the universe in the shaping of evolution upon this planet. In taking the *Twelve Steps of Ecological Spirituality*, we are maturing into the responsibility of being a co-creator. By going through the birth pangs that these steps presume, we will come, one by one, to a vision of the new land — *The Planet Earth in the Ecological Age*. Perhaps we, like Moses of the Hebrew tradition, will not ourselves ever fully enter therein. But, we can at least die knowing that we did our best to ensure that our children and their children have a living planet — a radiant planet — in which to live. What greater reward could life hold out to us? What greater purpose could we hope to realize in our lives? What greater comfort could we experience than this comfort? We are giving our lives to reshape the life of the whole.

As in Step Three, we come to the practical problem of how we shall go about taking Step Seven. The following is a simple formula which ideally should be spoken in the presence of another person, but, if you prefer, can be said alone. It should be done after much thought about our deluded habits, and after naming the worst of them out loud. This formula is merely a suggestion for those who have not come up with one of their own.

O———————————, Originating Mystery, Creator and sustaining will of the universe, I am willing that you should have all of me, the functional and dysfunctional, the addicted and free. Please remove from me all habits of thought, attitude, and deed that impede the emergence of your creativity in and through me.

Please remove from me anything that obstructs my usefulness to all humans, all species, to the entire creation. Please bring to birth in me attitudes and talents that will promote the birthing of the future. Strengthen me as I give my life as food for a starving world.

From here, we go on confident that we will be given all we need to create the future. But as we build the future, we must also begin to repair the present. This great challenge will be the subject of Steps Eight and Nine.

CHAPTER EIGHT

The blood which runs in us is born of the blood of our Earthly Mother. Her blood falls from the clouds; leaps up from the womb of the Earth; babbles in the brooks of the mountains: flows wide in the rivers of the plains; sleeps in the lakes; rages mightily in tempestuous seas.

The air which we breathe is born of the breath of our Earthly Mother. Her breath is azure in the heights of the heavens; soughs in the tops of the mountains; whispers in the leaves of the forest; billows over the cornfields; slumbers in the deep valleys; burns hot in the desert.

The hardness of our bones is born of the bones of our Earthly Mother, of the rocks and of the stones. They stand naked to the heavens on the tops of mountains; are as giants that lie sleeping on the sides of the mountains, as idols set in the desert, and are hidden in the deepness of the Earth.

The tenderness of our flesh is born of the flesh of our Earthly Mother; whose flesh waxes yellow and red in the fruits of the trees, and nurtures us in the furrows of the fields.

Our bowels are born of the bowels of our Earthly Mother, and are hid from our eyes, like the invisible depths of the Earth.

The light of our eyes, the hearing of our ears, both are born of the colors and the sounds of our Earthly Mother; which enclose us about, as the waves of the sea a fish, as the eddying air a bird.

. . . you are one with the Earthly Mother; she is in you and you in her. Of her were you born, in her do you live, and to her you shall return again. Keep, therefore, her laws, for none can live long, neither be happy, but he who honors his Earthly Mother and does her laws. For your breath is her breath; your blood her blood; your bone her bone; your flesh her flesh; your bowels her bowels; your eyes and your ears are her eyes and her ears.

I tell you, unless you follow the laws of your Mother, you can in no wise escape death.

Essene Gospel of Peace[1]

STEP EIGHT: WE MAKE A LIST OF ALL PERSONS, ALL OTHER SPECIES, AND ALL THE LIFE SYSTEMS OF THE PLANET THAT WE HAVE HARMED AND BECOME READY TO DO EVERYTHING IN OUR POWER TO HEAL THEM ALL.

So far we have admitted our powerlessness over the cultural addiction of *consumerism*. We have acknowledged that there is an Originating Mystery responsible for the emergence and evolution of the universe. We have made a decision to surrender our lives and our wills to this Originating Mystery in order to get ourselves out of the way of that evolving Mystery. We have examined ourselves and listed all our dysfunctions of thought, attitude, and deed. Having done so, we confided the content of those lists to another person. Next, we identified and listed the habits of soul formed by years of consumer behavior, and then, we humbly asked that the Originating Mystery remove those habits. By now we should have begun to experience certain changes in ourselves. Having experienced these changes, it is time to become active — we can go out and enter into the work of renewing the Earth, without fear of burnout or despair. The creative energy of the whole universe is behind us. We are able to ask ourselves this question: What can I do?

If we have done a thorough job on all of the preceding Steps, we should begin to find that we have vast, fresh, and unexpected powers at our disposal. This new source of power will enable us to begin to proceed toward a response to the evils that confront us and our planet. We will also have begun to achieve a new openness to this power source and will begin to find ourselves able to access this power within our own selves. It will begin to dawn on us that each of us contains the entire history of the universe, recorded and present, in the very fabric of our beings. Having realized our *Original Selves*, we will begin to have a wider vision, and we will begin to feel our oneness with the whole universe/Earth/life process. Our fragmentary thinking will end. Our fragmentary personalities and self-images will *re*knit and begin to become whole again.

Freed from denial and guilt, able to look ourselves and others in the eye and empowered by a new creativity, we can now begin to remedy our individual and the global situation. That remedy will begin by listing the ways in which we have hurt ourselves. We cannot hope to befriend the Earth and universe until we have befriended ourselves. So, again, we need to ask some questions. How have I hurt my body by my addictive illusions over the years? How have I injured my ability to think clearly? How have I injured my heart, my primary habitat — the place from which I live my life? How have I injured my womb, or any woman's womb, by not understanding that the human womb is a habitat? How have I injured my deepest values? What beliefs have I crossed? Returning to Step Four, we can consider the seven dysfunctions there listed and ask, How have I injured myself because of them? Remember to write all of the answers down — make a list. Am I ready and willing to change my behavior toward myself?

Next we will want to consider our relationships within our family of origin. How have I injured my parents? How have I injured my sisters and brothers? As soon as we ask ourselves these questions, our feelings are likely to go on the defensive. We will want to justify ourselves or consider the ways in which these people have hurt us, but our purpose here is not to count the offenses of others. Rather, we will want to acknowledge what we have done and be ready to heal the damage. Am I ready to repair whatever damage I have caused my mother, my father, and my sisters and brothers? How about grandparents? How about uncles, aunts, and cousins? Am I ready to try to heal all the damage I have caused?

Am I ready to try to heal all relationships within my present family? Am I ready to approach my spouse and express true and authentic sorrow for whatever pain I have caused? If I am divorced or separated, can I contact my ex-spouse(s) and do the same? Am I ready to make amends to my children? Am I ready to make contact with any children I might have ignored or abandoned and attempt to mend the breaches in those relationships? Can I at least write to them? An authentic expression of sorrow can often open doors that have been sealed for years.

Am I ready to make amends to people I have hurt in the workplace? Have I injured others for my own gain? Have I been willing to injure other families in order to "get ahead"? Have I been dishonest as a worker? Have I been callous or greedy as a manager? Am I willing to bow or kneel before those over me for some petty advantage? Do I stand up for what is right even though I might lose for having done so? Am I willing to apologize? Am I ready to change my ways at the workplace? Am I ready to use my work as a way of serving others? Does my work serve others or serve to threaten the well-being of others?

Have I injured anyone in my community? Have I been selfish in my pursuit of sexual gratification? Have I injured my own family or other families as a result of that selfishness? Have I seen others as "tools to be used" or as people to be served? Have I, in any way, compromised community good in favor of my own perceived private good? Am I ready to heal whatever harm I have done to anyone? How about members of my church or temple? How about members of my religious community? How about members of clubs, civic, professional, or educational bodies I have belonged to? Am I ready to make amends for harms done to one and all?

Sometimes our lives directly affect the lives of people at the state, national, and even international level. How have I injured people, perhaps many people, by my dishonesty, greed, or lust for power while in public office? Have I supported programs that promote fear, partisanship, or unreasonable private profit? Am I responsible for policies that threaten or kill born or preborn people, animals, or both? Has my life had a negative effect on the people of my state, my nation, or the world? Why? Am I ready to change my thinking, my attitudes, and my deeds?

As I mentioned earlier, all traditions of religion and spirituality offer a wealth of help with these questions. It behooves us to consult our own tradition as well as other traditions within the global spiritual tradition of the human. However, we are also confronted with evils that are peculiar to our own time . . . evils that are at a different order of magnitude than those that can be answered by the wisdom of the past. It falls heavily upon our shoulders to confront these evils and to formulate an ethical response to them. This is not easy — never before have people been forced to look into the face of evils of such daunting proportions. But, remember, if we have done our work well, we will not be facing these evils alone. We will be supported by the Originating Mystery — the birther and sustainer of the entire universe. If the Originating Mystery can engender the whole, then that same Mystery can recreate the whole. We do not face evil alone.

THE FIVE ADDICTIONS TO DEATH

We are coming to the end of the line personally and globally through our rejection of the feminine side of God. Addicts manifest an extreme form of this desecration in our culture, but they are also potential catalysts for the rebirth of the feminine. Not only are they individuals carrying the unconscious of their forebears. As human beings in the history of mankind, they are also living out what is unconscious in the social environment. We can remain blind to our personal shadow until we look into the starving eyes of an anorexic or alcoholic we love; we can also remain blind to the collective shadow until we turn on television and look into the eyes of a starving child.

In a technological civilization geared up for its own heady destruction, we are destined to become the victims of an outworn patriarchal consciousness so long as we collude in equating femininity with biological identity. That kind of consciousness is propelling not only individuals but the whole planet into an addiction to power and perfection, which, viewed from the perspective of nature, can lead only to suicide. Feminine consciousness dare not be limited to unredeemed matter or unconscious mother. The realization that a neurosis has a creative purpose applies globally as well as personally, and surely, in an age addicted to power and the acquisition of material possessions, the creative purpose must have something to do with the one thing that can save us—love for the Earth, love for each other—the wisdom of the Goddess. Responsibility belongs in the individual home, in the individual heart, in the energy that holds atoms together rather than blows them apart.

— Marion Woodman[2]

In *Ecological Spirituality* we are formulating a position that speaks in defense and in support of all life and of all life systems. We trust that the Originating Mystery inherent in all matter will cause life to self-organize, self-evolve, and self-regulate in benign and appropriate ways. Further, we believe that what we humans need to do is to allow the process to evolve. If we remove the blockages that threaten the whole of life, the Earth will do the rest. The most obvious blockages I have called the five addictions to death.

The Death of the Earth: *Nuclearism*

Never before has a culture been confronted with the ability to destroy all of life on Earth. Never before has one species had the ability to convert the bio-planet into a bier-planet. A city? Yes. A nation? Yes. Even a culture? Yes. But never the whole of life — human, animal, and vegetative. Never! *Nuclearism* is the suicide component of the addicted culture; it is the temptation to self-abort the human species along with all other life. Governments have fingered and continue to finger the guns that are held at all of our heads. Many of us are so frozen with the terror and denial that surround this reality that we seldom, if ever, allow it into consciousness long enough to do anything about it. Many more of us are relaxed about the situation because of recent changes in the relationships between the super powers, but the weapons remain nonetheless.

Seldom, if ever, do we hear our preachers confront this unprecedented evil head on. Seldom, if ever, do we hear them encourage us to make this issue a personal one, as though our own deaths, along with all that lives, are not personal or religious issues.

Am I ready to allow planetary suicide to become a personal and religious issue for me? Am I ready to make my children's future my concern? Am I ready to acknowledge my own responsibility for bringing to an end that which threatens all that lives as well as the conditions necessary for life itself? Am I ready to change my thinking about nuclear weapons and about nuclear power generally? Am I ready to look at the ways my life enhances the escalating madness of nuclearism?

The apocalyptic psychology of an addicted culture—a psychology that anticipates the divine revelation in one blinding bolt of insight—could on a planetary scale foreshadow a holocaust.

— Marion Woodman[3]

The Death of Species by Chemical Solution: *Pollutionism* The In-*Toxic*-ation of All Life

The addiction to consuming is fueled by overproduction. All production depends upon the materials of the Earth, all production has a certain amount of pollution attendant to it. When we overconsume, we do so at the expense of the whole planet. The resultant poisoning of the Earth's systems is the direct result of our own actions. Am I ready to acknowledge the relationship between *my* overconsumption and *my* poisoning of *my* planet? Am I ready to admit that the poisoning affects everything that lives? Am I ready to begin to héal the damage by being willing to consume only what I really need? Am I ready to change my habits so that all beings might live?

The Death of Life's Original Plan: Genetic Engineering and other "Bio-technologies" — the Human in the China Closet

We have a sacred obligation to say no.

— Jeremy Rifkin[4]

Since the 1950s we have learned more about genetics than we ever knew before in the entire history of the human. Each year we learn more than we knew in all the years since the fifties combined. Next year we will learn more than all we know now in the wonderful study of life. In fifty years it will seem as though we knew nothing whatsoever this year. In a hundred years it might seem as though we had barely begun to know much now. Perhaps we should wait before we tamper with a code that has been responsible for the transmission and sustenance of such a marvelous diversity of Earth-beings? Perhaps we should leave the unfolding of life to the Originating Mystery? Am I ready to speak for and as all of life — past, present, and future — by speaking out against genetic engineering? Am I ready to insist that no one knows enough about life to tinker with ours and our children's genes? Am I ready to challenge all experts who think they have the right to toy with the future evolution of life on Earth? Am I ready to make the issue of genetic engineering a personal one? Am I ready to do it now?

The Death of Habitat: Destroying the "Context for Life"

Scientists and conservationists are urgently calling for worldwide action to slow the accelerating mass extinction of animal and plant species. Many of them warned this loss threatened future human food and drug sources and, according to several speakers, might even threaten the current level of civilization.

His own [Dr. Edward O. Wilson of Harvard] estimate of species that are now vanishing each year is "10,000 and increasing."

Norman Myers, a consultant on environment and development, said an impending "extinction spasm" was likely to produce "the greatest single setback to life's abundance and diversity since the first flickerings of life almost four billion years ago."

If the current trend continues, Dr. Ehrlich says "humanity will foreclose many of the direct economic benefits it might have withdrawn from Earth's once well-stocked genetic library." Among the possibilities that might be foregone is a cure for cancer from some organism as yet undiscovered. Worse, he said the genetic losses would cause the entire ecological system on which humanity depends to falter.

"Humanity will bring upon itself consequences depressingly similar to those expected from a nuclear winter," he warned, including famine and epidemic diseases.

— *New York Times*[7]

Currently we are eliminating thousands of species of living beings every year — eliminating a species is not like eliminating an individual being within a species. When we destroy a species, we destroy its chance to reproduce itself again, and, we eliminate those species that feed upon it. We kill them all, absolutely. No one knows how long we can go on removing threads from the fabric of life before the fabric itself collapses. It might be too late already, but we don't know that. We do know that the Originating Mystery was responsible for the emergence and evolution of all life on this planet. We also know that human life is utterly dependent on these other plant and animal life forms for its own existence and functioning. Put bluntly, whatever we do to other species will ultimately happen to us!

Am I ready to admit that I need all the other species in order to survive? Am I willing to admit that all other species have the right to habitat? I am a member of that species wherein the Earth attains reflexive consciousness of herself. Am I willing to begin to accept responsibility for all of life, for the whole planet? Am I ready to ask myself how my life contributes to *The Great Slaughter?* Am I ready to change my behavior in order to allow for the healing of all of life? Am I ready to do all I can to heal all of life?

The Death of Love: The Destruction of Born and Preborn Human Young

The death of love is surely *the* psychic epidemic of our times. Since the word love was itself cheapened by its commercial use in the selling of products since the late sixties, love itself has been dying. In its absence, we find the culture obsessed with and becoming addicted to sexual behaviors that are beginning to appear to be deeply maladaptive. Human love, like everything else in the "consumer society," has been desacralized. Having reduced our understanding of love to a physical phenomenon, we have allowed the deeper reality — the psycho-spiritual reality of love — to atrophy. Consciously or unconsciously we have extended our reductionistic and materialistic view of reality to include even our own persons. We seem to be forgetting the cosmological and mystical dimensions of our love.

The following questions must be asked: Are we, as a species, forgetting how to rear human young? Could this malaise spring from the fact that we have given ourselves the right to kill preborn human young in utero in the same way that we have given ourselves the right to kill thousands of species each year? Is not abortion what we are doing to the whole Earth process? Haven't we even toyed with the idea of global thermonuclear abortion? By giving ourselves permission to eliminate that which is inconvenient, do we not cheapen our whole view of living beings? Presently we find ourselves awash in a psychic epidemic of sexual, physical, emotional, and spiritual abuse of our own young! We are aborting them in all of those ways and in others. We believe we have the right to abandon them when our marriages and their problems seem too difficult. The matter is an epidemic at the species level.

As fewer and fewer people take the deeper dimensions of love seriously, dimensions that include morality, responsibility, commitment, and integrity, it becomes more difficult for others to do so. Many of us feel unsupported in our struggle to sustain family life. The result of all of this is the loss of real community. The "loss of community" is another way of saying the death of love.

The universe blossomed forth from Mystery. The Earth blossomed forth from the unfolding dynamics of the universe, and life blossomed forth from the Earth. Human life blossoms forth from the womb of women. Human conception and birth are functions of the universe/Earth process. As such, they are functions of the Originating Mystery. In the human, conception is a spark thrown by bio-cultural evolution. If we are to befriend the evolution of the whole, we might begin by befriending the evolution of the human.

Throughout this book I have emphasized the need to change our thinking about nuclear, environmental, and species extinction issues. In Steps Eight and Nine I am going to give some extra space to dealing with what I call the "ecology of abortion." In deep ecological thought, we must include human behavior. I would like to look at this most difficult and divisive of issues from the point of view of ecology.

The human womb is the first habitat of all human beings and the family is the second. If these habitats are not safe and healthy, the beings growing therein seldom develop properly. Each of us alive today was allowed to spend the time we needed to grow in the primary habitat of the womb. Those of us who intend to defend the right of the animals and plants to their habitat might choose to examine our relationship to human habitat. If we are to be consistent in our claims for protection of habitat, should we not begin by examining our relationship to the human womb, the first habitat of us all, and to the family, the second habitat of us all?

Make a commitment to be the person, who transmits notions of peace, love and prosperity to others. Enlist in the army of the Mother, whose fight it is to restore balance. May humans die by natural causes only! May the planet and Her creations know death only at Her discretion. May She be merciful in Her judgment!

— Luisah Teish[6]

It is often said that a woman has the right to choose to end a pregnancy. Many men believe that they have the right to coerce a woman into doing so as well. When a woman does so, or a man coerces her to do so, it is said that they are acting as the Great Mother Goddess. Because the Great Mother kills as well as births, women, especially, have the right to choice with respect to preborn human young. In that both men and women share in being both the Great Mother — anima, the feminine — and the Great Father — animus, the masculine — what if the Mother in the preborn's father chooses life? Has the Mother spoken?

Many, I suspect, have trodden this same path through the mind. Those millions of Christians who make a special place in their hearts for the Virgin Mary possibly respond as I do. The concept of Jahweh as remote, all-powerful, all-seeing is either frightening or unapproachable. Even the sense of presence of a more contemporary God, a still, small voice within, may not be enough for those who need to communicate with someone outside. Mary is close and can be talked to. She is believable and manageable. It could be that the importance of the Virgin Mary in faith is something of this kind, but there may be more to it. What if Mary is another name for Gaia? Then her capacity for virgin birth is no miracle or parthenogenic aberration, it is a role of Gaia since life began. Immortals do not need to reproduce an image of themselves; it is enough to renew continuously the life that constitutes them. Any living organism a quarter as old as the universe itself and still full of vigor is as near to immortal as we ever need to know. She is of this Universe and, conceivably, a part of God. On Earth she is the source of life everlasting and is alive now; she gave birth to humankind and we are a part of her.

— James Lovelock[7]

By her many names over the centuries on different continents and in different cultures, the Mother Goddess is always the planet and her biosphere. The human, as a species, is the Mother drawn up — Assumed — into self-reflexive consciousness. Self-reflection is the "god" born of the Virgin Mother. Seen in this way, the God in all of us, male or female, is the self-reflexive function with its "free will" or choosing dynamic. Both the Great Mother, feminine, and the Great Father, masculine, are present in all men and women.

"Choice" then, as well as other self-reflection dynamics of the psyche, represents the God dimension of the human and not the Goddess. Spontaneous abortion, miscarriage, is indeed a function of the Goddess. When an apple falls, She has spoken. When a mother cat eats her birth-defective young, She has spoken. Matri-focal religions focus on the Sacred as Mother. Patri-focal religions emphasize the view of the Sacred as Father. Mainline patri-focal religions in the west have traditionally stood against the practice of abortion. Has this all been a mistake? Or, do we all have something to recognize here?

Because of the "New Story" and *Greenspirit*, old questions are being asked in new ways. Could the choice to abort be a pathological expression of the God dynamic in all of us? Could this whole predisposition toward abortion be a symptom of the larger cultural pathology? Could it be yet another example of the cultural abuse of women because of the pathological masculine or "choice" dynamic in us all? And is this masculine the true, the authentic masculine, or is it the missing masculine, the emptiness, the *orphanism* at the core of the western psyche? Certainly what we experience as patriarchy all around us cannot be the genuine masculine! Perhaps, however, the core symbol system of western religions still contains the seed of what really is the authentic masculine! When we abort, are we mistaking the voice of cultural pathology, of orphanism, of addiction, for the voice of our Father?

If the choice to abort is in fact a masculine dynamic, is it possible that abortion itself is just another form of warfare? It is accomplished by an intrusive entry into the habitat of the womb with the express intention of killing. It allows men and not women to be sexually irresponsible; the women and not the men are cornered into the ultimate choice. It is presided over by a nearly all-male medical establishment that performs abortions on women for very lucrative personal gain for men. Could the table of abortion be a pathological form of the abandoned male altar of sacrifice? Could the aborting doctor be a pathological form of the male sacrificial priest? Could abortion, horribly, provide the missing lamb of sacrifice? More horribly, could the preborn be replacing the missing Christ of sacrifice? In our nearly mythical obsession with material progress over the last three centuries, have we as a culture unknowingly regressed spiritually from the Christian Mass back to human sacrifice?

So, am I ready to ask these new questions? Am I ready to amend my relationship to my own morality and sexuality? Is abortion a "green" function? Does not true choice take place prior to conception for both men and women? Except in the cases of rape and incest, do we not choose to enter into the sexual dynamics of life? That choice is a moral one, one that must be learned again and again in each generation. It is passed or not passed from parents to children. In the human, morality can be thought of as a niche in that moral choices guide the human species toward behaviors that are adaptive for the overall life and health of the whole species. It is not extrinsic, but a biologically grounded instinct that springs forth as culture in the self-reflexive animal.

Once we choose to enter into the reproductive dynamics of sexual play, we enter into the biospiritual dynamics of the Great Mother — Earth. Should a pregnancy result, has that preborn human not then a right to be considered a Child of the Goddess, a citizen of Earth, regardless of what country it might be born in? Does not that citizen hold the same claim to soil, air, and water as the female human who carries her and the male human who sponsored her? Is not the authentic masculine posture, individually and culturally, one of Father to the child and Husband to its mother? Is not the genuine masculine attitude toward human young one of protection and nurturance for child and mother rather than to war on one and exploit the other? Is not default in these matters a default on the genuine masculine, individually and culturally?

To say that the human mother has a more superior claim to the nutritive functions of the planet than does the preborn child is to again value conscious over preconscious life. Is this not the abuse of the feminine in us all by an overvaluing of the masculine in us all? Does this not further exascerbate the hyper-patriation of the culture? Men who pressure women into abortion not only destroy their own sons and daughters, but also murder the souls of women. Is this not warfare? Is this not masculine violence at its root? These are questions that threaten us all. Still, if we are to take the whole culture into therapy, do we not need to ask them? So, am I ready to rethink my relationship to the death of love?

Symbolic of the pathology that presently torments the psyche of western culture is the sharp polarization of politics and religion into the so-called left and right. To vote for the "left" is to vote against both nuclearism and pollutionism and for some consideration for the poor and helpless, but to vote for the left most often means a vote for the legal support of abortion. A vote for the right means a vote for protection of preborn humans. But a vote for the right most often means a vote to support nuclearism and the plundering economy, a grotesque maldistribution of wealth, an outright and shameless disregard for the poor, and often an open hatred for women who've had abortions. *Greenspirit* proposes a third position: decency toward all living things.

Having considered these addictions to death, we have begun to look at the problems that are uniquely our own. Planetary death by human agency is our concern. Any ethical response to the problem must begin with the realization that soil, water, and air are the primary referents for all of reality. Every decision we make must include these three referents. Anything or anyone who hurts them hurts us, each of us, as well as all our preborn or born children. We are able to end life. Death is a natural function of the planet; no-birth is not. Humans can create the condition of no-more-birth. We cannot look to the past for answers to this monstrous reality. We must find the answers in the quiet of our own hearts, and be ready to change our thinking. We must be ready for the Originating Mystery to reveal the truth of life to each and every one of us. Legality or illegality is no longer the question. We have before us a choice between life and death. The planet, her plants, her animals, and her preborn or born humans are alive or they are not.

To become ready is to recognize that any change of thinking must begin to lead toward a change of being. Am I willing to rethink some of my priorities? Am I ready to drop all my prejudicial defenses and look again at all issues that I have decided "once and for all"? Am I willing to allow change in my beliefs? Am I willing to change my job? Am I willing to change my social circle? These questions threaten all of us to the core. This is why we need groups. We need community. To ask these questions alone is to risk falling into despair.

Am I ready to rethink my position concerning human life? If I decide that abortion is a dysfunctional behavior, am I ready to do what I can to amend my relationship to the preborn? Am I willing to reconsider my relationship to all other species of living beings? Am I ready to speak in the name of all life? Am I ready to rethink the whole notion of genetic engineering? Am I willing to give genetic hegemony back to the planet? Am I ready to rethink my position on nuclearism? Am I willing to do what I can to reverse the addiction to biocidal and geocidal armaments? Am I ready to do what I can about detoxifying the planet? Am I willing to make the health of the soils a primary referent for all of my activities as a person? Am I willing to make the waters of Earth another of my primary referents? Am I willing to do the same concerning the air?

STEP EIGHT is taken by writing out a list of all harms we have done to humans, to other species, and to the planet. Having done so we ask ourselves if we are ready to begin to heal them. If we are ready to take the following pledges, we have accomplished the openness called for in Step Eight. We will then be ready to proceed to Step Nine.

1. *I am no longer willing to injure myself in any way.*
2. *I am no longer willing to injure my fellow humans in any way.*
3. *I am no longer willing to injure my fellow species in any way.*
4. *I am no longer willing to injure our soils in any way.*
5. *I am no longer willing to injure our waters in any way.*
6. *I am no longer willing to injure our air in any way.*

CHAPTER NINE

In Step Nine, we go into action. We make the move to become an active part of the healing of our planet. We begin to give ourselves away for the health of the whole. In doing so, many of us will discover for the first time that this giving of ourselves was what we have longed for all of our lives, from the deepest centers of our beings. Furthermore, we discover that our addiction to consuming was one result of not having given ourselves away for something bigger than ourselves in the first place! We tried to fill the emptiness of our orphaned interior lives with junk . . . and we became junkies . . . and built a culture choking on junk.

As we begin to move out past the empty lie of addiction, we begin to feel meaning permeate our lives again. We begin to be filled with the marvelous power of hope. We join with others in the great work of renewing the Earth, and in doing so, we begin to experience community again. These are just some of the benefits of being *"whole-y"* people again, of having reawakened to our place in the universe, of having reawakened to life and to our Earth.

As we once again learn to live within the context of the life systems of our planet, we begin to feel more alive and healthier. The problems we face somehow become more manageable. We see and feel — sense — that we are moving toward a refreshed life and a renewed planet. We become "verbs" again, active agents of our fate rather than "objects" — victims — of the choices of others.

Beginning with ourselves, and then moving outward in concentric ripples, we begin to heal the ravages left in the wake of our addiction to *consumerism.* How do we heal ourselves? Diet is a good place to begin. A visit to our local health food store is a place to start. Further, we can look into chiropractic, massage, and other alternative health techniques. We can learn to dance, to do yoga, or t'ai chi. We can take more time for rest and walks on the shore or in the woods.

We can begin to study what we feel like studying again. We can choose to move out toward our *original dreams* for ourselves. These dreams are grounded in our *Original Selves*. They are, therefore, the will of the Originating Mystery for us. We can avail ourselves of psychotherapy in order to heal the habitat of our hearts — our feeling lives. We can change jobs. We can give ourselves permission to do what we want to do rather than what we "should" do or what pays most. We can look around at life again and at values and activities we have shelved. We can look again at the religion we rejected years ago or at others. We can look again at people we rejected years ago and make time for friends. We can laugh again.

We can realize that we are not machines but body/fields — body/souls. In rereading Step Six, we can remember to be gentle toward all phases of ourselves, visible and invisible, physical and psychic. It is difficult to learn to be gentle with ourselves. The rat-race of consumerism can make us feel self-indulgent when we are gentle with ourselves, but we must make an effort to do so. It is only in doing so that we will come to feel the needs of others. Those who try to help others without learning to nurture themselves often practice pity, manipulation, and control in the name of ministry or compassion. They never learn to need and often feel contempt, conscious or unconscious, for the needs of others. The saccharine mask of ministry cannot hide that contempt — the body might smile but the soul betrays a grimace. The following prayer, applied to one's self first and foremost, can be a great help in the application of its principles to others.

Addressing the Originating Mystery with whatever name we choose, we say this:

Make me a channel of your peace . . .
    that where there is hatred, I might bring love . . .
    that where there is wrong, I might bring the spirit of
       forgiveness . . .
    that where there is discord, I might bring harmony . . .
    that where there is error, I might bring truth . . .
    that where there is doubt, I might bring faith . . .
    that where there is despair, I might bring hope . . .
    that where there are shadows, I might bring light . . .
    that where there is sadness I might bring joy.
O Universal Mystery grant that I might seek
    to comfort rather than to be comforted . . .
    to understand rather than to be understood . . .
    to love rather than to be loved.

For it is in self-forgetting that I find.
It is in forgiving that I am forgiven.
It is by dying that I awaken to universal life.

Let's consider the prayer line-by-line.

Make me a channel of your peace, that where there is hatred,
I might bring love . . .

To be a channel means that we are opening ourselves to allow something to flow through us. We are trying to remove all blockages within us so that the Originating Mystery can make us whole, healthy, and creative again. Our job is always to cooperate with the Originating Mystery in making us and our planet new. So, where do I feel a lack of peace? How can I provide that peace? Where do I feel hatred toward myself? How can I bring love and healing to those places in me?

that where there is wrong, I might bring the spirit of
forgiveness . . .

Where have I wronged myself? Why is it that I cannot or will not forgive myself. How do I need to change so that I can forgive myself? Have I done Steps Four and Five in a thorough manner?

that where there is discord, I might bring harmony. . .

Where is there discord in my body, my mind, my field/soul? What can I do in order to restore harmony to these diseased areas?

that where there is error, I might bring truth. . .

Am I still lying and denying? How can I be more honest with myself?

that where there is doubt, I might bring faith. . .

Do I trust myself? If not, why? What will it take for me to trust myself? Why do I deny myself faith in the Originating Mystery? What prejudices are still blocking my way?

that where there is despair, I might bring hope. . .

Am I still feeling desperate? Why? What do I need to do in order to empower myself? What will make me hopeful? Can I act upon the answers that arise?

that where there are shadows, I might bring light. . .

How about my own shadow, my own repressed self? Can I allow myself to be fully in the light? Who tells me who I can be? Can I allow myself to be myself? There's only one of me. . . no one has the model of me, except me. Am I willing to do my part to redeem the skotosphere, my part of the pollution of the thought life of Earth?

> that where there is sadness, I might bring joy. . .

Am I sad? Why? What can I do to feel that sadness honestly and then let it go? Do I even want to be joyful, really?

> O Universal Mystery grant that I might seek to comfort rather
>   than to be comforted. . .

Do I, can I comfort myself? Or, am I totally dependent on those surrounding me for my comfort? Am I resentful when they do not?

> to understand, rather than to be understood. . .

Have I come to understand myself? Am I able to stop explaining myself to everyone? Am I able to accept myself, my history, and my wounds? Has self-understanding brought me to self-compassion?

> to love rather than to be loved. . .

Am I able to allow myself to have what I need? Am I always waiting for approval from someone "out there"? Can I give to myself so that I have something to give to others? Do I understand the difference between this kind of self-love and self-centeredness?

> For it is in self-forgetting that I find.

Am I ready to forget what I look like in the eyes of others? Am I able to be myself from the inside out? It is in forgetting my false self, my persona that I find my real, my *Original Self*.

> It is in forgiving that I am forgiven.

When I truly forgive myself I feel forgiven. To know that I am forgiven is not enough. Do I feel forgiven? After I have admitted and amended my wrongs, have I forgiven myself? It is only when I forgive myself that I can begin to forgive all others.

> It is in dying that I awaken to eternal life.

The *Twelve Steps of Ecological Spirituality* call for a death and rebirth. We die as an old, addicted self and awaken as our Original Selves. Having done so, we find ourselves in a new planet in a new universe that glistens everywhere with the life of the Originating

Mystery who willed it into existence. Truly, we awaken to a new heaven and a new Earth.

Having gone at least some of the way toward a new, more gentle relationship with myself, I can move outward to others. Beyond the field of myself lies the field of my family of origin. In Step Nine I go out to each member, one and all. I contact them in person, if possible; if not, then by phone or letter. In each case my only purpose is to admit what I have done and to ask if anything is required of me in order that the damage be healed. We will find that in many cases an apology will be sufficient, but, if we can repair damage — physical, emotional, or financial — we do so. If anyone refuses to allow us to do so, we do not argue, bow, beg, kneel, or scrape. We simply go on to the next person.

However, in this context, there is a cardinal rule that we must apply to each and every situation. *IF WE HAVE HARMED SOMEONE AND THEY ARE UNAWARE OF IT, WE REVEAL THE TRUTH ONLY IF REVEALING IT HURTS NEITHER THE PEOPLE CONCERNED NOR OTHER PEOPLE. NEVER DO WE RELIEVE OUR OWN GUILT AT THE EXPENSE OF OTHERS.* We have no right to inflict pain on anyone in order to lessen our own. In such a case, we might want to do something good for the person in question without him/her knowing why. There are cases where we should say or do nothing at all. Here there is room for discernment, caring, and great sensitivity. Perhaps we can consult someone for advice whose opinion we trust. If we have made proper amends to ourselves, we will know what to do.

Having dealt with all members of our family of origin, including uncles, aunts, cousins, and grandparents, we will want to move out into our present situation. If we are in a religious community, we will want to consider all of our relationships there. If we are married and have children, we will want to consider our spouse and each child one at a time. If we have experienced divorce(s), we will want to consider our ex-spouse(s) and all of our children. By now we should have had some experience of the wonderful relief of forgiveness and will want to go onward and outward.

Next, we will want to consider people in the workplace and those with whom or for whom we work. Have I hurt or cheated anyone? I contact them and free myself from guilt and remorse. I do the same with members of my immediate community, with those elsewhere in my state, nation, and the world. My purpose is to attain freedom from guilt and remorse *for me*. How about those who are dead? I ask the Originating Mystery to communicate my sorrow to them. If I wish to be free, I must go out to anyone and everyone I have harmed.

Has the culture I live in done damage to the native people? Perhaps it's time to make the pain of these people my concern? Am I able to foster the recovery of these people in some way? Perhaps I should do so. Sometimes just reading the historical truth of their situation can begin the amends. Some of us might know an individual who is a survivor of genocide — a Jew, a Black American, a Native American, or a person practicing a prepatriarchal religion. Apologizing to one such person can heal us. If we feel we should, then we should. If we have made some progress in all these areas, we might be ready to become active in confronting the *Five Addictions to Death*. Remember, however, if we have not begun to clear up our own backyard, we might be wise to begin there. Each of us knows where we should begin. The important thing is to begin somewhere. Then we will have the authority to go on to wider problems.

BREAKING OUR FIXATION WITH THE FIVE ADDICTIONS TO DEATH

Healing The Cultural Hemorrhage: Speaking on Behalf of "the Throw Away Human"

> Then from behind came a woman, who had suffered from a hemorrhage for twelve years, and she touched the fringe of his cloak, for she said to herself, "If I can only touch his cloak I shall be well again." Jesus turned round and saw her; and he said to her, "Courage, my daughter, your faith has restored you to health." And from that moment the woman was well again.
>
> Matt. 9:20–22[1]

The final stage in the healing of our relationships with all humans will be to heal our relationship to the preborn members of our own species. Until we heal our relationship to self, to family, to community, to nation, and to species we cannot go on to deal, effectively at least, with the problem of species extinction and the other blockages. But, when we first deal with the former, we can go on to the latter with authority and calling power. If we still think we have the right to kill within our own species, who will find convincing our attempts to save the members of others?

As the Earth continues to become toxic, we begin to notice a rise in the rate of birth defects. This is due, at least in large part, to the "stickiness" of some of the chemicals recently introduced into the biosphere. These man-made chemicals tend to attach themselves to chromosomes in human, animal, and plant cells. New genetic material can only reproduce itself out of those materials present in living cells. Thus, as we ingest these chemicals in our air, water, and food, they fix themselves onto the genetic strands and become part of the genetic code. As this happens, the code is interrupted by these chemicals resulting in birth-defective young.

With the spectacular development of in utero technologies, we become more and more able to see into the womb process as well as to detect which preborn humans are defective. If we dispose of the defective ones, we destroy the evidence of our poisoning of the Earth and of ourselves. In doing so we silence these warnings of the Great Mother. The very signs that could serve as a warning of our impending catastrophe are destroyed. Do we not need our birth-defective young to remind us of what we are doing? Are they not the messengers of Earth, warning us to stop while there is yet time? Are they not the prophets of the womb, the prophets of our Mother? Can we not hear what they are saying of the not-very-distant future? To kill them is to remain in denial that we are killing ourselves and aborting the whole planet of her life. Are not these messengers of the Goddess especially deserving of her air, water, and food?

In these last two chapters, we have said much about the ecology of abortion. Having said what we've said, many might still be unconvinced that we should reconsider the issue in this context. But what if we were to discover that abortion actually accomplished the opposite of its intended purpose as a birth-control mechanism? What if we discovered that the practice of abortion actually enhanced population numbers globally? In his book *The Presence of the Past*, Rupert Sheldrake says this:

The specific nature of the fields, according to Weiss, means that each species of organism has its own morphogenetic field, although fields of related species can be similar. Moreover, within the organism there are subsidiary fields within the overall field of the organism, in fact a nested hierarchy of fields within fields.[2]

What if the entire human family does indeed function within a single field of organization or soul? Races then, would be subsidiary fields nested within the larger species field. Individuals can be thought of as single fields nested within the racial fields. If this is true, then could the pinching off of an individual field in one place result in the emergence of another or others in places of less resistance? If so, it would probably express itself as a higher fertility in places like Africa or India where the lack of contraceptive technologies creates a zone of less resistence in the overall human species field. Is this one reason why birth rates drop in highly industrialized societies? Rather than being a termination of pregnancy, could abortion actually function as a sort of pruning? If so, then we would be causing more, and not fewer, human "buds" to appear!

To be part of any dialogue concerning abortion, one condition is required: to *not* have been aborted. This is obvious! Had our parents been given, or had they taken the power to make that choice, then we would not be here to discuss it. It might be wise to detach from the legal versus illegal polarization. That battle has been fought; abortion is legal almost everywhere, whether or not we think it should be. In **Greenspirit** we're encouraged to go on to the deeper question: Do I *really* believe that my parents should have had the "choice" over my life that many of us presently claim to have over the lives of the preborn? Do I really claim the *right* to that choice? The legal right is a fact. The real question we need to ask ourselves is this: Do I really believe I have the moral right to that choice? And, is that choice sound ecology for the overall health of the culture and therefore of the planet in which the culture is nested? Each of us must answer that question in the quiet of the human heart — appropriate action will evolve from the heart.

If we are to befriend the Earth, we must understand that nothing is "just an object." The whole universe/Earth process emerged from mystery, the whole is mystery and is destined to be mystery. To see why, we must first befriend ourselves — the human family. There should be no "power over" anyone — the woman, the man, or the girl or boy in utero.

So, what can I do about abortion? First of all, I can seriously question the current rhetoric and euphemisms concerning "pro-choice." Everyone *does* have the choice, whether or not it is a legal choice! Instead I can ask my own heart, "What do *I* really believe?" Then, if I find that in my heart of hearts I believe it is wrong, I can stand on that, act on that. I can begin to value birth and share my belief with others. Again, legality or illegality is not the question. If it is illegal and millions are killed each year, what has been accomplished? On the other hand, if it is legal and no one is killed, then it is over! In a culture that views birth as sacred, appropriate morality would surround reproduction. When men take responsibility for their reproductive capabilities and begin to offer women the support they need when a surprise pregnancy occurs, the right to an abortion would become obsolete. The right to birthing would replace it. Let's not fight abortion; let's value women; let's value birth.

We can also get involved in the Ovulation Method of natural family planning. It is a Goddess-Mysticism in its own right and is as effective as the pill. Also, there is adoption — a tribal mechanism that can channel "unwanted children" into human families where they are wanted. Adoption is the way in which the human family receives its own. We can sacralize the role of midwife into priestess-hood. That is a step only women can take, a ritual only women can enact.

The Right to Habitat: Renewing the "Context for Life"

Humans are not abstractions that have their being and functioning separate from *this* planet. In the second chapter of Genesis in the Hebrew Bible, humans are said to be formed of the dirt of this planet. They are animated by the breath of God. As such, they are "divine dirt."

> Yahweh God fashioned man of dust from the soil. Then he
> breathed into his nostrils a breath of life, and the man became
> a living being.   Gen. 2:8[4]

We say the same thing when we say that the Originating Mystery self-organized the soils of the planet and became living beings.

All life arises from the soils of the planet. All life depends on soil, water, and air. All life depends also on all other life. The "Solarvores," the green plants, "eat" and store sunlight. Herbivores eat the green plants. Carnivores eat the herbivores. Omnivores, such as the human, eat plants, herbivores, and carnivores as well. The whole of life could be summed up as the sun/Earth system eating itself. Whatever species we eliminate from the chain, we do so at our own peril. When we destroy their habitat, we abort those species.

What can we do? We can make the small move from doing nothing to doing something. We can move from being part of the problem to being part of the cure. We could call our local Audubon society and get a list of all local environmental groups and join one as a volunteer. We could take a one-semester course in ecology at a local college. We could read one book on ecology. We could press for legislation that requires anyone who uses state or national parks to show proof that they belong to an environmental group and thereby require that anyone who uses the environment is also serving it elsewhere. We can inform ourselves concerning the condition of the environment in our community. We can take this book and start a **Greenspirit** group. We can do something!

Protecting the *Original Plan*: No Genetically Engineered "Frankensteins" Please!

Experts depend on our ignorance and feelings of inadequacy arising out of it in order to operate without our mandate. Tampering with genetics is tampering with life; it concerns us all. Who do you trust with the evolution of life? Is there anyone you trust to that extent? If not, then you and I must make genetic engineering a personal issue.

It is not terribly difficult to understand, in a general way, everything that is now known about genetics. A single, simple book by Theodosius Dobzhansky or another author can open us up to the wonder of the evolution of life . . . and . . . to the hellish dangers of tinkering with that evolution. Once we have even the most modest understanding, we begin to feel empowered about talking to others. We can contact governmental representatives and request information on all governmental research into genetics. Chances are that an elected official will know less than you do about genetics. When you sense that you are on level ground with him or her, you can begin some general questioning. Door after door will open if you begin to inform yourself. The more informed you become, the more you will know what you need to do. We must declare loudly that we want no Frankensteins in ours or in any species!

Ending *Pollutionism*: Learning to Clean Up After Ourselves

Love thy species as thyself.
— Nicholas Georgescu-Roegen[5]

One does not have to go far to find something to do concerning pollution. The whole planet is polluted to a greater or lesser extent.

You can begin right in your home by reading labels. What am I pouring down the kitchen sink, the bathroom sink, the toilet, the bathtub/shower, the washing machine? Whatever goes down our drains goes into the life systems of the planet. What am I doing with my cans, bottles, plastics, metals, and newspapers? All are recyclable.

Preparatory to the Jewish feast of Passover — *Pesach* — comes an intense cleaning of the home. All leaven — *Chametz* — is looked for and cleaned out of the house. When every grain of leaven and every crumb of leavened bread is removed, that house and its people are in proper relationship to the feast. Perhaps yearly at the time of *Pesach*, we could all pass over into proper relationship to the planet by cleaning our homes of all chemicals. If no poisons go down our drains, no poisons will enter our rivers. That simple action could go a long way toward healthier water. Healthier water will not abort aquatic species. A house in proper relationship to the planet has passed over to proper relationship to the solar system and, therefore, to the universe.

Beyond that, we can contact groups such as Greenpeace. They use volunteers and will also know of many other groups who do so as well. If we make a move to help, if we even inquire, the door will open. We don't have to "do it all" ourselves either. We need only do something. If we all do *something*, *everything* will change.

Ending *Nuclearism*: Rebirthing True Security

It makes me so mad—it's such a male thing—
Competing with each other to see who's got the biggest bomb.
— Lifton and Falk[6]

No one should have any trouble finding a peace group to join. Thousands are popping up globally, or, our local churches often have groups as well. Any one of them can connect us to many more groups that have organized to express disgust for the grinning evil of nuclearism. We can write letters to the heads of government expressing our revulsion for those who continue to arm and praising those who speak out against the madness. It's not what we do, but rather, if we do anything at all. To do nothing is not neutral, it is a mandate to our leaders to return to the buildup.

In all five addictions to death, the underlying dynamic is a fixation with violence and death. It amounts to the attempt to deal with life's problems and complexities by applying deadly solutions. Western culture is a culture in love with death — the death of itself and of everyone and everything else. We are all, whether we are men or women, part of it too. Addiction is merely a symptom of that love of death; or, the love of death is a symptom of addiction — both are true. We must befriend ourselves, the whole human family, the whole Earth, and the universe; we must choose life in all of its manifestations. Chapter nine is a step out of the dead land and a step into life. It is our "Passover" from death to birth, from "The Great Slaughter" to *decency*.

STEP NINE is accomplished by beginning to heal all the relationships that we listed in Step Eight. Then, when we can take the following pledges, we are ready to move on to Step Ten.

   1. You will no longer injure me!
   2. You will no longer injure my fellow humans!
   3. You will no longer injure my fellow species!
   4. You will no longer injure my soils!
   5. You will no longer injure my water!
   6. You will no longer injure my air!

"You" in this case stands for anyone . . . *and* . . . everyone. *Step Nine is a call to action.*

CHAPTER TEN

The honest man looks into himself and in his daily acts maintains constant respect to his given word that his deeds fall not below it. If he have failed in something, he dare not slacken in the attempt toward it; if he have erred, he dare not carry the error to the extreme; his words accord with his acts and his conduct with his words as one who turns to compare them with scruple. The essence of honesty is that it springs from the heart.

— Confucius[1]

STEP TEN: WE CONTINUE ON A DAILY BASIS TO GO ON EXAMINING OUR THINKING AND OUR ACTIONS AS TO WHETHER THEY FOSTER OR IMPEDE THE EMERGENCE OF LIFE. WHERE THEY IMPEDE THIS EMERGENCE, WE ADMIT IT AND BECOME WILLING TO BE CHANGED.

As we have said over and over again, our purpose is to remove all impediments to the evolution of life. Each of the *Twelve Steps of Ecological Spirituality* is designed to help us toward this end. In Step One we let go of control over the addiction itself. In Step Two we let go of prejudice concerning the involvement of some sort of intelligence in the evolution of psyche/matter. In Step Three we abandon ourselves to the evolution of this intelligence inherent in matter. In Step Four we list all our blockages to this evolution. In Step Five we admit the truth concerning these blockages. In Step Six we become ready to be healed. In Step Seven we ask for this healing. In Step Eight we acknowledge that our lives have had some negative impacts upon other people, upon other species, and upon the life systems of the planet. In Step Nine we go out to all of these and attempt to set things right. In Step Ten we integrate all of the above into our daily spiritual practice of an ecological life.

We begin each day with a moment of surrender. We admit to ourselves that we are utterly powerless over an addicted society. We acknowledge that there is an evolving intelligence and that that intelligence can, *if allowed*, restore our proper relationship to all of creation. We therefore surrender our day to this Originating Mystery, however we might name it. Then, we begin our day knowing that we are on the surest ground of all. We are embraced by the wisdom of the universe/Earth process.

At night, we spend a few minutes going over our day. What have we done to harm the created order? What persistent habits of illusory thought, attitude, and behavior cause us to go on damaging others? Are we willing to be changed? Have we injured anyone or anything today? Are we prepared to apologize, or, in some other way repair the damage done? Can we do so now, or tomorrow?

Few of us have ever wanted to make self-criticism a daily practice. We must do so if we want to survive. Change requires discipline. We can no longer afford to just drift along allowing tomorrow to take care of itself. We no longer have a guaranteed tomorrow to depend upon. If there is to be a future, we must create it.

We begin by admitting what is wrong today, and if possible, by rectifying it today as well. One of our main problems is that we have not been able to see clearly who we really are today. Too often we see ourselves as inferior or second rate. Too often we have looked at ourselves in disgust. But this mode of self-appraisal, while posing as humility, has often been the source of a horrendous compensating pride. We have had to mask our denigration with pride and then mask our pride with denigration of ourselves. "Fallen people" become "chosen people." We have seldom had the chance to see clearly or ask this question: "Who am I?" We must begin to answer that question by understanding that all people, all animals, all plants, and all minerals are chosen or they would not be here.

Denigrating ourselves in the name of "humility" has become the main focus of some religions. Many of us are trained to think of ourselves as "stained" from conception. At many church services we repeat over and over again that we are unworthy and sinful. To compensate for this, we are offered the sentimentality of "I'm O.K., You're O.K." Trite attempts, such as "God doesn't make junk," do little or nothing at all to cover over our deep sense of futility. Be clear; none of this has anything whatever to do with our *Original Self*, which is the whole vision of who we are, but to contact our *Original Selves*, we must become totally honest.

Our Original Selves were present some sixteen billion years ago when the fireball flared forth from nothingness. We were present when the turning and burning galaxies took their shape. We were present when the sun/planets system emerged, the bio-planet Earth taking its place three planets out from the sun. We were there when life emerged on this planet and articulated itself into myriad varieties of species that can only be described as beauty upon beauty, wonder upon wonder. We were there when the flowers came and when the humans came on the scene. I don't mean that we were there watching. What I mean is that we are intrinsic to this universe and were born with it in the same way that a woman is born with all her eggs. It might be years before a person emerges from one of those eggs. It was some sixteen billion years before we emerged from the cosmic egg, but we were there.

With the emergence of humans, the beauty and goodness of the universe awakened into self-reflection. With self-reflection came choice, and choice presupposes the possiblilty of error. But choice likewise presupposes the ability to change one's mind, to choose again, to reinvent oneself. Beauty was more original than error. Goodness was more original than error. Error can be turned into choice once it is recognized as error and named. So, let's be whole and complete in our look at ourselves. Always, we must remember how good we really are. Then we can afford to look at error and name it.

We are equally off the mark when we try to ignore either our goodness or our weakness. An overemphasis on goodness creates self-delusion and inner blindness, and an overemphasis on weakness creates rigidity. By "owning" our goodness, we have the healthy ability to own our weakness without having it crush us. When we own our mistakes, we break the power of denial. By breaking the power of denial, we open ourselves to the creativity of the universe process. When we claim our creativity, we become empowered as people. In becoming empowered and remaining empowered, we can rise to a sustained confrontation of the malaise that afflicts western culture.

In spite of all our foibles, we are still the awesome event of the fireball arriving at consciousness of itself. We are immanent mystery, rising out of ultimate mystery from which all things emerge into being. We make our mistakes and often, and we must learn to admit and confess them often. But we are not ontologically stained any more than any part of nature is ontologically stained — nature emerges pristine and glistening out of the mystery of mysteries, and so do we. We are nature conscious of herself. The whole created order is one of unfolding beauty, extravagance, and pleasure, and so are we. It's no wonder that our instincts sometimes over-reach their intended purpose and even draw us into addiction. We live in such bountiful beauty here on our garden planet. We are the children of this planet, and, like all children, we often grab for too much of what, in good measure, is healthy for us. In Step Ten we admit our bad choices, rectify them, and go on.

We must mature as a species and as a culture. We must come to understand our proper place in the scheme of things. We must take responsibility for our actions and our choices. In doing so, we take responsibility for our own well-being, as well as for the well-being of other species and our whole planet. When this happens, the great flowering universe blossoms in us and through us. This takes place when we see ourselves clearly, honestly, and humbly. Doing so requires that we acknowledge both our strengths and our weaknesses.

What about evil? Intelligent evil did not seem to be present in the universe until the emergence of the human. True, there seems to be a certain violence in the whole universe process, but evil seems to arise from choice — from free will gone awry. Evil happened in Germany when the choice was made to act on anti-Semitic feelings. The deeper question becomes: What denied or repressed portion of the collective German psyche was operating beneath consciousness engendering the anti-Semitic bias?

Intelligent evil, it seems to me, arises from the individual and collective phases of the human shadow that are the denied portions and contents of the self, which I have called the *skotosphere*. The human creates the *devil*. When I say creates, I do not mean "fabricates." The devil is not a construct — it is real. What I mean is that we engender what we fear most. What we fear most we deny. That denial introjects the fear into the unconscious phase of the psyche — the planet — until it becomes collective. When it becomes collective, we experience the fear as "out there," thus giving it an Earthly as well as a cosmic dimension. It is then that we begin to speak of nature as "fallen." It is our own denial that engenders the "father of lies." If there is an original flaw in us, it is this propensity for denial.

Denial pollutes the healthy thought life of the *noosphere* with the venom of the skotosphere. As the skotosphere becomes prevalent, we begin to speak of the presence of evil. It is our powerlessness over this evil that we actually admitted to in Step One. Because we are loathe to see the evil as indigenous to ourselves, to the "choices" we have made, we project it onto others as well as onto the planet herself. Our denied disgust for our own mistakes, individual and collective, is experienced as disgust for others as well as for life itself. By emptying ourselves we are doing our part to begin to cleanse the skotosphere from the noosphere, thereby replacing disgust for life with the zest for life.

Having done this in a radical way in Step Four and Five, we then continue the process in Step Ten. When we make internal emptiness a permanent condition of our lives, we will begin to see clearly again. It is then that we will see evil and goodness clearly. In seeing goodness clearly again, we will reawaken to the beauty and goodness of life, to the honesty of the planet and to the truth of the universe. It is then that we will be able to celebrate life again, and that celebration of life is the main function of the human. We are the celebration of the universe. We are the ecstacy of the universe. We are the heart of the universe. We are the exultation of the Earth and the locus of her compassion.

We must stand sentinel over our own condition of emptiness. We are powerless over others as well as over the addicted culture, but we can watchdog our own small portion of that culture. In his book *People of the Lie*, M. Scott Peck gives us four traits of the personality that signify a slippage into denial, repression, and evil. We can ask ourselves each day if we are exhibiting any or all of these four traits:

(a) consistent destructive, scapegoating behavior, which may often be quite subtle.
(b) excessive, albeit usually covert intolerance to criticism and other forms of narcissistic injury.
(c) pronounced concern with a public image and self-image of respectability, contributing to a stability of life-style but also to pretentiousness and denial of hateful feelings or vengeful motives.
(d) intellectual deviousness, with an increased likelihood of a mild schizophreniclike disturbance of thinking at times of stress.[2]

We should not panic if we see signs of all four in ourselves. The very ability to look at the problem is proof positive that none of the traits has a tyrannizing hold on us. Only those in complete denial will not see any of the traits in themselves.

We experience more fear in the vicinity of large urban centers for the same reason that we experience greater concentrations of entropy — material pollutants — in those same areas. Where greater concentrations of population are present, there will be greater concentrations of the psychic smog of the skotosphere. When we live in such places, we begin to feel evil as omnipresent, because it is. We are in it. We are all introjecting lies, until the *Lie* becomes collective. We can imagine it to be similar to the way we all contribute to a poisoned river by our individual flushings. Then each of us looks at the river and bemoans the state it is in. When each of us becomes responsible for the individual "flushings" of denial, the cultural river will run clean again.

When evil is unnamed, it has free rein — we have no way to deal with it. In this book I have named it the skotosphere. It is the collective human shadow of a culture . . . of our species . . . and therefore, of the planet. It is a product of consciousness in the same way that morality is a product of consciousness. When we default in morality, we create the skotosphere. When we exercise morality, we create the noosphere and healthy cultures. Collective denial leads to evil, but collective confession leads to psychic health. This cannot be "proven." In order to understand it we must do it. If we are to survive as a culture, the western human must return to the practice of confession — owning up.

Happily, the skotosphere is a small obstacle for the tremendous powers of the expanding universe, a wisp of smoke before a tornado. As we begin to see through the smoke we can begin to perceive that the kingdom of our happiness is in our midst. It is the planet Earth — the Goddess, the Great Mother, our Mother. She is everywhere present to us, patient and waiting for us to open our eyes, to come out of our addicted coma. She is waiting for us to help cool her fever — the "greenhouse effect." She is waiting for us to clear away the smoke of our delusions and gaze again into her beauty which is our beauty. We are the eyes of the Earth. In us she reflects upon herself. In her, we gaze into a mirror. Can we daily prepare ourselves for a vision of such splendor? Or must we go on destroying her, and thus ourselves, because we cannot?

Can we calmly admit our mistakes without becoming obsessed with guilt? Can we begin to practice psychic hygiene daily? Can we invite and allow the universe to blow away the haze of our shadows so that our vision will be healed? Can we manage the vision of our own beauty? Of each and every others' beauty? Of the Earth's beauty? Can we withstand the beauty of the animals again? Can we leave them in their habitat again? Can we stop imprisoning their beauty in zoos? Can we meditate on the ultimate mandala — the picture of the Earth in space? Can we begin to see and feel the awesome depth of a universe of power and beauty that was born of the beauty and power of the most splendid event of all time and timelessness? Can we befriend ourselves? Others? The Earth? The universe?

This is how we reinvent the human. We begin to honor our need for confession, apology, and restitution. It will represent a beginning of peace with ourselves, peace with each other, and peace with all the Earth. Always, we must remind each other that we are making progress at realizing the fullness of our power and beauty — progress at creating the future. We must not be afraid of validating each other. We all need encouragement. We all need to be told that we are growing. This validation is the positive basis for a renewal of authentic community.

Once again we are going to review the twelve categories of individual and collective dysfunction listed in Steps Four and Eight. However, this time we will be looking to validate the progress we have made in each of them. So, we will be asking different questions this time.

1. EGOCENTRICITY

Go placidly amid the noise and haste, and remember what peace there may be in silence. As far as possible, without surrender, be on good terms with all persons. Speak your truth quietly and clearly; and listen to others, even the dull and the ignorant; they too have their story.

— Desiderata

Where has my concern for self opened outward to embrace concern for others? Where has my concern for the human opened outward toward concern for all species? Where has my concern for all of life opened further into concern for the planet and her soil, water, and air? How have I grown in friendship with the Earth? How have I grown in friendship with the universe?

2. LOVE OF MONEY

Keep interested in your own career, however humble; it is a real possession in the changing fortunes of time.

— Desiderata

How has my desire that I have money opened outward into the desire that all people have the basics of life? How have I turned my money from service to myself only, toward service of others? How have I employed my money toward enhancing the life and health of all species of living things? Where have I tempered my desire to take by desiring to give of myself toward the health of soil, water, and air? How have I come to see money as a way to serve the whole of creation?

3. SEXUAL SUPERFICIALITY

Neither be cynical about love; for in the face of all aridity and disenchantment it is perennial as the grass.

— Desiderata

Where has my desire for sexual gratification opened out into an authentic concern for the well-being of all members of the opposite sex as well as for all homosexuals? Where has my desire for sexual pleasure opened outward into a desire to be pleasure's source? Where has sexual greed become a gentle concern for my and others' bodies? How far have I come toward realizing that sexual union in all species is a function of the universe? Have I begun to be concerned for the bodies of animals, fish, and birds? Am I coming to love the body of the Goddess, Earth?

4. VIOLENCE

Avoid loud and aggressive persons, they are vexations to the spirit.

— Desiderata

How have I learned to be gentle with myself? How have I learned to resolve conflicts with others without violating them? Have I learned to be sensitive with other species, taking from them no more than I *need*? How have I made my life encouraging rather than discouraging to the rest of life? How have I become gentle in my interactions with the planet? How has my life become life's blessing?

5. OVEREATING/DRINKING

Beyond a wholesome discipline, be gentle with yourself.

— Desiderata

How has my desire for food and drink become the desire that all people have enough to eat and drink? How have I minimized the damage I cause to other species by taking only what I need? How have I concerned myself with the health of water so that the fish will prosper? How have I enhanced this little plot of Earth, my body, by changes in my diet?

6. ENVY

If you compare yourself with others, you may become vain and bitter; for always there will be greater and lesser persons than yourself.

— Desiderata

How have I been doing in contenting myself with what I have? Have I accepted myself as I am, as my *Original Self*? In what instances have I succeeded in not comparing myself to someone else? Where has my envy turned into good will toward others? Have I come to see that the good of others is really my good as well? In what ways have I rejected competition as a basis for relationship? Can I see the gains of all nations as my gain?

7. APATHY

Nuture strength of spirit to shield you in sudden misfortune.

— Desiderata

In what ways have I triumphed over my own apathy? How have I stopped being lazy? How has my renewed enthusiasm affected those nearest me? How have I awakened to the needs of my community? How have I awakened to the needs of all people? How have other species entered my concern? How have the soil, the water, and the air become a personal concern of mine?

8. REAWAKENING TO LOVE

You are a child of the universe, no less than the trees and stars; you have a right to be here.

— Desiderata

In what ways have I changed my relationship to preborn humans? What are the ways in which I have chosen to value birth and family? How have I spoken on behalf of the preborn and on behalf of the family?

9. DESTRUCTION OF SPECIES / HABITAT

What have I done to end the *Great Slaughter* of the species? What steps have I taken to guarantee all living beings the Divine Right to habitat?

10. DESTRUCTION OF THE ORIGINAL PLAN

And whether or not it is clear to you, no doubt the universe is unfolding as it should.

— Desiderata[11]

Have I made genetic engineering and other biotechnologies my concern? How? What have I done to claim my children's right to a genetic endowment, untampered with by experts? What have I done to claim that right for all living beings?

11. DESTRUCTION OF SPECIES BY CHEMICAL SOLUTION

Exercise caution in your business affairs; for the world is full of trickery. But let this not blind you to what virtue there is; many persons strive for high ideals; and everywhere life is full of s/heroism.

— Desiderata[12]

What have I done to purify the soil, water, and air of the planet? What have I done to protect terrestrial, aquatic, and flying animals, and insects from industrial poisoning?

12. DESTRUCTION OF ALL LIFE ON OUR PLANET

With all its sham, drudgery and broken dreams it is still a beautiful world. Be careful. Strive to be happy.

— Desiderata[13]

In what ways have I come out of hiding concerning the nuclear threat? How have I made the safety of *my* planet *my* concern?

If we see progress in any area of the above twelve categories, we are growing. If we are growing, the Earth and the universe are evolving. Whatever we do, or do not do, affects the whole. In a short time we will begin to see progress not only in ourselves, but in others, and in the quality of life generally. In seeing, we will begin to have hope again.

We have embarked upon the great project of reinventing the human at the species level. We will begin to see that we can live in appropriate relationship to the life systems of the planet. Our fear about the future will begin to subside as we shoulder our responsibilities as sentinels of life on Earth. The natural world, in its entirety, will begin to rejoice with us. Earth's fever will go down, and all of life will increase in fluorescence and radiance. That radiance will be the ambiance in which the human and all species will bathe. We will have moved into the *Ecological Age* of human/Earth relationship.

As self-appraisal becomes a habit, we will begin to change. Others will become curious as they perceive that change. As many choose to change, a new kind of community will be born. A new human community, yes, but also a new community among the species of the Earth will emerge. There will be those who assent to what we are doing but who will be slow to change. Even just a change in attitude will be a positive sign for the whole of life. Some will refuse to budge; let them be. It takes only five percent of a culture to believe an idea in order for that idea to become embedded and rooted in that culture. It takes only a twenty percent assent on the part of a culture to make an idea unstoppable. Invite everyone but never exhaust yourself pleading with the stubborn. You are the yeast that will cause the bifurcation — the change of direction of the whole human family. If you are getting better, then "things are getting better."

We must also understand that it is okay to make mistakes, to be, or to have been wrong. We can make the practice of the fine art of the apology a permanent function of our personalities. Few, if any, of us are saints; we all make mistakes. We are seeking growth and change, not perfection. We have the right to be imperfect and we must claim that right. But, we can apologize . . . to ourselves . . . to others . . . to the whole. And . . . we can choose not to be experts.

When people cannot apologize, great violence can often be done to themselves as well as to others. Just imagine what would happen, for example, if an American President apologized to the Native Americans and to the Black Americans during an inaugaural address? What if the Pope apologized on behalf of all men to all women? What if an American President apologized to the Soviet Union for having interfered in their revolution? We have seen what has happened since the Soviet Union apologized to Hungary, Poland, Czechoslovakia, and Afghanistan. What if all industrial nations apologized to all nonindustrial nations for having plundered their natural resources, for polluting the whole planet, and for holding the whole planet hostage to the terrorism of a nuclear technology gone mad? What if we all apologized to the preborn dead of our species? What if you apologized to someone whom you don't think deserves an apology?

Great healings come about whenever someone bursts through the armor of pride with an apology. When we are sorry, let us all learn to say so. Let us all be humble enough to change, remembering that there are those who are simply without good will. With them, we offer our apology and move on; they are in their own hell. We must be compassionate toward them all. They, too, are ensnared by pride; they can neither apologize nor forgive. They are more to be pitied than despised.

We might want to go over Steps Four and Five once or twice a year. However, it is just as important that we "check in" with ourselves each and every day. If during the day we become uncomfortable, we can stop what we are doing and ask ourselves why? Have I been wrong? Am I defending myself? If so, I can admit the truth, first to myself and then to the person or people concerned. If we have harmed the animals or the planet, we can admit that and again become willing to be changed.

Remember, whenever we deny any of our feelings, we begin again to erect a barrier between ourselves and the rest of creation. In doing so, we begin to block the splendor of the emergent mystery within us. We must remain open and denial-free, otherwise, we put a halt to the unfolding of beauty, of creativity, of the emergence of that universal mystery from whom we emerge into being. We are the hearts and hands of that *mystery*. When we are blocked, compassion disappears from the face of the Earth. When we form a fist, evolution stops; but when we once again open our hand in friendship, the great flower blossoms forth from our palm.

We feel the pain of all that we have been and done. We feel shame at motives late revealed. We become aware that we did much, and often, to the harm of others. We can see that what we often thought was virtuous was in fact ignorance. We have had the approval of fools and have given the approval of fools. We have gone from wrong to wrong. But now, we have a program of recovery. The *Twelve Steps of Ecological Spirituality* can help us so that we can begin to move through life with the grace of dancers. We have failed, but we can choose to change. We can all choose to be vents for the emergence of the happiness that is in our midst. We can all become midwives to life, midwives to the Earth, and midwives to the universe.

We can take STEP TEN by setting aside a few minutes of each day in order to sit and consider our relationship to all of life, remembering to consider and to value our progress.

CHAPTER ELEVEN

I would like to begin this chapter with a long quotation from the writings of Sri Ramakrishna. It has about it the tone of tolerance we shall need if we are ever to establish peace among humans. Any lasting peace must begin with mutual respect for our different languages of the divine. While it is, admittedly, a lengthy piece, I think it really sets that tone and sums up this entire chapter.

God has made different religions to suit different aspirants, times and countries. All doctrines are only so many paths; but a path is by no means God Himself. Indeed, one can reach God if one follows any of the paths with whole-hearted devotion. One may eat a cake with icing either straight or sidewise. It will taste sweet either way.

As one and the same material is called by different names by different peoples, one calling it water, another *eau*, a third *aqua*, and another *pani*, so the Everlasting-Intelligent-Bliss is invoked by some as God, by some as Allah, by some as Jehovah, and by others as Brahman.

As one can ascend to the top of a house by means of a ladder or a bamboo or a rope, so diverse are the ways and means to approach God and every religion in the world shows one of these.

As a young wife in a family shows her love and respect to her father-in-law, mother-in-law, and every other member of the family, and at the same time loves her husband more than these; similarly, being firm in thy devotion to the deity of thy own choice, do not despise other deities, but honor them all.

Bow down and worship where others kneel, for where so many have been paying the tribute of adoration the kind Lord must manifest himself, for he is all mercy.

The devotee who has seen God in one aspect only, knows him in that aspect alone. But he who has seen him in manifold aspects is alone in a position to say, "All these forms are of one God, and God is multiform." He is formless and with form, and many are his forms which no one knows.

The Saviour is the messenger of God. He is like the viceroy of a mighty monarch. As when there is some disturbance in a far-off province, the king sends his viceroy to quell it, so whenever there is a decline of religion in any part of the world, God sends his Saviour there. It is one and the same Saviour that, having plunged into the ocean of life, rises up in one place and is known as Krishna and diving down again rises in another place and is known as Christ.

Every man should follow his own religion. A Christian should follow Christianity, a Moslem should follow Islam, and so on. For the Hindus, the ancient path, the path of the Aryan sages is the best.

People partition off their lands by means of boundaries, but no one can partition off the all-embracing sky overhead. The indivisible sky surrounds all and includes all. So common man in ignorance says, "My religion is the only one, my religion is the best." But when his heart is illumined by true knowledge, he knows that above all these wars of sects, and sectarians, presides the one indivisible, eternal, all-knowing bliss.

As a mother, in nursing her sick children, gives rice and curry to one, and sago arrowroot to another, and bread and butter to a third, so the Lord has laid out different paths for different men suitable to their natures.

Dispute not. As you rest firmly on your own faith and opinion, allow others also their equal liberty to stand by their own faiths and opinions. By mere disputation you will never succeed in convincing another of his error. When the grace of God descends on him, each one will understand his own mistakes.

— Ramakrishna[1]

STEP ELEVEN: WE CONTINUE THROUGH PHYSICAL-MENTAL-SPIRITUAL DISCIPLINES TO SO CHANGE OURSELVES AS TO IMPROVE OUR OWN ABILITY TO FOSTER THE EMERGENCE AND HEALTH OF THE WHOLE CREATED ORDER.

As we have said many times now, we, as individuals and as cultures, are part of the wonderful unfolding of beauty and creativity that began with the fireball. This unfolding continues in us and will continue long after our individual and collective tenures on this planet have come to an end. Once we understand this, it becomes easier to see why we must find a *way* in which to maximize our openness to the Originating Mystery in order to pass life on in its integrity and multiformity. The history of culture provides us with many such ways, offered to us from many cultures and from many times. In our own time, when we have access to so many ways, we have come to know them together as the *Global Spiritual Tradition of the Human*. In whatever culture we presently find ourselves, we will all be enriched by knowing something about each of the ways that make up the whole spiritual, cultural, and religious tradition of the human.

We have said that the whole universe emerged out of Mystery. We have called this Mystery the Originating Mystery. People everywhere, sensing this Mystery, have named it by many different names. No one name or theology captures everything there is to say about the Mystery. Nor do all the ways and names combined tell the whole story either. The Mystery, by definition, is greater than the whole universe and is everywhere present in it. That is why we rely on the term Originating Mystery. After we have said all we can say, the Mystery goes on emerging, goes on flooding from the Uncreated, potential state, into actuality. Yet, the Mystery remains mysterious. The human mind searches for its source. Reason rebels at the idea of an uncaused universe. We might well disagree as to the name and nature of that source, but we can agree to allow the Mystery to be mystery, choosing to call it/him/her or whatever we will.

So, while realizing that we have told the "New Story" in part already, we shall repeat the whole story again in chapters eleven and twelve. In chapter eleven, we shall look at the story as a way to see how the past brought us to our present point in space/time. We will see how all the ways of the past brought us to the present. Then we shall move on to looking at our way into the future, which will gather up the past for our use in the present as well as in the future. Chapter twelve will be a look into possiblities for that future. Now, let's review the "New Story," this time including all the ways of the one way — the *Global Spiritual Tradition of the Human*.

From the dark nothingness of the Originating Mystery, there flared into being some sixteen to twenty billion years ago, a stupendous eruption of energy. Within seconds the energy cooled into matter and the evolution of the universe was underway. Vast clouds of primordial energy/matter began to self-organize in space. This self-organization is a property of matter, an invisible function of the universe that we call gravity. As atoms began to form from subatomic particles, which themselves had formed from the cooling of energy, the other three forces — also invisible — of the universe, electromagnetism, the strong and weak forces, exhibited themselves. These early structures are called "proto-galactic nebulae."

Self-organization seems to be a function of invisible fields associated with all matter, from the tiniest subatomic particle to the most complex beings, humans included. As subatomic fields interact, they can coalesce to form new atomic fields. When atomic fields interact and join together, a molecular field is evoked, and when many molecular fields join, a mega-molecular field is evoked. At some point, mega-molecular fields began to join to become cells. Cellular fields interact in the field — soul — of an organism. Organism-fields interact to form species fields. The fields of several species interact to form *eco*systems. Ecosystems fields can co-function to form *bio*regional fields. Bioregional fields interact within the planetary field of the Earth. The Earth, the planets, and the sun interact within the field of the solar system, and the solar system interacts in the greater field of the Milky Way galaxy. Galaxies interact gravitationally throughout the whole universe. All visible organization arises out of invisible fields, and these invisible fields remain mysterious.

So the universe swelled into being and is swelling still. Everything in the expanding universe is rushing away from everything else in the universe as it expands. But everything in the universe is also attracted to everything else, and thus the rate of expansion is controlled, held together, so that everything doesn't just fly apart randomly as in the explosion of a hand grenade. Imagine the tummy of a woman newly pregnant, and imagine that we cover her tummy with polka dots before she begins to show her pregnancy. If we could film her tummy using time lapse photography over nine months and then watch it speeded up, we would see that as her tummy skin stretched, the polka dots would move further and further away from each other all the while being held together by her skin. Imagine that the polka dots are galaxies in an expanding universe and that her skin is the attractive pulling-back we call gravity. Just as the pregnant woman is more than her tummy and the new life dwelling therein, so, too, is the Originating Mystery more than the universe that arises out of him/her/it.

So we can imagine the early galaxies as great vortices of turning gases. In each of them, smaller vortices began to form. As these smaller vortices gained mass, they were able to attract more and more hydrogen to themselves. In time, many such vortices formed in all galaxies. Then, as more and more hydrogen atoms became sucked into smaller and smaller spaces, these atoms began to bounce off one another at increasing velocities. As this happened, they also heated up to higher and higher temperatures. Eventually, the temperatures got so high that the hydrogen began to fuse to form helium. When this happened, gigantic quantities of matter were converted into energy and stars were born.

If we compare the beginning of a star to the beginning of a human, then the beginning of fusion could be thought of as stellar conception. Hydrogen atoms join together and something new is born. It was in this way that our sun came into being, but, the sun is a second generation star. That means that it is a star formed of the remains of a dead first generation star. Let's look at the sun from its conception through its life span, to its death, and its rebirth into our present source of life.

Fusion is the beginning. As fusion continues, the star gives off greater and greater amounts of energy, and as this happens, greater and greater amounts of hydrogen are converted into helium. After many years all the hydrogen is used up. When this happens, the star flares up in a last hurrah giving off incredible amounts of energy until it completely exhausts itself in the grand spectacle. Then, the ashes of the exhausted star collapse upon themselves. An ember in your fireplace has the same life span, until it becomes dust.

But, the star is different. Its implosion goes on until all of the ashes gather into a dense center of intense mass. As this happens, the ash is converted into all the metals and minerals that we associate with life on Earth. Calcium, magnesium, zinc, and so on, and finally gold are formed in the tightening fist of the contracting star. When this contraction can grow no denser, when everything is drawn tighter and tighter still, it explodes in one grand finale, bequeathing itself — body and field — into space, becoming vast clouds of metal-rich dust.

No sooner has this dust spread out than it begins to feel the tug of gravity pulling it together again, but the metal-rich dust of this second birth has a different potential than the original hydrogen. This dust has the potential to form planets, and the planets have the potential to birth life. Life has the potential to walk, run, fly, bark, laugh, love, compose symphonies, and reflect on the fact that it can do so. So, the dust begins to spiral again, and within the spirals, smaller vortices begin to appear. In time, a star is born again.

This is how the sun/planets system came into being. We can imagine a gigantic cloud of metal-rich dust turning and gathering itself to itself in the darkness of space. This disk had a huge central nucleus, or core, around which the remaining dust rotated. The core of the nebula — dust cloud — kept on gathering mass as it drew more and more matter to itself. In fact, it managed to pull more than ninety percent of the cloud to itself leaving only ten thin bands of matter moving around it. Chances are the sun had not yet ignited. Like us, the solar system was formed in the dark.

Within each of the ten thin bands, smaller eddies of matter began to organize themselves. It is wonderful to reflect upon the fact that all of this self-organization was accomplished by invisible forces inherent in matter. As these smaller eddies grew in size they grew in mass as well, and began to draw each other in and subsume one another. The larger an individual eddie became the greater became its ability to subsume more and more. Eventually, the eddies became planets with other eddies becoming the moons of these planets. At this time, the sun probably attained sufficient mass to begin to burn. Here was the solar dawn.

Each of the planets tried to become a little sun, but lacking sufficient mass they could not and eventually became satellites of the sun — the planets. The third planet out from the sun began its unique adventure, which includes me as I write this and you as you read it. Having tried to become a sun, she got only as far as being molten, boiling matter, and slowly she began to cool.

For millenia vast tantrums of matter shot up from her. Steam rose from these hot fonts and dissipated its heat into space. The water vapor began to form clouds around the planet. When the clouds cooled, the rains came. This rain helped to cool the surface which in turn created more and more steam. In time a veil of mist surrounded the entire planet. The rains continued and the cooling continued until a thin crust began forming around the whole surface of the planet. By now, the sun was brilliant and the moon was cooling down to rock.

Still, the lava tantrums continued to shoot jets of molten rock up through the crust. Here and there the crust failed and split, and glowing rock shone through, but, never again would the entire crust disappear. The surface of the Earth was forming, and great wrinkles began to form in the crust as cooling caused contraction. Think of an apple forgotten in the refrigerator and discovered in the spring. The Earth became wrinkled in the same way. These wrinkles became troughs that collected the rains — the oceans had begun to form.

By now the moon was hot only in her center, but the moon hadn't sufficient mass to hold onto her veil. It disappeared in the winds of space leaving only silent rock devoid of air, water, and soil, and devoid of life until Earth life walked upon her surface in 1969. The moon, nonetheless, had mass, sufficient mass to exert great gravitational attraction on the Earth. This attraction caused, among other things, the pull upon the oceans of Earth that we call the tides.

For millions of years, the tides rocked and sloshed. Metal-rich minerals from the planet's own self mixed with these waters to form the saline broth of the oceans. All the while the sun went on impregnating the planet with energies. At some point, perhaps three billion years ago, perhaps because intense lightning pierced the sea womb, the mineral broth sparked into life — a cell was born. Remember this whole unfolding — from the fireball to the galaxies, the formation of the sun and Earth, and the emergence of life on Earth — is one process, one function of the Originating Mystery from which they all in turn emerged.

The cell began dividing into new cells and these did the same until the sea was swarming with life. Later, they began to come together into aggregates or communities and to divide their functions within the community. Some joined to become the mouth of the community, and others grouped to become swimming appendages. Others became sensing appendages, and still others became the reproductive functions of the community. In time, these communities achieved sufficient specialization to become organisms.

Some of these organisms became fixed to the ocean floor and became plants, and soon the ocean floor was teeming with life. Fish began to swim in great swarming schools. Life was in full bloom. Some of these plants began to creep ashore and to colonize the land. These, in time, gave themselves as food for walking fish that ventured from the water. When this happened, the reptiles were born. Plants and reptiles covered the Earth. Some evolved into flying creatures. Now, the whole planet was boiling with life in the water, on land, and in the air.

Plants developed the ability to receive, capture, and store sunlight. We call this talent photosynthesis. Herbivores, as hungry for sunlight as anything that lives, ate the green plants and stored their energy in their flesh. When carnivores evolved, they too were hungry for solar energy. They ate the herbivores. The whole planet/sun marriage was feasting upon itself. Animals changed and evolved. Some became extinct but many more evolved from the Originating Mystery to replace them, and from this outpouring of being came the mammals.

The family tree of the mammals branched off in many directions, and from the mammals came a branch known as the primates.

Among the primates are the monkey, gorilla, chimpanzee, and the human. The human was in many ways the weakest and most vulnerable of all the primates, but the human possessed a new and special type of consciousness heretofore unknown on the planet. Humans could self-reflect — not only could they know, they could also know that they know. Now, life on Earth could self-reflect. The human was that being in which the Earth, but also the universe, could reflect upon itself. The Originating Mystery had engendered a new dimension to life on Earth.

We can imagine the first humans, barely erect and terrified by the dangers and beauty of the Earth and sky, frightened by the animals, enchanted, scared, and allured. A new sound came into being on Earth when the human arrived: laughter. Laughter is the cry of the human, a sound known only to us. Imagine the wonder they must have felt huddled together in the face of a hurricane or tornado. The helplessness they felt, and we feel, when the Earth quakes beneath our feet. We can still feel their questions because they are our questions as well. Where does all this come from? What am I? What is all this? Who makes the storms? Who makes it rain? What is the blinding light in the sky, and where does it go at night? What is the shining face in the night sky and what are the many points of twinkling light? Did they, too, wish upon a star?

This wondering at the Earth, the universe, and ourselves seems to be the primary function of the human. Like all of life, humans are totally dependent upon the sun/Earth relationship for survival, but unlike the animals, humans can know that and wonder about it. Animals kill to eat; so must the human, but the human can conceive of killing just to kill. Humans respond to beauty and terror. Humans can also cause beauty and terror. The human can imagine not being human. The human can imagine animals and plants as being human. The human can imagine not needing the planet . . . to our peril!

The response to all this wondering is called religion. The word comes from the Latin *religio* — to relink, reconnect, remember. Religion seems to be a way to reconnect to and remember the overwhelming whole of who we really are . . . the Originating Mystery, the fireball, the galaxies, the sun and Earth, and all life drawn up into self-consciousness. Religions are attempts to befriend the universe and the Earth. Religions are an attempt to befriend the Originating Mystery:

You are my friends
if you do what I command you.
I shall no longer call you servants,
because a servant does not know
his master's business;
I call you friends,
because I have made known to you
everything I have learnt from my Father.
John 15: 14–15[2]

Religions offer ways or paths by which people can do this. Religions
are the ways humans live on Earth. Most of them give specific
guidance gained from individual and collective human experience.
They are ways to fruitful relationships with other humans, all of
life, with the Earth, the universe, and the Originating Mystery
from whence they all emerge into being. And, they are all true
especially within the context of the culture in which they emerge.
Religions grow out of cultures and cultures grow out of religions.
Termite colonies grow with termites and termites grow within
colonies. Herds are comprised of cattle and cattle are born in
herds. Schools are comprised of fish and fish are born into schools.
Religions are the psychic ecology of humans, they are biological
niche externalized as culture. Humans are born in culture.

The Great Ways are to an extent true even beyond the cultures
in which they shaped themselves and that were shaped by them.
Each of them is most truly understood when seen in the context
of all the others. We don't fully understand "pantherness" when
we see a panther in a zoo. We begin to understand pantherness
when we know the panther within the context of the other animals
and plants that make up the panther's true environment. A panther
in a zoo is to some extent an abstraction. Panthers do not belong
in such a separate state.

In the same way, we cannot fully understand a Christian or
a Jew separate from Christianity or from Judaism. Nor can we
understand western nations separate from Judeo-Christian teachings or eastern nations separate from Hindu-Buddhist teachings.
Furthermore, we cannot fully understand any religion separate
from all the others in that only when we gather them together do
we have the *Global Spiritual Tradition of the Human* — the whole
cultural experience of the human species.

The rose is most beautiful, most completely a rose, when all of
its petals are present. Pluck one or more of the petals and the rose
begins to be diminished in beauty — it begins to lose its roseness.

A single petal has its own peculiar beauty, but it is an abstraction; it cannot exist separate from the context of the whole rose. This seems to be true of the *Global Spiritual Tradition of the Human*. All the ways belong to us all; they are all parts of our collective spiritual endowment. Each of us might follow only one. Perhaps it is only possible to follow one, but that one is richer for being seen within the context of all the others.

Whatever path we might follow, it is crucial to remember that none of them is an extrinsic imposition from the past fabricated by people in the past to enslave us here in the present. Religions, on the contrary, are products of consciousness and consciousness is a product of the planet. Religions are the ways in which people live on Earth. They are the languages of the Originating Mystery speaking to each of us in every culture. Again, culture is, for the human, biological niche externalized. Cultures contain the dos and don'ts that guide us through life's passages.

The remainder of this chapter will concern itself with brief looks at several "Ways." They are all Ways that have brought us to the present. Then, we will look at a Way that can lead us from the impasse of the present and into the future.

THE GLOBAL SPIRITUAL TRADITION OF THE HUMAN

Many Ways: One Mystery

As we have said, religions are functions of self-reflexive consciousness, while self-reflection itself is a function of the planet. Religions provide an external landscape reflecting the internal landscape of the human psyche. This externalized landscape can be thought of as the niche of the human. Because religions are a product of the Earth, to speak of the "religions of man" does not go deep enough; we must speak of the religions of the Earth. The *Global Spiritual Tradition of the Human* belongs to the Earth, and therefore to us all, and, because it is niche, we can learn much about our relationship to the Earth by looking to the religions of the Earth.

In all religions of the Earth are recorded guidelines concerning, what I call, the three great relationships:

1. The human/Universe or human/Originating Mystery
2. The human/Earth, human/species
3. The human/human

In all religions of the Earth, these three relationships are shown to be of one process — a holy and unbroken development beginning with the fireball and continuing to this moment in space/time. Each religion adds some insight into the one great epiphany of being, and sheds light on how the human is to live most creatively within it. So, beginning with a brief look at tribal/shamanic religion, we shall proceed to an equally brief look at the great classical religions that have shaped civilizations as we know them. In order to be brief, I shall focus only on showing that the *three great relationships* are commented on in them all. This outline of the *Great Ways* within the *Global Spiritual Tradition* is meant simply to tempt the reader to explore each of them further.

The Tribal/Shamanic Tradition — Native Americans

When Europeans came to North America, they found the land virgin and pristine despite the fact that it had been peopled for some thirty to fifty thousand years. Now, after only some three hundred years, the North American continent is a "running sore" of devastation. The time has come when the Euro-American must apologize to the Native American and ask this question: "Will you teach us how to live here?" The history of this continent did not begin in 1776. Hopefully, that date will not go down in history as the year it became terminally ill. We Americans must tune in to the deeper history of this continent before we poison and/or bomb it and ourselves into lifelessness. If we are ever to be at home here, if we are ever to become native to this place, we must come to an experience of the indigenous way that is the human ecology of North America. To do so, we must listen to the land through the ears of the native people. The "Indians" are the ears and mouth, the heart and mind of the land mass we call North America.

Native American spiritualities are so plentiful, so multiform, as to be a treasure chest for anyone wishing to befriend the Earth and universe. There are spiritualities to fit the eco-structures of all bio-regions of the continent, coastline, plains, river bank, lakes region, mountains, and so on. To study the tribes of any locale is to learn about the land they live in.

While many tribes had specific religious ceremonies, most natives experienced their lives as a single epic ritual of birth-life-death and rebirth. Their religion was "*now*," the connection was to "this place," to "these animals," and "these people." In this, the native experience had certain affinities with Zen or Gestalt. This living ritual was not acted out by humans for humans only, but was experienced within the context of the animals, planet systems, nonliving beings, spirit world, and universe. These, of course, are all one anyway, and native spirituality is one of participation with all that is.

Native Americans experienced a unitive knowledge of a "Wakan-tanka,"— the unifying spirit of all being — comparable to the Hindu, Brahman, or the Christian Holy Spirit. Wakan-tanka was the all-animating spirit, the context in which everything has its being.

> One thing we know which the white man may one day discover: Our God is the same God.
>
> — Chief Seattle[3]

The various gods/goddesses were all worshipped as variant aspects of this one numinous reality. Native Americans saw clearly what it has taken western science until now to realize, namely, that all things — animals, rocks, trees, and stars — have a common origin and a common destiny, and that all beings living and nonliving have souls. They knew, and know, that humans do not live in isolation from other beings in theory or in fact. All are one in the grand dance of the one spirit: Wakan-tanka or Manitou.

The Human/Universe Relationship

These four ribbons hanging here on the stem are the four quarters of the universe. The black one is for the west where the thunder beings live to send us rain; the white is for the north, whence comes the great white cleansing wind; the red one is for the east whence springs the light and where the morning star lives to give men wisdom; the yellow for the south whence come the summer and the power to grow.

— Black Elk[4]

All living creatures and all plants derive their life from the sun. If it were not for the sun, there would be darkness and nothing could grow. Yet the sun must have the help of the Earth. If the sun were to act upon animals and plants, the heat would be so great that they would die, but there are clouds that bring rain, and the action of the sun and Earth together supply the moisture that is needed for life. The roots of a plant go down, and the deeper they go the more moisture they find. This is according to the laws of nature and is one of the evidences of the wisdom of Wakan-tanka.

— *Touch the Earth* [5]

The Human/Earth, Human/Species Relationship

The white people never cared for the land, or deer or bear. When we Indians kill meat we eat it all up. When we dig roots we make little holes. When we build houses, we make little holes. When we burn grass for grasshoppers, we don't ruin things. We shake down acorns and pinenuts. We don't chop down the trees. We only use dead wood. But the white people plow the ground, pull down the trees, kill everything. The tree says, "Don't. I am sore. Don't hurt me." But they chop it down and cut it up. The spirit of the land hates them. They blast out trees and stir it up to its depths. They saw up the trees. That hurts them. The Indians never hurt anything, but the white people destroy all. They blast rocks and scatter them on the ground. The rock says, "Don't. You are hurting me." White people pay no attention. When Indians use rocks, they take little round ones for their cooking . . . How can the spirit of the Earth like the white man? . . . Everywhere the white man has touched it, it is sore.

— *Touch the Earth*[6]

The following are all from Chief Seattle's letter to the United States government in 1851:

Every part of this Earth is sacred to my people. Every shining pine needle, every sandy shore, every mist in the dark woods, every clearing and humming insect is holy in the memory and experience of my people . . . . We are part of the Earth and it is part of us. The perfumed flowers are our sisters; the deer, the horse, the great eagle, these are our brothers. The rocky crests, the juices in the meadows, the body heat of the pony and man — all belong to the same family . . . . The shining water that moves in the streams and rivers is not just water but the blood of our ancestors . . . . The water's murmur is the voice of my father's father. The rivers are our brothers, they quench our thirst. The rivers carry our canoes, and feed our children . . . . And what is there to life if a man cannot hear the lonely cry of the whippoorwill or the arguments of the frogs around the pond at night? . . . The air is precious to the red man for all things share the same breath, the beast, the tree, the man, they all share the same breath . . . . The wind that gave our grandfather his first breath also receives his last sigh . . . . Teach your children that we have taught our children that the Earth is our mother. Whatever befalls the Earth befalls the sons of the Earth. If men spit upon the ground, they spit upon themselves. This we know: the Earth does not belong to man; man belongs to the Earth.[7]

The Human/Human Relationship

We may be brothers after all. We shall see.

— Chief Seattle[8]

And while I stood there I saw more than I can tell and I understood more than I saw; for I was seeing in a sacred manner the shapes of all things in the spirit, and the shape of all shapes as they must live together like one being. And I saw that the sacred hoop of my people was one of many hoops that made one circle, wide as daylight and as starlight, and in the center grew one mighty flowering tree to shelter all the children of one mother and father. And I saw that it was holy.

— Black Elk[9]

On every continent, in every culture, there exists a substrata of religious experience that is part of the *tribal/shamanic* experience. I have mentioned the Native American experience as the tribal/shamanic religion of the continent on which I live. The reader is encouraged to explore the equivalent "native" zone of his/her cultural psyche.

Hinduism

Hinduism is a religion of vast variety and tolerance. Even in the Vedas, Hinduism's oldest scriptures, it is made clear that the different religions are but different languages that God has used to speak to the human heart. Hindus believe that the truth is *one*, but that people call it by many names. Hinduism is the model of religious tolerance, the archetype for our concept of the *Global Spiritual Tradition of the Human*. From the Hindu point of view, anyone practicing any religion in sincerity and surrender to God is, in fact, a Hindu.

But it does not matter what deity a devotee chooses to worship. If he has faith, I make his faith unwavering. Endowed with the faith I give him, he worships that deity, and gets from it everything he prays for. In reality, I alone am the giver.

— *Bhagavad Gita*[10]

One can only wonder what the world would be like if all religions practiced that sort of tolerance.

The Hindu name for the divine and all-permeating Intelligent Mystery, which is co-extensive with the universe, is Brahman. Brahman is transcendent of the universe in that Brahman preceded the universe and is its source and ground. Brahman is also immanent in that all beings take their rise from, are sustained by, and ultimately return to Brahman to be born again. As such, these three faces of Brahman — creator, sustainer, and destroyer — are called Brahma, Vishnu, and Shiva respectively. As with all the thousands of Hindu gods and goddesses, Brahma, Vishnu, and Shiva are aspects of Brahman and not separate entities. There are no separations in Hinduism:

> Know this my Prakriti
> United with me:
> The womb of all beings.
> I am the birth of this cosmos:
> Its dissolution also.
> I am He who causes:
> No other beside me.
> Upon me these worlds are held
> Like pearls strung in a thread.
>
> I am the essence of the waters;
> The shining of the moon;
> OM in all the Vedas,
> The Word that is God.
> It is I who resound in the ether
> And am potent in man.
> I am the sacred smell of the Earth,
> The light of the fire,
> Life of all that lives,
> Austerity of Ascetics.
> — *Bhagavad Gita*[11]

OM, — chanted *aaa-uuu-mmm* — the sacred syllable of Hinduism, is said to be the sound of the universe, the sound of evolution. By a lucky chance "OM" is also the initials of the Originating Mystery! To chant the OM is to come into union with the whole. The Atman is the Hindu notion of a soul. The Atman is Brahman in the individual being. The human Atman is Brahman caught up into self-reflection. The purpose and goal of living for the Hindu is to realize the ontological oneness of Brahman and Atman. Once this is realized the individual is no longer limited by the notion of an individual self, but experiences his/her self as one with the *self* of the whole universe. The ego splits open like a seed and reveals itself as a branch on the great tree of the universe.

The Hindu notion of spiritual evolution is called "reincarnation." Reincarnation is the slow progress made by the individual Atman through many births and deaths, until it finally realizes its identification with the whole in the moment called "Nirvana."

Nirvana is the ecstatic, unitive experience, wherein one realizes oneness with the whole. That particular insight was experienced by Jesus when He realized that He and the Father were one.

> The Atman is the light
> The light is covered by darkness:
> This darkness is delusion.
> That is why we dream.
> When the light of the Atman
> Drives out our darkness
> That light shines forth from us,
> A sun in splendor,
> The revealed Brahman.
> — *Bhagavad Gita*[12]

To feel Brahman in all things is to feel *with* all things — to have compassion. It is this reverence for all life that makes vegetarianism so widespread among Hindus. When we truly feel *with* the very Being of all beings, a deep sensitivity washes over us, and we begin to want not to hurt anything.

> Who burns with the bliss
> And suffers the sorrow
> Of every creature
> Within his own heart,
> Making his own
> Each bliss and each sorrow,
> Him I hold highest
> Of all the yogis.
> — *Bhagavad Gita*[13]

There are four major yogas, or ways to God in Hinduism. They appeal to different types of people. They are:

1. Jnana: the path of the intellectual, the mind's road to God
2. Bhakti: the path of the lover
3. Karma: the path of work
4. Raja: the path of psychological experience

This is not the place to go into each of these in any depth, but, in order to give the reader the flavor of Hindu spirituality, I list here the eight steps of Raja yoga:

1. The Five Abstentions: from injury, lying, stealing, lust, and greed
2. The Five Observances: cleanliness, contentment, self-control, studiousness, contemplation of the divine

3. Asans: in *Hatha Yoga* toning of the body by stretching positions called "asans"
4. Control of the breath
5. The closing of the windows of the senses to the outside world
6. Concentration: bringing the mind to rest
7. Meditation: practice of making conscious contact with Brahman
8. Samadhi: realization of Brahman leading to nirvana.

— *Religions of Man*[14]

The Human/Universe Relationship:

Arjuna, I am the cosmos revealed, and its germ that lies hidden.
. . . this very day you shall behold the whole universe with all things animate and inert made one within this body of mine. Then the son of Pandhu beheld the entire universe, in all its multitudinous diversity, lodged as one being within the body of the God of gods.

— *Bhagavad Gita*[15]

The Human/Earth, Human/Species Relationship

My energy enters the Earth
sustaining all that lives:
I become the moon
Giver of water and sap
To feed the plants and the trees.
Flame of life in all,
I consume the many foods,
Turning them into strength
That upholds the body.

Bhagavad Gita[16]

Prakriti, this vast womb,
I quicken into birth
With the seed of all life:
Thence O son of Bharata
The many creatures spring.
Many are the forms of the living,
Many the wombs that bear them;
Prakriti, the womb of all wombs
And I the seed-bearing Father.

— *Bhagavad Gita*[17]

The Human/Human Relationship

May He protect us both. May He take pleasure in us both. May we show
courage together. May spiritual knowledge shine before us. May we never
hate one another. May peace and peace and peace be everywhere.

— *Upanishads*[17]

Buddhism

As Christianity came from Judaism, so Buddhism came from Hinduism. Buddhism arose in India in the fifth century BC. It was the
result of the spiritual insights of a prince named Siddharta Gautama, who lived from 563 to 486 BC. He was raised as a Hindu but
broke with Hinduism as an adult. Gautama made a personal search
for peace and salvation for himself but wound up attaining it for
millions. Following his enlightenment, he came to be called
Buddha, which means the "enlightened one." In time, his teachings
became the basis for one of the world's great religions. The best
way to describe Buddhism is to call it a philosophy accompanied
by a therapy designed to apply that philosophy to individual life.
Buddhism is also a religion in that it is a mysticism — a way to
experience the Originating Mystery by which we are all created
and sustained in being.

The way of the Buddha begins with the acceptance of *The Four
Noble Truths*. Without the acceptance of these, the therapy, called
The Eightfold Path, cannot be applied to the individual life. They
are:

1. Suffering is universal
2. The cause of suffering is craving
3. The cure for suffering is the elimination of craving
4. The way to eliminate craving is to follow *The Eightfold Path*

So suffering is inescapable . . . it is part and parcel of the whole
universe process. But, we can maximize or minimize our suffering
by maximizing or minimizing our craving. Craving is attendant to
all addiction. When we are craving for things, for people, for
advantages, we suffer whenever our demands are not met. What
we think will make us happy is precisely what increases our share
of suffering. Suffering ends when we cease to crave.

We might wonder, "All right, but how do we stop craving,
especially if we live in a culture built on craving?" Craving is good
for the economy! Buddha would answer, "Try my Eightfold Path."

The Eightfold Path

1. Right knowledge
2. Right intention
3. Right speech
4. Right conduct
5. Right means of livelihood
6. Right effort
7. Right mindfulness
8. Right concentration

For Buddhists, the practices of self-discipline lead to a life of good works and inner peace. Right speech and right conduct, in particular, are spelled out in a practical Way called *The Five Precepts*:

1. To abstain from the taking of life
2. To abstain from the taking of what is not given
3. To abstain from all illegal sexual pleasures
4. To abstain from lying
5. To abstain from the consumption of intoxicants.

Zen Buddhist monks follow the first five precepts in the same way a monk would do in any of the three major vehicles of Buddhism — 1.) Mahayana, 2.) Hinayana, and 3.) Theravada. Zen Buddhist monks follow an additional five precepts in order to further reduce craving for things, pleasures, privileges, status, or anything that would increase pain and its blinding delusions, which block out the radiance of *mind*, inherent in all space/time. They are:

6. To abstain from speaking of the misdeeds of others, but to be understanding and sympathetic
7. To abstain from praising oneself or condemning others
8. Resolve never to withhold spiritual or material aid to anyone
9. To abstain from becoming angry and to exercise control
10. To abstain from reviling the three treasures — the Buddha, the Dharma, and the Sangha.

The Human/Universe Relationship

The nature of the Absolute is neither perceptible nor imperceptible; and with phenomena it is just the same. But to one who has discovered his real nature, how can there be anywhere or anything separate from it? Thus, the six forms of life arising from the four kinds of birth, together with the great world-systems of the universe with their rivers and mountains, are all of one pure substance with our own nature. Therefore it is said: "The perception of a phenomenon is the perception of the Universal Nature, since phenomena and Mind are one and the same." It is only because you cling to outward forms that you come to 'see,' 'hear,' 'feel' and 'know' things as individual entities. True perception is beyond your powers as long as you indulge in these.

— Huang Po[19]

The Human/Earth, Human/Species Relationship

Such a man who does his duty is tolerant like the Earth, like a stone set in a threshold; he is like a lake without mud;

— *The Dhammapada*[20]

Forests are delightful; where the worldly find no delight, there the detached will find delight.

— *The Dhammapada*[21]

The Human/Human Relationship

All men tremble at punishment, all men love life; remembering that thou art like unto them, do not strike or slay.

— *The Dhammapada*[22]

He who though richly adorned exercises tranquility, is quiet, subdued, restrained, chaste and has ceased to injure all other beings, is indeed a Brahman, an ascetic, a friar.

— *The Dhammapada*[23]

Confucianism

More a philosophy than a religion, Confucianism holds out to us insights of enormous value without ensnaring us into conflicts over ritual or practice. I think of Confucianism as a cultural therapy in that Confucius seemed always to focus on the rectitude of the individual as being of value only within the greater context of a more perfect, or even the perfect, society created as the sum of the rectitude of its individuals. In our present context, this notion of a cultural therapy accomplished by the change of individuals is of supreme value.

Confucius offers us an ancient model similar to the one used throughout this book. Beginning with the individual, who is encouraged to look straight into the heart, healing goes out in concentric circles to the family of such an individual. From the family the healing energies of truth/sincerity ripple outward to the village, from the village to the province, and from the province to the country. Confucius tells us that this rippling of cultural health makes us partners with the Earth and with heaven. How?

If we continue our circles beyond the individual culture, we can say that when the countries are healthy, the planet will be healthy. Thus, the people will be in harmony with the planet. Being in harmony with the planet, we are in harmony with the solar system, with the galaxy, with the universe, and with the Originating Mystery from which all things emerge into being. Thus, the healing energies beginning with the individual end with the universe, and can then be seen to be the universe itself healing itself — all healing energies are cosmic/divine. Remember, it all begins with individuals! The *Twelve Steps of Ecological Spirituality* only become a cultural and planetary therapy by first being an individual therapy.

Like Confucius, we have recognized over and over again the importance of tradition. Truly, the action of all our steps has been a relinking with tradition — cultural tradition, biological tradition, geological and cosmological tradition. The entire Confucian system rests upon the need to build on tradition, handed down and reverenced by succeeding generations. Because science has given us the New Story, we can go all the way back to relink to the beginning. In doing so, we can rebirth not only ourselves but our cultures and the planet. Again, we can spark the *Second Western Renaissance*.

Confucius begins by looking into the heart:

It is said in the K'ang Proclamation; He showed his intelligence by acting straight from the heart.   — *Confucius*[24]

Confucius tells us that this looking straight into the heart evokes certain fruits within the human, and therefore, of course, in the culture. These fruits are four in number:

1. Jen: Jen means human-heartedness. It is the sense of respect or reverence that humanity is able to express, not only toward itself, but likewise toward all other beings, living and nonliving. Jen could be defined as a universal compassion. To incarnate Jen is to befriend the self, humanity, life, the planet, and the universe.
2. Chun-Tzu: This is the opposite of pettiness, the opposite condition of puniness of soul. It is the ability to see the whole picture, and thus to subordinate one's desires to the good of the whole. In fact, the health of the whole comes to be seen as one's own greatest good. Again, it represents the befriending of the whole *as* one's self, and then acting accordingly.
3. Li: Li can be translated as appropriateness. To be appropriate one must see the whole and the self within it. When this is seen, one sees oneself in true size. Once we see ourselves in proper size, we can value our contribution while not overvaluing our own importance.

4. Te: Te can be translated as power, but, it is not a power over others as much as an empowerment from within. Te is spiritual power — the ability to call people forth because they hear the voice of authority coming from within. A person with Te leads by authenticity rather than by force.

The Human/Universe Relationship

What heaven has disposed and sealed is called the unborn nature. The realization of this nature is called the process. The clarification of this process is called education. You do not depart from the process even for an instant; what you depart from is not the process. Hence the man who keeps rein on himself looks straight into his own heart at the things wherewith there is no trifling; he attends seriously to things unheard. Nothing is more outwardly visible than the secrets of the heart, nothing more obvious than what one attempts to conceal. Hence the man of true breed looks straight into his heart even when he is alone. Happiness, rage, grief, delight. To be unmoved by these emotions is to stand in the axis, in the center; being moved by these passions each in due degree constitutes being in harmony. That axis in the center is the great root of the universe; that harmony is the universe's outspread process. From this root and in this harmony, heaven and Earth are established in their precise modalities, and the multitudes of all creatures persist nourished on their meridians. — Confucius[25]

The Human/Earth, Human/Species Relationship

This Earth that bears you up is a handful of sand, but in its weight and dusky large, it holds The Flower Mount and Dog Mountain without feeling the weight of them; Huang Ho, the river, and the oceans surge and the Earth loses not a drop of their waters, holding them in their beds, containing the multitude of their creatures.

Mount Upholder that you now look upon is but a fold of rock amid many, a pebble, and on its sides grow the grasses and trees, sheltering wild fowl and the partridge, the four-footed beasts and stags; gems are hidden within it abundantly that were for delight or for commerce.

This water is but a spoonful mid many; it goes forth and in its deep eddies that you can in no wise fathom there be terrapin and great turtles, monsters, crocodiles, dragons, fish and crustaceans to make rich whomso will seek with a bold eye into their perils. — Confucius[26]

The Human/Human Relationship

The Meaning of, "World Order [bringing what is under heaven into equilibrium] is rooted in the good government of one's own state," is this: If those in high places, respect the aged, the people will bring filial piety to a high level; if those in high places show deference to their elders, the people will bring their fraternal deference to a high level; if those in high places pity orphans, the people will not do otherwise; it is by this that the great gentlemen have a guide to conduct, a compass and square of the process.

If you hate something in your superiors, do not practise it on those below you; if you hate a thing in those below you, do not do it when working for those over you. If you hate something in the man ahead of you, do not do it to the fellow who follows you; if a thing annoys, you from the man at your heels, do not push it at the man in front of you. Do not in relations with your left-hand neighbor what annoys you if done at your right, nor in relations to your right-hand neighbor what annoys you if done at your left. This is called having a compass and a T-square of the process.

— Confucius[27]

Taoism

Lao-tzu, the founder of Taoism, lived sometime in the sixth century before Christ. Little is known about him. In fact, there are many scholars who question the fact of his having lived at all. Legends have it that he was born about fifty years before Confucius, and according to Confucian tradition, there was a meeting between the two. The name Lao-tzu was given him by his disciples as a sign of affection and respect. It means something along the lines of the "Old Man" or the "Old Master."

There is a legend that tells us that Lao-tzu was the keeper of the Royal Archives during the Chou Dynasty, but he grew weary of his post and retired. Journeying to the west, he came to the mountains at the northwest border of China. He was recognized by a guard who would not allow him to leave China until he had committed all of his wisdom to writing. So, he sat down and wrote the *Tao Te Ching*. When it was finished, he is said to have left the country never to be seen again.

The word Tao means "way" or "path." As such, however, it has three meanings that are all different aspects of its one, singular essence. Its first meaning is "Ultimate Reality" or "Originating Mystery" or "Ultimate Source." In this context it refers to the ultimate ground of the universe. In its second meaning it refers to the way of the universe and of nature. As such, it refers to the Intelligence inherent within the unfolding forms of the universe, the emergent solar system and Earth, the immanent intelligence within all that lives, the way of things. Its third level of meaning is the way that humans should live and act in union with the universe/Earth/life process. So, Tao is the way of all that is. Tao is source, process, and wisdom. In Tao, the way of the universe, the way of the Earth, the way of life, and the way of culture are one way.

The Human/Universe Relationship

> Between heaven and Earth
> There seems to be a bellows:
> It is empty, and yet it is inexhaustible;
> The more it works, the more comes out of it.
> No amount of words can fathom it;
> Better look for it within you.
> — *Tao Te Ching*[28]

or

> Tao can be talked about but not the eternal Tao.
> Names can be named but not the eternal name.
> As the origin of heaven and Earth it is nameless:
> As "the mother" of all things it is nameable.
> So, as ever hidden, we should look at its inner essence:
> As always manifest we should look at its outer aspects.
> These two flow from the same source, though differently
>   named;
> And both are called mysteries.
> — *Tao Te Ching*[29]

or

> There was something undefined and yet complete in itself
> Before Heaven-and-Earth,
> Silent and boundless,
> Standing alone without change,
> Yet pervading all without fail.
> It may be regarded as the Mother of the world.
> I do not know its name;
> I style it "Tao";
> And in the absence of a better word call it "The Great."
> — *Tao Te Ching*[30]

The Human/Earth, Human/Species Relationship

> Does anyone want to take the world and do what he wants
>   with it?
> I do not see how he can succeed.
> The world is a sacred vessel, which must not be tampered
>   with or grabbed after.

To tamper with it is to spoil it, and to grasp it is to lose it.
— *Tao Te Ching*[31]

or

All things will grow of themselves.
When they have grown and tend to make a stir,
It is time to keep them in their place by the aid
of the nameless Primal Simplicity,
Which alone can curb the desires of men.
When the desires of men are curbed, there will be peace
And the world will settle down of its own accord.
— *Tao Te Ching*[32]

The Human/Human Relationship

He who knows men is clever;
He who knows himself has insight.
He who conquers men has force;
He who conquers himself is truly strong.
— Tao Te Ching[33]

or

The sage does not take to hoarding.
The more he lives for others, the fuller is his life.
The more he gives, the more he abounds.
The way of heaven is to benefit, not to harm.
The way of the sage is to do his duty, not to strive with
    anyone.
— *Tao Te Ching*[34]

or

Know the masculine,
Keep to the feminine
And be the Brook of the World.
To be the Brook of the World is
To move constant in the path of Virtue
Without swerving from it,
And to return again to infancy.
— *Tao Te Ching*[35]

or

The Spirit of the Fountain dies not;
It is called the Mysterious Feminine.
The doorway of the Mysterious Feminine
Is called the root of Heaven and Earth.
— *Tao Te Ching*[36]

or

Cultivate Virtue in your own person
And it becomes a genuine part of you.
Cultivate it in the family,
And it will abide.
Cultivate it in the community,
And it will live and grow.
Cultivate it in the state,
And it will flourish abundantly.
Cultivate it in the world,
And it will become universal.
— *Tao Te Ching*[36]

Judaism

Hear, O Israel, the Lord our God is one. You shall love the Lord your God with all your heart, with all your soul, with all your might. These words which I command you on this day shall be in your heart. You shall teach them diligently to your children. You shall talk about them at home and abroad, night and day. You shall bind them as a sign upon your hand and they shall be as frontlets between your eyes and you shall inscribe them on the doorposts of your homes and upon your gates.
— Deut. 6: 4–9[38]

Though religious practices among Jews vary widely, generally, the unifying feature among all Jews is this belief, "Hear O Israel, The Lord your God is One." Judaism contributed a radical monotheism to the *Global Spiritual Tradition of the Human.* In its insistence on the fact that there is one God and that God is Spirit, the Jews gave the world a special clarity of vision beyond all the gods and goddesses and to the one Originating Mystery of which they are all aspects. The Jews called that one mystery "Yahweh."

This one mystery, Yahweh, reveals himself in three ways through:

1. creation
2. history — ongoing creation or evolution
3. human goodness/creativity.

The religious practices of the Jews center around eight Holy Days. The first of these recurs every week and is called the *Sabbath.* It is a day of rest and reflection, and it begins at sundown on Friday and ends at sundown on Saturday. It is that day in which Jews reflect on the meaning of the other six days of the week. Work is suspended for this one day, not only for people, but for animals as well. So important is this weekly day for Jews that it is referred to as the "Princess" in their prayers. Beyond the weekly Sabbath, the Jews have seven Holy Days/periods.

Rosh Hashana: This is the Jewish New Year. It begins with the blowing of the shophar or ram's horn, and inaugurates a ten-day period of penance. It is a time for reflection on one's sins that should lead to confession and atonement to both God and man.

Yom Kippur: This is the holiest day of the year and it concludes the ten days of reflection spoken of above. It is a day of fasting, prayer, and meditation that culminate in confession and a request for God's pardon. It is concluded with the blowing of the shophar.

Sukkoth: This is a feast of thanksgiving or ingathering. It is commonly called the "feast of booths" or "feast of tabernacles" in memory of the impermanent dwellings in which Jews lived during their forty years of desert wandering. It begins five days after Yom Kippur and lasts five days. It is a joyful time of celebration of the harvest as well as a reminder that Yahweh is the God of nature.

Hanukkah: This is the feast that commemorates the rededication of the temple of Jerusalem following its desecration by Antiochus Epiphanies of Persia. Because lighting of candles is associated with the feast, it has come to be called "feast of lights." The emphasis of Hanukkah is upon religious freedom and loyalty.

Purim: This is also called the "feast of lots." It commemorates a story from the Book of Esther in the Hebrew Bible. It is the story of a man named Haman, who was influential in the Persian government, and his plot to kill the Jews. Because of the daring and clever intervention of Esther, Haman ends up hanging from the very gallows he had built to kill the Jews. It is a joyful feast and one that is associated with the giving of gifts.

Pesah: This is the famous "Passover" of the Jews from Egyptian bondage into freedom. It is sometimes called the "feast of unleavened bread," due to the use of bread in the Seder meal — the central celebration of this feast. It was this Seder meal that became in the Christian tradition, the Sacrifice of the Mass.

Shabuoth: Sometimes called the "feast of weeks," Shabuoth is known to many non-Jews as Pentecost which means fifty days. It occurs on the fiftieth day after Passover. It was originally a spring harvest festival, which later came to be considered the birthday of Judaism. It celebrates the day on which Moses was given the tablets of the Ten Commandments by God on Mt. Sinai.

So now, we can look at Judaism through the Three Great Relationships.

The Human/Universe Relationship

In the very first lines of the *Tanakh* — Hebrew Bible — it is claimed that Yahweh is the agent of the creation of the universe (heavens) and of the planet Earth.

> In the beginning when God created the heavens and the Earth . . .
>
> — Gen. 1:1[39]

Having done so, Yahweh would prepare the Earth for life and would then bring forth life in all of its manifestations. Between Genesis 1:1 and 1:11 there is an intuitive or poetic story of how the planet was formed and prepared for the advent of life. In understanding that this is "story," we need not get ensnared in the twofold traps of:

1. Fundamentalism — insisting that the story is literally true
2. Skepticism — insisting that because the story is not scientifically true, it is therefore untrue.

These two, equally extreme, cause us to miss the real truth, which is intuitive truth, the truth of story.

The Human/Earth, Human/Species Relationship

> Then God said, "Let the Earth bring forth vegetation: every kind of plant that bears seed and every kind of fruit tree on Earth that bears fruit with its seed in it." And so it happened: the Earth brought forth every kind of plant that bears seed and every kind of fruit tree on Earth that bears fruit with its seed in it.
>
> — Gen. 1:11–12[40]

Next, of course, came animal life. That, too, is part of the story, part of the one creation of Yahweh:

> Then God said, "Let the water teem with an abundance of living creatures, and on Earth let birds fly beneath the dome of the sky." And so it happened: God created the great sea monsters and all kinds of swimming creatures with which the water teems, and all kinds of winged birds. God saw how good it was and God blessed them saying, "Be fertile and multiply, and fill the water of the seas; and let the birds multiply on the Earth."
>
> — Gen. 1:20–22[41]

Then God said, "Let the Earth bring forth all kinds of living creatures: cattle, creeping things, and wild animals of all kinds." And so it happened: God made all kinds of wild animals, all kinds of cattle, and all kinds of creeping things of the Earth. God saw how good it was.

– Gen. 1:24–25[42]

The Human/Human Relationship

Then God said: "Let us make man in our image, after our likeness."
God made man in his image;
in the divine image he created him;
male and female he created them.
God blessed them saying:
"Be fertile and multiply; fill all the Earth. . . ."

— Gen.1:26–28[43]

The Way of the Jews is best described by the Ten Commandments. They are said to have been given to the Hebrew prophet/patriarch, Moses, by Yahweh Himself on top of Mt. Sinai. The central ethic of Judaism is summarized within them.

The Ten Commandments

1. I am the Lord your God. You shall not have strange gods before me.
2. You shall not take the name of the Lord in vain.
3. Remember to keep holy the Sabbath.
4. Honor your father and your mother.
5. You shall not kill.
6. You shall not commit adultery.
7. You shall not steal.
8. You shall not bear false witness against your neighbor.
9. You shall not covet your neighbor's wife.
10. You shall nor covet your neighbor's goods.

Christianity

Christianity grew out of Judaism in the person of Jesus of Nazareth. After His death He came to be called the "Christ," which means "annointed one." Annointing among Jews is a sign of kingship, and Jesus was claimed by His followers to be "King of the Jews" as well as "Son of God."

He was the son of a carpenter named Joseph and was himself a carpenter. He only lived for about thirty-three years, and his teaching career was concentrated in the last three years of His life. He had a small band of followers, who walked with him around the countryside, healing the sick and befriending the poor and power-less. He proclaimed the immanence of God in teaching that "the Kingdom is in our midst." Roman authority feared His power among the people. The Jews feared His spiritual authority; he is said to have been able to convince people to give up their lives and follow Him simply by inviting them to do so! It seems that even His own family thought Him mad:

> When his relations heard of this, they set out to take charge
> of him; they said, "He is out of his mind."
> — Mark 3:21[44]

In the final week of His life, Jesus was tried under Roman law at the instigation of the Jewish hierarchy. He died by crucifixion on the day Christians call "Good Friday." A condemned criminal was crucified on either side of Him.

For Christians, however, the end of Jesus' life was really the beginning. The Christian doctrine of Resurrection holds that Jesus rose from the dead and lives a different kind of life — a life that is co-extensive and co-present throughout the universe. In the opening verses of the Gospel of John, Jesus becomes identified with Yahweh as the creator of the universe. During His life He identi-fied Himself in the same way in saying: "I and the Father are One."

In His rising from the dead and returning to the Father, He became identified by St. Paul as the Cosmic Christ, co-extensive with the universe, alive in all that lives, present as well in non-living creation. As co-extensive with the universe, alive in all of the created order whether cosmological, geological, biological, or cultural, Jesus is experienced as the Holy Spirit. Thus is the doc-trine of the Trinity explained.

The doctrine of the Trinity is the doctrine that says that while God is indeed one, as the Jews understood, God is nonetheless Triune — having three persons: Father, Son, and Spirit. Herein lies the great and mysterious teaching that separates Christian monotheism from both Judaic and Islamic monotheisms. This pro-found mystery can be illuminated somewhat by considering that the human, claimed by Jew and Christian alike as being made "in the image and likeness of God," is also triune and one at the same time. We are a creative intelligence, a body, and a spirit or soul. Still, we are, each of us, one nonetheless.

In the most traditional forms of Christianity, Catholicism, Ortho-doxy, and High Anglicanism, there are seven sacraments. Sacraments are special moments when the power of God is shown forth in special ways. They are:

Seven Sacraments

1. Baptism — ritual washing and "splicing into" the death and Resurrection of Jesus
2. Confirmation — a ritual sealing with the "Fire of the Holy Spirit"
3. Eucharist — ritual eating of the Body and Blood of Jesus
4. Marriage — ritual bonding of man and woman in the sacrament of sex
5. Annointing — ritual healing with vegetable oils
6. Confession — ritual "emptying of the self" of sin
7. Holy Orders — marriage of celibates to the whole Church.

The basic teachings of Christianity are best summed up in one of Jesus' sermons called "The Sermon On The Mount." It is recorded in the fifth chapter of the Gospel of Matthew in the New Testament portion of the Christian Bible or Holy Book.

> How blessed are the poor in spirit: the kingdom of Heaven is
>   theirs.
> Blessed are the gentle:
>   they shall have the Earth as inheritance.
> Blessed are those who mourn:
>   they shall be comforted.
> Blessed are those who hunger and thirst for uprightness:
>   they shall have their fill.
> Blessed are the merciful:
>   they shall have mercy shown them.
> Blessed are the pure in heart:
>   they shall see God.
> Blessed are the peacemakers:
>   they shall be recognized as children of God.
> Blessed are those who are persecuted in the cause of
>   uprightness: the kingdom of Heaven is theirs.
> Blessed are you when people abuse you and persecute you
>   and speak all kinds of calumny against you falsely on my
>   account.
> Rejoice and be glad, for your reward will be great in heaven;
>   this is how they persecuted the prophets before you.
> — Matt. 5:3–12[45]

The Human/Universe Relationship:

> In the beginning was the Word:
> the Word was with God
> and the Word was God.
> He was with God in the beginning.
> Through Him all things came into being,
> not one thing came into being except through him.
> What has come into being in Him was life,
> life that was the light of men;
> and the light shines in darkness,
> and darkness could not overpower it.
> — John 1:1–5[46]

Similarly, in St. Paul's letter to the Colossians he says this:

> He is the image of the unseen God,
> the first-born of all creation,
> for in him were created all things
> in heaven and on Earth:
> everything visible and everything invisible,
> thrones, ruling forces, sovereignties, powers—
> all things were created through and for him.
> He exists before all things
> and in him all things hold together,
> and he is the Head of the body,
> that is, the Church.
> He is the beginning,
> the first-born from the dead,
> so that he should be supreme in every way;
> because God wanted all fullness to be found in him
> and through him to reconcile all things to him,
> everything in heaven and everything on Earth,
> by making peace through his death on the cross.
> — Col.1:15–20[47]

The Human/Earth, Human/Species Relationship

He also said, "What can we say the kingdom of God is like? What parable can we find for it? It is like a mustard seed which at the time of its sowing is the smallest of all the seeds on Earth; yet once it is sown it grows into the biggest shrub of them all and puts out big branches so that the birds of the air can shelter in its shade."   — Mark 4:30–32[48]

Jesus summoned the crowd and said to them: "Hear me all of you, and try to understand. Nothing that enters a man from the outside can make him impure;"   — Mark 7:14[49]

I warn you then: do not worry about your livelihood, what you are to eat or drink or use for clothing. Is not life more than food? Is not the body more valuable than clothing? Look at the birds in the sky. They do not sow or reap, they gather nothing into barns; yet your heavenly Father feeds them . . .   — Matt 6:25[50]

The Human/Human Relationship

Then the King will say to those on his right hand, "Come, you whom my Father has blessed, take as your heritage the kingdom prepared for you since the foundation of the world. For I was hungry and you gave me food, I was thirsty and you gave me drink, I was a stranger and you made me welcome, lacking clothes and you clothed me, sick and you visited me, in prison and you came to see me." Then the upright will say in reply, "Lord, when did we see you hungry and feed you, or thirsty and give you drink? When did we see you a stranger and make you feel welcome, lacking clothes and clothe you? When did we find you sick or in prison and go to see you?" And the King will answer, "In truth I tell you, in so far as you did this to one of the least of these brothers of mine, you did it to me."   — Matt.25:34–41[51]

But I say this to you who are listening: Love your enemies, do good to those who hate you, bless those who curse you, pray for those who treat you badly. To anyone who slaps you on one cheek, present the other cheek as well; to anyone who takes your cloak from you, do not refuse your tunic. Give to everyone who asks you, and do not ask for your property back from someone who takes it. Treat others as you would like people to treat you.
                                        — Luke 6:27–32[52]

And now a lawyer stood up and, to test him, asked, "Master, what must I do to inherit eternal life?" He said to him, "What is written in the Law? What is your reading of it?" He replied, "You must love the Lord your God with all your heart, with all your soul, with all your strength, and with all your mind, and your neighbor as yourself." Jesus said to him, "You have answered right, do this and life is yours."
                                        — Luke 10:25–28[53]

With respect to the acceptance of different ways within the *Global Spiritual Tradition of the Human*, we can see the following quotations as guides to what Jesus might say if we were to ask Him now:

John said to Jesus, "Teacher, we saw a man using your name

to expel demons and we tried to stop him because he is not
one of our company." Jesus said in reply: "Do not try to stop
him. No one can perform a miracle in my name and at the
same time speak ill of me. Anyone who is not against us is
with us."

— Mark 9:38–40[54]

In my Father's house there are many dwelling places;

— John 14:2[55]

> And there are other sheep I have
> that are not of this fold,
> and I must lead these too.
> They too will listen to my voice,
> and there will be only one flock,
> one shepherd.
>
> — John 10:16[56]

Islam

Of all the major religions of the Earth, Islam is the youngest. It
was founded by the prophet Muhammad. Unlike the founder of
Christianity, Muhammad made no claims whatever to divinity. He
considered himself a prophet of the one God, Allah. The word
Islam means "surrender." Therefore, we have much to learn from
Islam concerning the *Twelve Steps of Ecological Spirituality*. A
Muslim, then, is one who surrenders to God.

Like Jews and Christians, Muslims trace their origins back to
the Patriarch, Abraham. Islam, however, traces its ancestry in
Abraham, not through his sons Isaac or Jacob, but through Ishmael. Ishmael was born to Abraham by Hagar, who, after his birth
was sent away with him to Canaan. This whole story is recorded
in the Tanakh. (See Genesis 16–20)

In the year 570 AD, twenty-five centuries after Ishmael, Muhammad was born in Mecca. Things were in a considerable state of
decadence. There was much gambling and drunkenness, as well
as a very corrupt and lucrative trade in idol worship, which passed
for religion. Women were very poorly treated, and the rule of
might was the only law of the day. But, a new idea came with the
birth of Muhammad.

After a painful boyhood caused by the loss of both his father
and grandfather, Muhammad finally went to work as a shepherd
for his uncle, Abu Talib. Early on his reputation for honesty earned
him the name "Al Amin," which means the honest one. On coming

to maturity, Muhammad went to work for a widow named Khadija, whom he married and with whom he fathered four daughters and three sons. The marriage was a happy one.

Khadija was a strong support for the prophet's growing vision. For years he visited a cave in Mt. Hira in order to meditate. One evening during the month-long Ramadan fast, while he was meditating he felt a presence who he came to believe was the angel Gabriel. From that evening on, the angel Gabriel began to relate a message to Muhammad from Allah. This message became a book, Islam's holy book — the Koran.

In Mecca Muhammad met with a great deal of resistance from the organized religion of the day. His new message was in direct confrontation with the corrupt practices of the day and threatened the income from the temples. However, in the city of Medina about two hundred miles away, a following of Muhammad began to grow. Muhammad's life was now in danger in Mecca so he fled to Medina. This flight to Medina is called "Hegira." It took place in the year 622 AD and this is the date usually considered as the beginning of Islam. In Medina Muhammad became famous, not only as a spiritual leader, but as a political leader as well. His rule was known far and wide for its deep sense of justice. After having fought to victory in Mecca, Muhammad died in 632 AD.

One of Islam's strongest points is its simplicity. The core insight into the proper relationship between God and man is captured in what is called the Five Pillars of Islam. These five pillars represent the way of Islam.

The Five Pillars

1. The Creed (shahadah): There is no God but Allah; Muhammad is his prophet.
2. Daily Prayer (salah): Moslems are required to pray five times daily.
3. Almsgiving (zakah): Every Moslem is required to give two to three percent of his earnings for the poor and for the temple upkeep.
4. Fasting (sawm): During the entire month of Ramadan, Moslems are expected to abstain from food, drink, smoking, and sexual relations from before sunrise until after sunset.
5. Pilgrimage (hajj): All Moslems must make at least one pilgrimage to the Kaa'ba at Mecca during their lifetime.

The Human/Universe Relationship

I swear by the turning planets and by the stars that rise and set; by the fall of night and the first breath of the morning; yet you cannot will, except by the will of Allah, Lord of creation.

— Koran[57]

I swear by the glow of sunset; by the night and all that it brings together; by the moon in her full perfection: that you shall march onward from state to state.

— Koran[58]

Many the marvels of the heavens and the Earth; yet they pass them by and pay no heed to them.

— Koran[59]

Allah conceives creation, then renews it. How is it that you are so misled?

— Koran[60]

The Human/Earth, Human/Species Relationship

By the heaven with its recurring cycles, and by the Earth, ever bursting with new growth . . .
  Surely worthier is He who made the heavens and the Earth. He sends down the water from the sky, bringing forth gardens of delight. Try as you may, you cannot cause such trees to grow.
  Surely worthier is He who has established the Earth and watered it with running rivers; who has set mountains upon it and placed a barrier between the seas.
  Allah's promise will be fulfilled. He gives being to all His creatures.

— Koran[61]

Allah has brought you forth from the Earth like a plant and to the Earth he will restore you. Then he will bring you back afresh. He has made the Earth a vast expanse for you, so you may traverse its spacious paths.

— Koran[62]

The sun and moon pursue their ordered course. The plants and trees bow down in adoration. He raised the heavens on high and set the balance of all things, that you might not transgress it. Give just weight and full measure. He laid the Earth for His creatures, with all its grain and scented herbs. Which of your Lord's blessings would you deny?

— Koran[63]

As a way of concluding this short section on Islam, I would like to mention a religion, which took its rise from Islam, but which is presently no longer considered part of the Moslem world. This religion began in the nineteenth century, and while it is still relatively small in numbers, it is global in both its perspective as well as in its membership. In the thirteen tenets of Baha'i are captured a model for the human/human relationship globally. These tenets present us with a succinct model of tolerance — a model for the *Global Spiritual Tradition of the Human.* So, while Baha'i is in no way attached to Islam, I add them at the end of the Islam section to represent its Human/Human relationship.

The Human/Human Relationship

1. There must be an independent search after truth, unfettered by superstition or tradition.
2. The pivotal principle and fundamental doctrine of the Faith is the oneness of the entire human race.
3. There is a basic unity of all religions.
4. All forms of prejudice, whether religious, racial, class, or national are condemned.
5. Harmony must exist between religion and science.
6. There is an equality of men and women, the two wings on which the bird of humankind is able to soar.
7. Compulsory education should prevail.
8. A universal auxiliary language should be adopted.
9. Extremes of wealth and poverty should be abolished.
10. A world tribunal for the adjudication of disputes between nations should be instituted.
11. Work performed in the spirit of service should be exalted to the rank of worship.
12. Justice, as a ruling principle in human society, and religion, as a bulwark for the protection of all people and nations, should be glorified.
13. The establishment of a permanent and universal peace should be the supreme goal of mankind.

— *Religions of the World*[64]

With a rediscovery of our relationships to self, to tradition, to life, to Earth, and to the universe, we will have done our part to promote the *Second Western Renaissance.* Having learned something about the *Global Spiritual Tradition of the Human* we will be able to discover the disciplines we need to continue our growth.

STEP ELEVEN is taken by searching out those disciplines in our own religion and in other religions that will help us to change in ways that will improve our ability to foster our own growth, as well as to foster the emergence and health of the whole of creation.

CHAPTER TWELVE

Before I flew I was already aware of how small and vulnerable our planet is; but only when I saw it from space, in all its ineffable beauty and fragility, did I realize that humankind's most urgent task is to cherish and preserve it for future generations.

— Cosmonaut Sigmund Jahn
German Democratic Republic[1]

Looking outward to the blackness of space, sprinkled with the glory of a universe of lights, I saw majesty—but no welcome. Below was a welcoming planet. There, contained in the thin, moving, incredibly fragile shell of the biosphere is everything that is dear to you, all human drama and comedy. What's where life is; that's where all the good stuff is.

— Astronaut Loren Acton[2], U.S.A.

STEP TWELVE: HAVING EXPERIENCED A REAWAKENING TO SELF, TO HUMANITY, TO ALL SPECIES, TO THE PLANET, AND TO THE UNIVERSE, WE TRY TO SPREAD THIS AWARENESS TO OTHERS AND TO PRACTICE THESE DISCIPLINES IN ALL PHASES OF OUR LIVES.

It is not enough to know about the whole. Many know the science of the whole, the cosmology, the geology, the botany, and the zoology. But, how many of us experience the whole? How many feel the turning galaxies? How many feel the Milky Way? How many feel the turning Earth and the night sky? How many of us experience ourselves as experiences of the whole? How many of us feel ourselves as "*cell*ves" within the divine body that swells into time and space? But that, in fact, is what we are!

To experience ourselves and each other as functions of the whole Earth and as functions of the whole universe, to experience the other species and all of life as functions of the whole and to experience the planet within the solar system, we must reawaken to the divine mystery from which they all emerge, in which they are sustained, and toward which they are destined.

Integrity is wholeness, the greatest beauty is
Organic wholeness, the wholeness of life and things, the divine
beauty of the universe. Love that, not man
Apart from that, or else you will share man's pitiful confusions
or drown in despair when his days darken.

— Robinson Jeffers[3]

The whole is a function of the Originating Mystery. Reawakening to the whole is reawakening to that mystery. To reawaken to Mystery is to reawaken to our own nature, to all of nature, and to the Earth.

Ztt! I entered. I lost the boundary of my physical body. I had my skin, of course, but I felt I was standing in the center of the cosmos . . . I saw people coming toward me, but all were the same man. All were myself. I had never known this world before. I had believed that I was created, but now I must change my mind. I was never created; I was the cosmos; no individual existed.

— H. Smith[4]

The *Twelve Steps of Ecological Spirituality* are designed to provide us with the experience of just that sort of reawakening, the *Second Western Renaissance*. But even as we feel the ecstacy of this reawakening, we will also begin to feel the horror of the present in the full impact of its deep pathology. Everywhere we will see, as though for the first time, the garish ruins of a culture bottoming out in addiction. What we thought was a wonderworld, in the drugged haze of our consumption, will turn out to be a waste-world of addiction with its cynicism and its trash.

We will feel the agony of fish, tortured every moment of their degraded lives in the chemical baths of our waste. We will be aghast at the idea of their eyes forced to stay open in the toxic soups that flow through their mouths and out their gills. We will feel the deaths of the millions, the billions of aquatic beings who couldn't make it and died . . . for nothing.

We will feel the billions of animals denied habitat because of our insatiable lust for more and bigger offices, gas stations, and car washes. We will feel their writhing confusion as they tried to escape bulldozers that peel up soils and wetlands. We will feel the hell of birds and animals burned to death in rainforests incinerated so that we could have cheaper hamburgers. We will feel the slow bleeding deaths of animals crushed, or worse, half-crushed as they ran frantic beneath our wheels. We will feel the slow agony of their cubs, chicks, and pups starving while they awaited their crushed parents' return.

We will begin to feel the desparation of animals forced to slaughter each other in fighting over habitat. Many animals are genetically mandated for the defense of territoriality. They have no choice but to fight to the bleeding death should evicted members of habitat stolen from them by "development" venture into habitat already occupied. If there was room for only one and another comes, one must die. Again, as that one dies, there is the slow death of the young waiting in the dens and nests. When we begin to feel the twisting agony of them all, we are awakening to the pain of the Earth. When we feel the moaning torment of the whole planet, we will begin to see what happened during the night of addiction and will begin to feel the dawn of being human again.

When we begin to feel the slow poisoning of the great birds, forced to breathe the "air" over our cities — when we feel their loss of dignity and numbers, we are awakening. When we become enraged to hear "important" business and political "leaders" talk glibly about bottom lines and profit margins, we are awakening. When we understand that "gross" is the perfect word to describe the National Product, we are awakening. The real bottom line is the agony of the poor, the animals, and the other life forms. The real bottom line is the desecration of *our* planet. The real bottom line is the degradation of *our* air, *our* water, *our* soils! The real bottom line is the ruination of the quality of *our* lives here on *our* planet. The real bottom line is not paid for by business and political types . . . the real bottom line is paid for by *us* and by *our* planet, the Earth. When we speak for the Earth, we are awakening.

Galaxies turn in us. Pulsars pulse in us. Quazars sing in us. We are the whole universe conscious of itself. We are the *spirit* — "Wakan-tanka," "Goddess," "Yahweh," "Allah," "Brahman," "Tao." Is it not an incredible privilege to know that we are that species in whom life celebrates itself? Does this not change the dead and gloomy hell of addicted culture into the hope of the brightest heaven? Shall we awaken to the heavenly garden in our midst? Or, shall we stand by and watch as we lose Paradise a second time?

This good Earth is our home; we are *not* just travelers here. If only we would open our eyes! We are in the Pure Land now! We are in the Promised Land now! We are in Eternity now! If we would only rise from the drugged sleep of *consumerism*, from the sad torpor of compulsive — and repulsive — buying, we would find ourselves at home with ourselves, at home among our own kind, at home among the animals in the garden, and at home on this blue jewel of a planet we call Earth. At home on Earth, we shall be at home among the stars. Earth is home. The Originating Mystery saw fit to allow us to evolve here. We live here . . . at home.

When we awaken to the agony and ecstacy of the whole, we will need to tell others. We could not contain ourselves if we tried. For in awakening, we are no longer that little self so concerned with our petty designs and problems. When we awaken, we realize that we are not separate "automatons," bouncing off each other. Instead, we realize that we are mysterious and gentle beings, together representing the whole of life, the whole universe. Then we can answer this question: "What is humankind for?" The human is caretaker of the *whole Earth* and of all life. That is who we are; that is our purpose. We are the periscope, the lighthouse of self-reflection, overviewing the whole garden of life. It is high time we begin to be who we are!

We begin to be who we are where we are. That is how we spread the awareness to others. In our families, on the job, at school, wherever we find ourselves, we begin to talk about these Twelve Steps — we begin to speak for and *as* the Earth. We invite a half dozen or a dozen people to go through these steps with us. We form small groups in our churches and temples. We form groups in our clubs and civic organizations. We begin now . . . here . . . where we find ourselves . . . but . . . we must begin!

Most important of all, we must go on practicing the insights gained from these Twelve Steps . . . in all phases of our lives. So, what are these insights? I call them the

Five Principles of Psychic Hygiene
1. *Surrender*: We must give up trying to confront unprecedented evils with just the force of the individual ego. Our surrender must be twofold:
   a. We must admit powerlessness over a culture gone mad.
   b. We must surrender to membership in the whole community of life.
2. *Decision*: We must decide to give ourselves away for the good of the whole. We do this by deciding to give ourselves to the Originating Mystery from which we have emerged.
3. *Confession*: We must empty ourselves not only of actions and attitudes that are poisonous to life, but we must allow ourselves to be emptied of the habits that produce such dysfunctional behavior.
4. *Restitution*: We must try to heal all harms done to self, to others, to life, and to the Earth.
5. *Carry the message*: We must tell others.

By keeping these five principles forever before us, we will make our reawakening permanent. We do so by practicing them in all phases of our lives. What are these phases?

First, if I practice these principles, I will discover myself, my true, authentic *Original Self*. I will begin to appreciate my uniqueness, the fact that I and each of us, as well as every being whatsoever, those gone and those to come, are all one-time events, unrepeatable. I will feel the fact that, in twenty billion years of universe history, there has been only one me. What was once the source of my loneliness will become the cause of my exultation, and that exultation will be expressed in the desire and willingness to bring forth all that I am. After all, I have my own song to sing! If I do not sing it, it will not be sung. Whoever I am, however limited or gifted, I have my gift to bring. **Greenspirit** is not for the eloquent only. **Greenspirit** is not for the rich, the powerful, or the educated only. **Greenspirit** is for anyone who wishes to be a part of it. I am necessary to **Greenspirit**, as well as to the whole of evolution, or I would not be here. Life is gushing through me. Freedom is gushing through me. What a vast dignity there is to it all!

This powerful experience of self-realization will overflow into all our other relationships. We will begin to feel kindred to all living beings — human, animal, and plant. This is the second phase of our awakening. As we sense the planetary and cosmic dimensions of our own personalities, we will sense our common divine origin and destiny. It will dawn on us that all other beings share in that origin and destiny. We will understand the unique value of every being, living and nonliving. We will begin to understand that our journeys are part of the one journey of life, of the Earth, and the universe. We will become big within and in our bigness there will be room for everyone. We will embrace all beings, befriending all, befriending the Earth and the universe.

We will begin to see that all life is food for life and that our lives, too, are food. We will understand that our lives are not our own only, that our lives and our creativity are also functions of the whole. We will understand that our love is not our own only but is the love of the planet, of the universe, and of the Originating Mystery out of which all emerged into being. We will discover that our true happiness lies not in what we can acquire but, rather, in what we can share. The mad illusion of addiction will be shattered. We will feel the evolution of the whole Earth within the depth of our own beings. We will understand that sin or violence can be defined as anything that militates against the growth and increase, the well-being, of the whole. A new reverence will dawn in us. We will cherish ourselves, each other, and all that lives. We will cherish the Earth.

When this overflowing takes place, when we feel this wellspring of new life bursting through us and bathing the whole planet, we will find a new love of the soil, the air, the water, and sunlight. We will become conscious and grateful for the wind we breathe and share with all that lives. When we drink, we will become conscious of the preciousness of fresh water and will want to protect it at all costs. When we are outdoors, we will cherish the warmth of the sunlight showering upon us, and when indoors, we will appreciate the stored sunlight that warms our homes. We will learn to thank the forests for those homes and the fields for the food upon our tables. We will thank the rivers for the cup of water that we drink. It is then that we shall become aware of the third phase of our awakening.

We will begin to become aware of the stars of the night sky, and to thank them for their beauty and mystery. We will begin to become conscious of the grand majesty of the turning galaxy through which we move. We will begin to feel the grand embrace of all galaxies as they hold each other and us in their gravitational embrace. We will begin to feel the slow "OM" of the expanding universe creating space and time fresh in every moment. Gratitude will begin to shine from every pore of us. We will walk in grace and bless all places that we enter. We will feel great pleasure just in being . . . and take an equal and shared pleasure in the beings of everyone and everything. We will cherish and celebrate the growth of the whole Earth knowing that it is our own. We will live life in the joy of true *Wholiness*.

The pain of all creation will be our shared pain. We will walk together, and together our lives will become food for a hungry world. We will be eucharist, thanksgiving — risked, broken, and shared together. And when death comes, we will know the peace of having experienced our true destiny, taking our place in the composting of Earth, sure to rise again at the next planting. We will know that our bodies, our minds, and our souls have been digested by a planet, fed for our having been here. We will know that our lives have blossomed into fruit that can be eaten by all of life. We will die knowing that we live. We will die truly human beings.

Is all of this the murmurings of a dreamer? Is it all impractical? Then, again, is planetary death by pollution or nuclear end practical? We know the way to death. This book represents a way to life. We, who have walked this way, have come to life. We create and recreate ourselves every time we take the journey that is Twelve Steps long. We are becoming. If there is a single word to describe the universe it is this one: *Becoming*. When we become, mystery becomes matter and matter becomes revelation. This book is the expressed joy and gratitude of one who has befriended himself, the Earth, and the universe.

There were two major purposes for writing this book. First, it was written in order that we might all come to know the "New Story" — the story that includes the universe, the Earth, life and conscious life, the human. It is our story, the shared family tree of each and every one of us. Second, it was written in order to help us all to break through the bondage of cultural addiction which, presently, is blocking the evolution of life on Earth. If it is effective, my great hope is that it will help to lead us all out of the wreckage of the present and into a new era of human/Earth relationship.

The tribal/shamanic age has come and gone. Tribes remain, however few, but no new tribes are forming. The age of the great classical religious cultures has come and gone. All of the great religions are still present among us, but no new ones seem to be forming. The Industrial Revolution has come and gone. The knowledge we have gained will remain with us and increase, but the great hope of a material wonderworld on Earth has betrayed itself. Instead, we have inherited a waste world. We find ourselves amid the ruins of the industrial infrastructures as well as amid the ruins of the natural world. What will the future bring? What will the *Ecological Age* of human/Earth relationship be like? Let's paint a few broad strokes using conclusions drawn from the writings of Thomas Berry.

Here is a brief glimpse into the future:

THE EARTH IN THE ECOLOGICAL AGE

1. Technologies have emerged under the sign of progress. "Progress" was supposed to remove our dependencies upon the natural world. Progress became the dream of a self-sufficient humanity, without need of relationship to anything outside of itself. The natural world was seen as dead and valueless in and of itself. Its only value lay in its utility to humans. In the Ecological Age, all human technologies will be seen as functions of Earth technologies.

Thus, human technologies will be shaped and fitted more appropriately into the life systems of the planet. They will be designed to enhance and utilize the air, water, soil, life and sunlight rather than to dominate, exploit and plunder them. Destruction of the natural world will be considered criminal and will be experienced as the second loss of Paradise.

2. Our pattern of life in the scientific/technological age has been human centered. The Earth and her life forms have had value only with reference to their utility. Hence, nature has had no legal rights in the face of unmerciful plundering and poisoning by human agency. In the Ecological Age, our life program will be Earth centered, life centered. We will experience ourselves as an invention of the Earth, as that being in whom the Earth community reflects upon and celebrates itself. We will find our norms of values, our source of healing, the governing principles of our societies, our education, nourishment and fulfillment of both body and spirit within the context of the whole Earth community.

3. In the present age, our technology rules over and dominates the whole biosphere. Nonhuman life has no rights in the face of human technologies. Nonliving matter is seen as dead. In the new pattern, "biocracy," the rule of life will govern the technosphere. Rather than seeing a product as the only focus of our concern, life, its reproduction and increase, and thus the reproducibility of products, will be our first concern. Life and the life systems of the planet will hold primary claims to our attention and concern and not products or machines or the wealth of a few.

4. In the present age, we have preferred monocultural situations. Technologies function best where predictability runs high, and where diversity and spontaneities run low. In the Ecological Age, diversity will be honored as a primary necessity for life and survival. An ecosystem or culture is more capable of survival the larger the number of its component species and ideas. The valuing of diversity among humans will begin with the valuing of the *Global Spiritual Tradition of the Human*, and the devaluing of any mono-cultural claims to the fullness of revelation.

5. The present mode of life is essentially a high entropy, high pollution producing system. There is a constant demand for higher energy flow, from an ever dwindling energy base. It is in this high entropy pattern that we discover the pathology of cultural addiction. Our desire to have sudden explosive satisfaction is (and

must be) followed by sterility and emptiness, disintegration and ultimately quiescence. This reveals the addiction syndrome in its full insidiousness. In the Ecological Age, life will be self-sustaining, experiencing constant renewal within the natural sequence of the planetary systems, sustained by the constant influx of energy from the sun. Natural systems produce a minimum of entropy. Human technologies will exist in cooperation with natural systems.

6. In the present age, science and technology are used to force the Earth to produce more than it can bring forth within the normal rhythms of its life process. Thus the Earth is growing sick and exhausted and even shows signs of impending death. In the Ecological Age, economic activity will again take place on a natural and human scale. The grandeur and wonders of the Earth systems will be valued rather than overcome. Humans will live locally, within the context of the *bio*region in a suitable relationship to the other life forms of the region, so that all component members of any given bioregion can interact creatively with one another. Western religions will be organized by *bio*cese rather than by *dio*cese, pointing to the age beyond the nation state.

7. In the present age the role of large amorphous urban centers has been exaggerated. These have come about as largely artificial environments divorced from any real relationship to the natural world, while they nonetheless exist at its expense. Within these urban sprawls, a disdain for the land-based mode of life has developed. In the Ecological Age, cities, large and small, will still be present in order to focus upon and activate the full range of human achievement, but a new form of village life also will emerge. These new villages will be in intimate relationship to the life systems of the planet. Here the village crafts will be developed along with the skills associated with the working of the land. Western religious orders will also play a crucial role here, as they renew their own roots to agrarian lifestyles.

8. The present age has been centralizing in its primary dynamic. Family scale ventures are extinguished in favor of the interests of gigantic, multinational corporations. Huge industries take over production as small craft activities die out. In commerce, education, professions, and government, the many are dependent on the few. In the Ecological Age, decentralizing forces would balance the centralizing forces. Especially in food production, in energy systems, and in human associations, a process of localization would

take place. From this would come progressive independence from undesirable controls from a distant authority.

9. Presently, national security depends on armaments capable of vast, even of total destruction. Military expenses have risen to such horrendous figures that many economies feel the parasitical and destabilizing effects of bloated military machines. In the Ecological Age, security will be based on human, moral, and ecological qualities. These qualities will help us discover ways of resolving conflicts without recourse to styles of conflict that threaten not only the human family, but all of life as well as the very conditions that make life possible.

10. Lastly, in the present age, employment is often sought in an industrial process that depends upon the destruction and exploitation of the Earth's resources. This only increases entropy or pollution, thus threatening the well-being of the employees themselves. In the Ecological Age employment will be provided in a more local, a more human/Earth enhancing context.

In short, the Ecological Age will represent a *Second Western Renaissance*, a reawakening to life, to Earth, to the universe. Already, small groups are forming that promise the emergence of a new era of human/Earth history. The "New Story" provides the context for cooperation between all cultures, between all peoples, between humans and all species, between life and the planet from which it takes its being.

The *Twelve Steps of Ecological Spirituality* provide a way out of the addiction that blocks this cooperation, as well as a way in which to live in the Ecological Age. Joined together in the awakening to our common origin and common destiny, we shall create the future. In doing so, we shall have created a new Earth, a new humanity, and a new universe. We can rejoice in our unity and shared life with all that lives. We will laugh again. We will have befriended ourselves. We will have befriended each other. We will have befriended the Earth. We will have befriended the universe.

Goffstown, N.H. January 4, 1991

APPENDIX

GREENSPIRIT PREAMBLE

Greenspirit is an organization of men and women who have accepted personal responsibility for the fate of the Earth. Members of *Greenspirit* come from any national, political, economic, or religious tradition, but *Greenspirit* as a whole is not allied or affiliated with any institution or entity whatsoever. The only requirement for membership is the desire to revitalize our relationship to life, thereby revitalizing our cultures and their relationships to each other and the Earth. There are no dues or fees for *Greenspirit* membership; we are self-supporting through our own contributions.

Our purpose is to come together to support and encourage one another in speaking for and as the Earth. In so doing, we hope to encourage and to support all forms of ecological, peace, and justice activism that speak in support of life.

We believe that the *Twelve Steps of Ecological Spirituality* will reveal to us the root cause(s) of our dysfunctional relationship with ourselves, others, other cultures, other species, and all the life systems of the planet Earth. Further, we believe that the *Twelve Steps of Ecological Spirituality* will provide a path that can help us to change these dysfunctional relationships.

Our hope is that through the practice of the *Twelve Steps of Ecological Spirituality*, we shall become morally regenerated ourselves, and thereby empowered to begin laying the foundations for a new human/Earth relationship. This new relationship will be grounded on the recognition that the primary referents of all reality are soil, air, and water — the life systems of the planet Earth. In recognizing our common ground, we hope to discover a new relationship of cooperation between individuals, nations, and cultures as we work together to renew the Earth in the emerging Ecological Age.

GREENSPIRIT SUGGESTED GROUP FORMAT

At each meeting a new chairperson should be elected to lead the meeting. If possible, the person leading should have been through **Greenspirit** before, or should have some knowledge of this book. Where this is not possible, just begin and discover your own way as a group. Each group is autonomous.

To open meeting: "We will open the . . . (name of group) . . . meeting of **Greenspirit** with a moment of silence for the Earth and for all of her creatures." (A long moment of silence should follow.)

Next, the chairperson, or someone else, reads the **Greenspirit** Preamble. Newcomers are introduced and the group process is explained.

Then the group shares the reading of the Step it is on at that time. It is suggested that each person read a paragraph until the chapter is completed. In a new group, it is suggested that the whole chapter be read before any sharing is done. In a seasoned group, it might be better to slow down and discuss questions as they arise. Each group will discover the best procedure for itself. At the end of each chapter, there is a short instruction for taking that Step. It is merely a suggestion. Nothing in **Greenspirit** is compulsory! The chairperson should always let people know that nobody needs to believe any one particular idea in this book in order to be welcome.

The book provides a guide and much food for thought. Some people may believe in one issue and not in another. That is perfectly acceptable. The book was written in an attempt to find common ground among people of different persuasions. There will be differences of opinion, but it is hoped that everyone will find something with which to grow and change. Everyone should be encouraged to share in the first person only. WE ARE IN **GREENSPIRIT** TO CHANGE OURSELVES. NOBODY CAN CHANGE ANOTHER'S MIND, AND WE SHOULD AVOID ALL ATTEMPTS TO TRY. WE ARE IN **GREENSPIRIT** TO SHARE HOW OUR OWN LIFE HAS BEEN DEGRADED AND HOW THE ORIGINATING MYSTERY, AS WE UNDERSTAND THE MYSTERY, HAS HELPED US TO CHANGE.

When the time to close the meeting arrives, pass a basket among the group for donations for refreshments, rent, and so on. A treasurer should be elected to collect and account for all monies. Should the group choose to contribute to the **Greenspirit** organization, it should come to a majority vote as to the amount.

When closing the meeting, the chairperson should say this:

"Can we close this meeting with another moment of silence?" During that silence s/he might say aloud: "May we be in peace. May our peace flow outward to all people. May our peace flow out to all the animals and plants of the Earth. May our peace embrace the whole planet." Then, remind everyone that if a person chooses to be anonymous, that request should be honored by everyone in the group. Wait a moment and say thank you and good-bye.

NOTES

Title Page

1. Henry David Thoreau, *Walden* (New York: Harper & Row, 1958).

Preface

1. Alcoholics Anonymous, *Twelve Steps and Twelve Traditions* (New York: A. A. Word Services, Inc., 1965). We are hereby acknowledging our obvious debt to A. A.'s 12 Steps.

Introduction

1. Anuradha Vittachi, *Earth Conference One* (Boston: New Science Library, Shambhala Books, 1989), 54.
2. Jeremy Rifkin, *Entropy* (New York: Bantam Books, 1981), 99.
3. Vittachi, 58.

Chapter One

1. Brian Swimme, *The Universe Is a Green Dragon* (Santa Fe, N.M.: Bear & Co. Books, 1984), 71.
2. Jeremy Rifkin and Ted Howard, *The Emerging Order* (New York: G. P. Putmam's Sons, 1983), 39–40.
3. Quoted from *Solid Waste Management Plan for the Town of Goffstown, New Hampshire*, December 1989.
4. Swami Prabhavananda and Christopher Isherwood, translation of *Bhagavad Gita* (New York: Mentor Books, 1944), 42.
5. M. Scott Peck, *People of the Lie* (New York: Simon & Schuster, 1983), 120.
6. Teilhard de Chardin, *The Divine Milieu* (New York: Harper Torchbooks, 1960), 40.

Chapter Two

1. N. J. Dawood translation of *The Koran* (New York: Penguin Books, 1956), Chap. 71: 17–20, 21.
2. Teilhard de Chardin, *Human Energy* (New York: HBJ Books, 1969), 83–84.
3. David Bohm, *Wholeness and the Implicate Order* (London and Boston: Ark Books, 1983), 191.

4. John G. Neihardt, *Black Elk Speaks* (New York: Washington Square Press, 1959), 1.

Chapter Three

1. Gregory Vlastos, quoted from *Beyond War Communicator's Guide* (Palo Alto, Calif.: 1985), 23.
2. Prabhavananda and Isherwood, 63.
3. Thomas Merton, *The Way of Chuang Tzu* (New York: New Directions, 1969), 40.
4. *The Jerusalem Bible* (New York: Doubleday & Co., 1966), 791.
5. Ibid.
6. Ibid.
7. C. G. Jung, *Collected Works* (Princeton, N.J.: Princeton University Press, 1957), Bollingen Series vol. 7, para. 218.
8. Ezra Pound, translation of *Confucius* (New York: New Directions, 1969), 101.
9. Dante, *The Inferno*. Translated by John Ciardi. (New York: Mentor Books, 1954), 74.
10. *U.S. Declaration of Independence*.
11. Danaqyumptewa translation of *From the Beginning of Life to the Day of Purification: The Hopi Story* (Los Angeles: Land & Life Inc., 1982), 2.
12. Jung, *Collected Works*, vol. 11, para. 390.

Chapter Four

1. Walter Brueggemann, *The Prophetic Imagination* (Philadelphia: Fortress Press, 1978), 49–50.
2. Pound, 173–4.
3. *New American Bible* (New York: Catholic Book Publishing Co., 1980), 885.
4. Irving Babbitt, translation of *Dhammapada* (New York: New Directions, 1965), 28.
5. Marion Woodman, *Addiction to Perfection* (Toronto: Inner City, 1982), 28.
6. Anna Cook, *You Are the Gift* (Cali.: Western Book/Journal Press, 1985), 50.
7. Thomas Aquinas, *Summa Theologica* (1985), Part 1, ques. 47, art. 1.
8. Cook, 49.
9. *New American Bible*.
10. Woodman, *Addiction*, 26.

Chapter Five

1. Erich Jantsch, *The Self-Organizing Universe* (New York: Pergamon Books, 1980), 301.
2. C. G. Jung, *Collected Works* 1 para. 484–91.
3. Jantsch, 296.

4. St. Paul, *Letter to the Philippians*, chap. 2: 6–9, *New Jerusalem Bible*.
5. Jung, *Collected Works*, vol. 17, para. 154.
6. Ibid., para. 155.
7. Ibid., vol. 4, para. 432.
8. Ibid., vol. 16, para. 503.
9. Ibid., para. 21.
10. Ibid., para. 135.
11. Ibid., para. 123.

Chapter Six
1. Thomas Berry, *The Riverdale Papers* (New York: Center for Religious Research). These are ten volumes of essays printed and copied by Thomas Berry himself. Many of the essays are available in a single volume, *The Dream of the Earth*, to be published by Sierra Club Books.
2. Rupert Sheldrake, *The Presence of the Past* (New York: Times Books, 1988), 97.
3. Ibid., 95.
4. Mary Rosera Joyce, *New Dynamics in Sexual Love* (Minn.: St. John's University Press, 1970), 59.
5. Marion Woodman, *The Pregnant Virgin* (Toronto: Inner City Books, 1985), 16.
6. Babbitt, 32.
7. Ibid., 34.
8. Ibid., 32.
9. Prabhavananda and Isherwood, 92.
10. Babbitt, 32.
11. *The New American Bible*.
12. Prabhavananda and Isherwood, 91.
13. Robert Jay Lifton and Richard Falk, *Indefensible Weapons* (New York: Basic Books Inc., 1982), 10–11.

Chapter Seven
1. Lifton and Falk, 112.
2. Jantsch, 248.
3. *The New American Bible*.
4. Stanley Gorsky, Trinity High School, Manchester, NH.

Chapter Eight
1. Edmond Bordeaux Szekely, *The Essene Gospel of Peace* (Costa Rica: International Biogenic Society, 1981), 9–10.
2. Woodman, *The Pregnant Virgin*, 138–9.
3. Woodman, *The Pregnant Virgin*, 139.
4. Jeremy Rifkin, *On Genetic Engineering* (Santa Fe, N.M.: Bear & Co. The Little Magazine), 20.

5. *New York Times*, 28 Sept. 1986, 28.
6. Luisah Teish, *Jambalaya* (San Francisco: Harper & Row, 1985), 201.
7. James Lovelock, *The Ages of Gaia* (New York: Norton & Co., 1988), 206.

Chapter Nine
1. *New American Bible.*
2. Sheldrake, 100.
3. *New American Bible.*
4. Nicholas Georgescu-Roegen, from *Entropy* by Rifkin, 269.
5. Lifton and Falk, 54.

Chapter Ten
1. Pound, 123.
2. Peck, 129.

Chapter Eleven
1. Quoted from Huston Smith, *The Religions of Man* (New York: Harper & Row, 1958), 86ff.
2. *The New American Bible.*
3. Chief Seattle, *Letter to the American President* (Mt. Carmel, Conn.: St. Ives Press, 1985).
4. Neihardt, 2.
5. T. C. McLuhan, *Touch the Earth* (New York: Touchstone/Simon & Schuster, 1971), 12.
6. Ibid.
7. Chief Seattle, Ibid.
8. Ibid.
9. Neihardt, 36.
10. Prabhavananda and Isherwood, 73.
11. Ibid., 70.
12. Ibid., 54.
13. Ibid., 67.
14. Smith, 54ff.
15. Prabhavananda and Isherwood, 91–92.
16. Ibid., 112.
17. Ibid., 106.
18. W. B. Yeats, and Shree Swami Purohit, *The Ten Principal Upanishads* (New York: Collier Books, 1937) 25.
19. John Blofeld, *The Zen Teachings of Huang Po* (New York: Grove Press Evergreen, 1958), 118.
20. Babbitt, 95.
21. Ibid., 17.
22. Ibid., 22.
23. Ibid., 23.

24. Pound, 35.
25. Ibid., 99–101.
26. Ibid., 185.
27. Ibid., 65–69.
28. John C. H. Wu, translation of *Tao Te Ching* (New York: St. John's University Press, 1961), 7.
29. Ibid., 3.
30. Ibid., 33.
31. Ibid., 41.
32. Ibid., 53.
33. Ibid., 49.
34. Ibid., 113–15.
35. Ibid., 39.
36. Ibid., 9.
37. Ibid., 77.
38. *New American Bible.*
39. Ibid.
40. Ibid.
41. Ibid.
42. Ibid.
43. Ibid.
44. *The New Testament of the New Jerusalem Bible* (New York: Image Books, 1986).
45. Ibid.
46. Ibid.
47. Ibid.
48. Ibid.
49. Ibid.
50. Ibid.
51. Ibid.
52. Ibid.
53. Ibid.
54. Ibid.
55. Ibid.
56. Ibid.
57. Dawood, *The Koran*, 17.
58. Ibid., 49.
59. Ibid., 47.
60. Ibid., 67.
61. Ibid., 86.
62. Ibid., 22.
63. Ibid., 19.
64. Lewis M. Hopfe, *Religions of the World* (London: Collier Macmillan, 1976), 297.
65. Berry, Ibid.

Chapter Twelve

1. Sigmund Jahn and Loren Acton, *Noetic Sciences Review,* Summer 1988.
2. Ibid.
3. Robinson Jeffers, "The Answer" from *The Selected Poetry of Robinson Jeffers* (New York: Random House, 1959), 594.
4. Smith, 149.
5. The entire last section, along with many sentences throughout the entire text, are taken from *The Riverdale Papers* of Thomas Berry nearly verbatim. I could not find a better way to say it than he did so I used his words in a slightly modified form.

Printed in the United States
1106000006B/79-99

9 781843 332855